Lost in Translation

Lost in Translation

The Book of Revelation:
Two Brides,
Two Destinies

by John Klein and Adam Spears
with Michael Christopher

Published by Covenant Research Institute, Inc.
© 2012 by John Klein, Adam Spears, and Michael Christopher

International Standard Book Number: 978–1-58930-283-9
Library of Congress Control Number: 2012903146

Cover by Ross Chandler, Chandler Photography, Bend, Oregon

Unless otherwise indicated, all Scripture quotations are from
New American Standard Bible® (NASB) © 1960, 1977, 1995
by the Lockman Foundation. Used by permission.

Additional Scripture quotations are from:

The Amplified Bible (AMP)
© 1965, 1987 by Zondervan Publishing House

The Holy Bible, New International Version (NIV)
© 1973, 1984 by International Bible Society,
used by permission of Zondervan Publishing House.

Complete Jewish Bible (CJB)
© 1998 by David Stern. Published by Messianic Jewish Publishers.

For information:
Covenant Research Institute
PO Box 8224
Bend, OR 97708
www.lostintranslation.org

Dedication

For all those who open these pages, may these three volumes be dependable sources of knowledge and understanding in the months and years ahead. And may they also be both a collective comfort and an ever-increasing inspiration.

Acknowledgments

The authors wish to thank Jodi Klein, Karren Spears, and Patricia Christopher for their unconditional support during the preparation of this manuscript – and the preceding two as well. Without their loyalty and commitment these three volumes simply would not have been possible.

Contents

Foreword

When the moment came for me to add my customary foreword — this time to Volume 3 — I spent at least three hours constructing various beginnings. But I eventually rejected every single one, because I suddenly remembered something I've been telling other writers and editors for more than 30 years.

"Stop trying to compose! Stop thinking about how you say it! Just pretend you're talking to your best friend and tell him what you want him to know, exactly like you'd do if he were sitting across the table from you!"

Then I'd usually add to the above by quoting some anonymous writer-teacher-editor, to the effect that "Nothing is ever written; it's always rewritten." Followed by my own grand conclusion: "You can re-arrange the words later but you can't fix something that hasn't been written yet!"

So let me be straight with you, just as I would if we were sitting in a room together.

First of all, like a lot of books I've worked on, this project isn't ending up the way it started out. It was supposed to be just one book, which was supposed to take about a year and a half to pull together. Now, ten years later my two co-authors and I are on the third volume. And I'm not quite sure that we won't need more volumes to deal with things we've brought up but not fully explored in these three.

Second, my wife, Patricia, has been a vital part of this project from the very beginning, and during those ten years, John Klein and Adam Spears have become our best friends. Our families have had dinners and lunches and coffee klatches together many times. We've watched their kids grow up. But most important of all, we've learned that they are exactly who they appear to be in these three books – highly intelligent, somewhat unconventional, outdoors-loving guys who are incredibly committed to passing on what they've learned about the book of Revelation after years of rigorous study, to anyone willing to see it from a non-mainstream perspective.

Third, I sincerely believe they understand the book of Revelation better than anyone who has ever written about it in the past – certainly for any mainstream publishers. I've read numerous other authors on the same subject and have worked with one or two as well, all of whom seem to come at Revelation from a Greco-Roman-Western mindset rather than the Hebraic perspective from which it originated.

In fact, as John and Adam explain over and over in these three volumes, the entire Bible was written down by Hebrew authors inspired by a Hebrew God, using Hebrew idioms that reflected Hebrew customs and Hebrew cultural understandings. In other words, it was keyed to a mindset that was relentlessly Hebraic on every level. And it still is.

It's just not possible to approach it, logically and productively, in any other way.

Michael Christopher
Bend, Oregon – 2012

Introduction

IN VOLUME 2 OF THIS THREE-VOLUME SERIES WE BEGAN EXPLORING THE book of Revelation from an Hebraic perspective, starting with its underlying structure. We then talked about its bare bones and began putting the meat on those bones while observing the three foundational principles essential to understanding Revelation:

First, the book of Revelation is a thoroughly Hebraic text.

Second, its basic structure mirrors the design of the master menorah.

Third, to obtain an accurate understanding of the book of Revelation the reader must have a working knowledge of the different types of covenant delineated in Scripture.

Next we introduced four groups, each containing seven events – the letters, the seals, the trumpets, and the thunders. We then ended Volume 2 with a discussion of the trumpets, followed by some comments on world events as they relate to prophetic, end-times occurrences. We also added "Where Are We Now?" and "Things to Watch for Next" sections, dealing with then-current events and highlighting a series of additional events to watch for against the overall backdrop.

With respect to Revelation's prophesied events, in "real time" in the early part of 2012, we now find ourselves near the middle of the Four Horsemen of the Apocalypse/First Four Seals, as detailed in Revelation 6. We anticipate that all four of the seal events will come to pass within world affairs in the immediate future. And, they will entail increased economic upheaval, war, famine, and devastating plagues.

In fact, most observers would agree that much of the above has already started. Most of the Middle East is currently in turmoil, with wars breaking out all over. The death of Muammar Gaddafi will be old news by the time you read this![2] Likewise, though we haven't necessarily seen any devastating plagues yet, every country in the world seems to be going through economic turmoil of one kind or another. In our own country, the officially acknowledged unemployment figures hover around 9 percent, while the real number is probably closer to 19 or 20 percent, or more. And no one is quite sure what will be the long-term consequences of public union negotiations in Wisconsin, Ohio, and other states as well. By the time you read this the "bad-things-a-coming" litany will almost certainly be much more advanced.

In Volume 2 we also anticipated a more aggressive Russia, China, and Iran, complemented by increased friendships between Russia and the Arab nations, including Iran and Syria. We further antici-pated that the Palestinians would continue to solidify and expand their alliance against Israel, balanced against a sometimes-faltering friendship between the US and Israel and further complemented by the continued rise of the European Union – not its collapse. Finally, we anticipated wavering relations between Turkey and the West, realigning Turkey with Russia and possibly with the Arab nations as well, with war continuing to escalate in the Middle East until it spreads worldwide.

In other words, at the time of this writing, the "first preliminary acts" of all the events listed above have continued to develop, exactly as predicted.

Where We Left Off

We left our Revelation narrative in volume 2 at the death and resurrection of the two witnesses (whom we suggested will be the prophets Enoch and Elijah), the blowing of the seventh trumpet, and the beginning of the rise to power of the False Messiah and the False Prophet. While these events are still somewhat distant compared to the events that are occurring today, the second half of Revelation will reveal to us the identities of these two evil beings. Later chapters in Revelation will detail their purpose and their ultimate demise.

Meanwhile, keep in mind two specific time periods: 1,260 days and 42 months. Together they equal seven years, the last seven years of the Great Tribulation. The first 3½ years (delineated by 1,260 days) include the time of the two witnesses (Revelation 11:3). The next portion of text we'll be exploring deals with the last 3½ years, delineated by 42 months (Revelation 13:5). As we will explain, this will happen when all the plans of the False Prophet, the False Messiah, and the whore of Babylon come to fruition . . . before they fail once and for all.

Going Sideways a Moment

While we were discussing the best way to describe the next chapters of the book of Revelation, God reminded us of the parable of the weeds:

> ²⁴Jesus told them another parable: "The kingdom of heaven is like a man who sowed good seed in his field. ²⁵But while everyone was sleeping, his enemy came and sowed weeds among the wheat, and went away. ²⁶When the wheat sprouted and formed heads, then the weeds also appeared. ²⁷The owner's servants came to him and said, 'Sir, didn't you sow good seed in your field? Where then did the weeds come from?'

> [28] "'An enemy did this,' he replied. The servants asked him, 'Do you want us to go and pull them up?' [29] 'No,' he answered, 'because while you are pulling the weeds, you may root up the wheat with them. [30]Let both grow together until the harvest. At that time I will tell the harvesters: First collect the weeds and tie them in bundles to be burned; then gather the wheat and bring it into my barn.'" (Matthew 13:24–30, NIV)

This parable is the perfect illustration of what has taken place throughout all of time, specifically highlighted in the book of Revelation. It also applies to all believers on a personal level, personifying the good and the evil that we battle daily in our lives. The Lord plants good seed in the soil of our souls and the Adversary comes behind Him and sows weeds. When the seed that God planted begins to grow we then struggle against the weeds that do their best to choke God's good things out.

Remember, though – as explained in both Volumes 1 and 2 – that the Hebraic text of the Bible operates on four levels simultaneously:

1. **P'shat:** The simple or literal

2. **Remez:** Parables, hinting

3. **Darash:** Discussion, commentary

4. **Sod:** Hidden, secret, mysteries

In addition, even as the Hebraic text applies on a personal level it also applies on a corporate or universal level as well. Thus God has planted good seed (i.e., "wheat") in the earth, represented by righteous followers of Him and His Word. For the last six thousand years this wheat has germinated and grown. But now, as the final events foretold in the book of Revelation begin to unfold it becomes apparent that the time of the Great Harvest is approaching.

However, during the same six thousand years the Adversary has secretly sown bad seed, represented by devils, demons, nephilim, and those men and women who follow the Adversary's evil ways, whether willingly or because they have been deceived. On the other hand, those last two categories should probably be combined. Only someone who's been deceived at one level or another could willingly follow Satan.

Thus many weeds have grown up among the wheat. But the Creator hasn't yet pulled up the weeds, because doing so would destroy the wheat along with them. Rather, He awaits the moment when He will harvest the wheat and the weeds together, at which time He will separate one from the other.

In other words, here is one possible insight into the age-old question: Why does a loving Creator allow evil and suffering into the world?

- First, God didn't create evil. Evil is what fills the void when God is removed from – or is not allowed to be present in – the lives and the institutions of humanity.

- Second, evil and suffering do not represent God's will, but they can be by-products of a creation that refuses to follow His holy and righteous ways. For Him to allow free choice He has to allow us the possibility of rejecting Him. Evil is the tragic result of that rejection.

- Third, evil and suffering will exist for only a season. For humanity that "season" equates to seven thousand years. For God those seven thousand years are like seven days. As the Bible tells us in II Peter 3:8 (NIV):

  > But do not forget one thing: With the Lord a day is like a thousand years, and a thousand years are like a day.

Even though it sometimes feels to us like God is running late, in reality He is always right on time – literally, more punctual than any other being or force in the universe. For Him the last six thousand years have been only a week of time. Now the Sabbath is coming and we should be rejoicing!

Don't Be a Weed

As we delve into the remaining chapters and verses in the book of Revelation, we should hang on to the above awareness – that God has planted good seed while the Adversary has planted bad seed. In the text of the book of Revelation that we've explored so far we've seen the growth of the wheat and hints of the coming harvest. In the remaining text we will also see the growth and destruction of the weeds.

The difference between the two is that the wheat is gathered into the storehouse, while the weeds are bundled up and thrown into the fire. Keep in mind, however, that in accord with ancient Hebraic custom there's one other group, representing a small bit of the harvest, that will yet be left. It's still out in the field. In the Old Testament it was called the "gleanings." More about that in chapter 4 in this volume.

Right now, let's take a moment and examine the patterns and biology of weeds. First, a dictionary definition of a weed is:

- A valueless plant growing wild, especially one that grows on cultivated ground to the exclusion or injury of the desired crop.

- Any undesirable or troublesome plant, especially one that grows profusely where it is not wanted.[3]

Typically, the seeds that produce weeds (the plants often known in the Bible as "tares") are blown into an area. Or, they're already in the ground from previous growing seasons. Or, as in the case of the above parable, they can be secretly planted by an enemy. And finally, in ancient times, victorious armies would come into the lands they'd conquered, cut down all the crops, and spread salt everywhere to make it impossible to grow anything except weeds.

(This reminds us of a story in the news, in March of 2011, about a pizza parlor owner who introduced mice into the kitchens of two or three of his rivals, hoping to destroy their businesses. His intent was to tare-ify their customers, but he wound up doing a tare-ible disservice to his own. It's hard to run a restaurant from a jail cell.)

But to get serious again, because weeds usually germinate ahead of most desired, domesticated plants, they tend to steal most of the nutrients and water in the soil. And when they're fully grown they even steal much of the sunlight as well.

More insidiously, the roots of a weed become interwoven and entangled within the root systems of adjoining plants, making it impossible to remove the undesired weeds without destroying the other plants as well. Once the two groups of plants have sprouted, the owner of the field has to allow them to grow together even though the presence of the weeds may stunt the growth of the others. Something is better than nothing.

They Don't Produce Anything Good

In Scripture, weeds are metaphors for sin, for evil humanity, for untruth, and for the nephilim, all of which are in league with – or promoted by – the Adversary. Weeds are *his* seed, *his* offspring, *his* perverse desires brought to fruition. Meanwhile, wheat is used many times in Scripture to refer to righteous men and women who follow God and truth (e.g., Matthew 3:11–12). In physical terms, weeds choke the life out of wheat. From a spiritual perspective, weeds choke the purposes and goals of God out of our lives.

We could even compare the seven letters to the seven congregations as a warning from God to avoid the weeds. Such weeds sprout both from within and without our own congregations and our own circles of friends and relatives. And ultimately, if we fail to avoid them they sprout from within our own souls.

In God's Word, both the soil and the wheat represent mankind and his endeavors, personally and corporately. Wheat is a people and a kingdom, but weeds are also a people and a kingdom. One grows striving to produce life while the other grows at the expense of the first. As in the above parable, God is the farmer planting wheat. Satan is the enemy, coming in secret to sabotage God's plan to grow a crop that will bring health and life.

This parallel of wheat and weeds (God's people and Satan's minions) is paramount to understanding the next few chapters of the book of Revelation. In Volume 2 we've taken you up the right side of the master menorah, which illustrates many details of God's kingdom and His people. Now we'll be traveling up the left side of the same master menorah, which gives insights into Satan's kingdom and those who follow his evil ways. We've learned about the wheat; now we'll be learning about the weeds.

To put it another way, the letters represent God's "grand theme." What we'll discover as we work our way up the left side of the master menorah will be Satan's grand scheme. As always, Satan will try to counteract whatever God is doing by inserting into our lives his own pathetic, copycat alternative to God's divine plan, hoping thereby to lure us away from God and into the pathway that Satan prefers (see Figure I-1).

Where We're Going

In this volume of *Lost in Translation* we will continue our adventure of discovery through the pages of perhaps the most mysterious yet the most important book of the Bible for those of us who might live through the end times. We will continue to explore and reveal God's plan for all of His creation – specifically, His Bride. We will also continue to identify and reveal the Adversary's role, his sinister schemes, and his ultimate fate at the hand of God.

At the same time we will examine certain portions of the books of Joel, Isaiah, Ezekiel, and especially Daniel, all of which are vital to a full understanding of the book of Revelation itself. Each of these portions of Scripture provides meaningful insights into the events of Revelation now unfolding – or likely to unfold in the coming years – before our very eyes.

The only request we make of you, our readers, is that you read Volumes 1 and 2 before you dive into this one, Volume 3. Otherwise, because these three volumes build on one another, some of what we say in the pages ahead might not be entirely clear and comprehensible.

Now . . . let's get started . . . again!

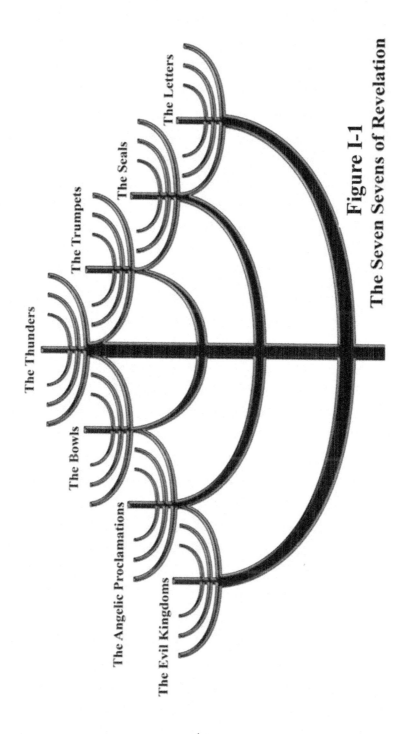

Figure I-1

The Seven Sevens of Revelation

The Thunders

The Trumpets

The Seals

The Letters

The Bowls

The Angelic Proclamations

The Evil Kingdoms

Chapter 1

Three Wars Ahead

BEFORE WE FOCUS ON SATAN'S WEEDS (THE SEVEN EVIL KINGDOMS), LET us first build up and extend our foundation a bit more, so we can put the events that follow in their proper context. At the end of Volume 2 of this three-volume series we focused on the events of the sixth trumpet, as detailed in Revelation 9:

> [13]The sixth angel sounded his trumpet, and I heard a voice coming from the horns of the golden altar that is before God. [14]It said to the sixth angel who had the trumpet, "Release the four angels who are bound at the great river Euphrates." [15]And the four angels who had been kept ready for this very hour and day and month and year were released to kill a third of mankind. [16]The number of the mounted troops was two hundred million. I heard their number.
>
> [17]The horses and riders I saw in my vision looked like this: Their breastplates were fiery red, dark blue, and yellow as sulfur. The heads of the horses resembled the heads of lions, and out of their mouths came fire, smoke and sulfur. [18]A third of mankind was killed by the three plagues of fire, smoke and sulfur that came out of their

mouths. [19]The power of the horses was in their mouths and in their tails; for their tails were like snakes, having heads with which they inflict injury.

[20]The rest of mankind that were not killed by these plagues still did not repent of the work of their hands; they did not stop worshiping demons, and idols of gold, silver, bronze, stone and wood – idols that cannot see or hear or walk. [21]Nor did they repent of their murders, their magic arts, their sexual immorality or their thefts. (Revelation 9:13–21, NIV)

A Great War Breaks Out

As the sixth trumpet was blown a great war broke out. It was a war between what appeared to be mythical beasts, allied with certain men who were riding atop the beasts and arrayed against the rest of mankind. One-third of mankind was destroyed by fire, smoke, and brimstone that came from these evil beasts.

The overlaying of end-times biblical prophecies on the master menorah increases our understanding of those events by connecting and expanding them. This helps explain certain events described in one prophetic biblical text versus another. Ezekiel 38–39 certainly substantiates this. This prophetic Old Testament passage is a detailed explanation of the events surrounding and including the sixth trumpet.

In addition we can coordinate most truths, including biblical, historical, and scientific facts, in this same manner by overlaying them on the master menorah. The seven covenants, Hebrew betrothal, the different types of fools, the attributes of light, and the four forces that govern creation[1] are all examples of this phenomenon. We will soon see how history (e.g., the seven evil kingdoms) fits on top of the master menorah as well.

In Volume 2 we concluded by describing the events of the sixth trumpet – a great war in which Russia and her allies attacked Israel, which is the same war mentioned directly above. Now, before we continue our study of Revelation, let's take a closer look at how these events are amplified in the book of Ezekiel.

> [1]And the word of the LORD came to me saying, [2]"Son of man, set your face toward Gog of the land of Magog, the prince of Rosh, Meshech and Tubal, and prophesy against him [3]and say, 'Thus says the Lord GOD, "Behold, I am against you, O Gog, prince of Rosh, Meshech and Tubal.
>
> [4]"I will turn you about and put hooks into your jaws, and I will bring you out, and all your army, horses and horsemen, all of them splendidly attired, a great company with buckler and shield, all of them wielding swords; [5]Persia, Ethiopia and Put with them, all of them with shield and helmet; [6]Gomer with all its troops; Beth-togarmah from the remote parts of the north with all its troops—many peoples with you.
>
> [7]"Be prepared, and prepare yourself, you and all your companies that are assembled about you, and be a guard for them. [8]After many days you will be summoned; in the latter years you will come into the land that is restored from the sword, whose inhabitants have been gathered from many nations to the mountains of Israel which had been a continual waste; but its people were brought out from the nations, and they are living securely, all of them. [9]You will go up, you will come like a storm; you will be like a cloud covering the land, you and all your troops, and many peoples with you." (Ezekiel 38:1–9)

Ezekiel 38–39 describes a great war between Israel and Magog. This passage includes a list of those who will ally themselves together in the sixth trumpet war:

- **Persia** – The Persians are believed to be descendants of Japheth (one of the three sons of Noah) through his son Madai (see Genesis 10:2). The center of the Persian Empire today is Iran. In ancient times the Persian Empire included western Asia between the Black Sea, the Caucus Mountains, the Caspian Sea, and the

Jaxartes River on the north; the Arabian Desert, the Persian Gulf, and the Indian Ocean on the south.

- **Cush/Ethiopia** – Cush, a grandson of Ham (one of the three sons of Noah), migrated south from Mount Ararat into Africa, specifically into Ethiopia, Sudan and southern Egypt.

- **Phut** – Commonly known as *Put* today, Phut represents the people who live in and around the nation of Libya in northern Africa. They are also descendants of Noah through his son Ham.

- **Gomer** – Listed in Genesis 10:2, Gomer is one of the sons of Japheth. Many scholars believe that Gomer's descendants became known as *Cimmerians*. During the 8th and 7th centuries BC they inhabited the region north of the Caucus Mountains and the Black Sea. Today this area would be in the Ukraine and part of Russia. Other scholars expand this area to include the steppes of Eurasia, which encompass the land mass from Hungary to Mongolia. Gesenius identifies the Gomerites as the Armenians. All the above opinions agree generally that the descendants of Gomer migrated to the north of Mount Ararat, but south of central Russia.

- **Togarmah** – Togarmah was the third son of Gomer and the grandson of Japheth, according to the Table of Nations in Genesis 10. Some scholars suggest that Togarmah today represents the peoples known as the Armenians, Georgians, and Turks. Generally, these peoples migrated to the land areas between the Caspian and Black Seas.

- **Magog/Gog** – The Hebrew construction of the word *Magog* would suggest that the *Ma-* combined with *gog* means "from the land of Gog." Magog is the second son of Japheth (see Genesis 10:2). Many scholars identify Magog's descendents as living in the land that lies to the north and east of the Black Sea, including also the lands north and northeast of the Caspian Sea. Today this would be Russia.

- **Meshech** – Genesis 10:2 lists Meshech as one of the sons of Japheth. Josephus provides evidence that equates the descendants of Tubal with the capitol city of Georgia, T'bilisi, which means "land of Tubal."

- **Tubal** – This name also occurs in the Table of Nations as another of the sons of Japheth. The Tubalite people lived in the area of the Black Sea. Many scholars believe that they gave rise to the Caucasian Iberians, the ancestors of modern Georgians. The word *Tubal* itself is also considered to be an ancient Georgian tribal designation.

The above people groups include the north and northeastern nations of Africa today, excluding Egypt. Their additional allies, coming from north of Israel, would include the nations of Iran and Turkey, all the nations around the Black and Caspian Seas, and the large nation that lies even farther north – Russia. We know that the descendants of Japheth migrated north and west from Mount Ararat in Turkey. They would eventually inhabit all of Europe, from the British Isles to the Caucus mountain range in Russia.

However, the descendants of Magog went north and settled in the area we now know as Russia. Many of the sons of Ham migrated south into Africa. So, in the second war in Revelation (the sixth trumpet war, Revelation 9:13–19) the descendants of Ham and Japheth will be attacking Israel. In contrast, in the first war represented by the red horse rider of the second seal (Revelation 6:4), the attackers are mostly Semitic peoples (Shem) with the exception of the Canaanites (Ham) and Assyrians (Japheth).

Today, it's not accidental that we see Turkey disassociating itself from its western allies, NATO and Israel, and beginning to shift alliances toward the Russian sphere. Expect that to continue as a fulfillment of prophecy.

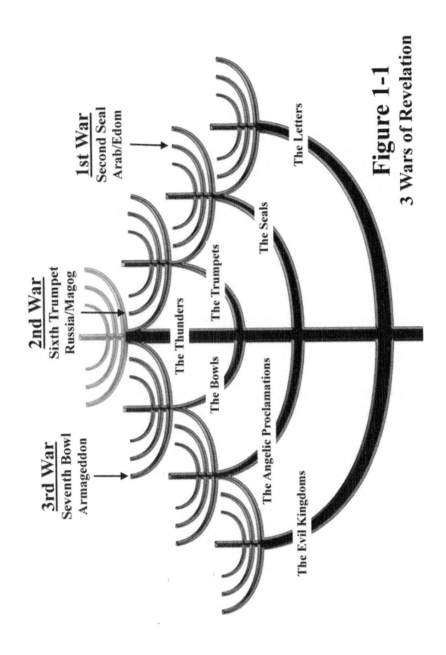

Figure 1-1
3 Wars of Revelation

1st War
Second Seal
Arab/Edom

2nd War
Sixth Trumpet
Russia/Magog

3rd War
Seventh Bowl
Armageddon

The Letters

The Seals

The Trumpets

The Thunders

The Bowls

The Angelic Proclamations

The Evil Kingdoms

The First Ring of Nations

The nations identified as allying themselves together to "come against Israel," in the three pre-millennial wars, are arrayed in three distinct geographic "rings" around the land of Israel itself. Logically enough, the nations within the closest ring attack first, while those in the second and third rings attack in that order. Thus Israel's end-times enemies arise from nations situated farther and farther out, until virtually the entire world gets involved.

As the world map shows, the allies within the first ring form a circle in the Middle East, with Israel at the center. Of course, Israel is the nation they will all attack, hoping to destroy it but intending to do so only *after* they have raped the land and pillaged its wealth.

Psalm 83 prophesies the second seal war and gives a list of the allies that attack Israel from the innermost ring in the end times. This is the first war of Revelation and is represented by the red horse rider back in Revelation 6, when the text introduces us to the seven seals.

> ¹O God, do not remain quiet;
>   Do not be silent and, O God, do not be still.
> ²For behold, Your enemies make an uproar,
>   And those who hate You have exalted themselves.
> ³They make shrewd plans against Your people,
>   And conspire together against Your treasured ones.
> ⁴They have said, "Come, and let us wipe them out as a nation,
>   That the name of Israel be remembered no more."
> ⁵For they have conspired together with one mind;
>   Against You they make a covenant:
> ⁶The tents of Edom and the Ishmaelites,
>   Moab and the Hagrites;
> ⁷Gebal and Ammon and Amalek,
>   Philistia with the inhabitants of Tyre;
> ⁸Assyria also has joined with them;
>   They have become a help to the children of Lot.
> (Psalm 83:1–8)

Psalm 83 is an excellent example of an Old Testament prophecy that provides incomparable insight into a briefly described future event foretold in Revelation 6:3–4. This ancient prophecy describes the same war that the Apostle John describes when he writes about the second horseman, the red horse rider who will take peace from the earth.

However, the list in verses 6 through 8 does not match the list of Israel's attackers in Ezekiel, making it clear that these passages refer to two different wars. Whereas Ezekiel's list includes peoples and nations that surround the Middle East, the allies mentioned in Psalm 83 circle Israel as well but are located in immediate contact with Israel's borders.

This latter group of allies, listed in Psalm 83, includes:

- **Edom** – Arabs – and yes, the Arabs descended from Esau, not Ishmael. These people today make up most of the populations of the nations that constitute the Middle East, except for Turkey, Iran, and Egypt. Thus, most of those who currently surround Israel are Edomites/Arabs.

- **The Ishmaelites** – Bedouin and Kurds. These people do not constitute any nation today, but have genetically mixed with those living in the nations surrounding Israel. The Kurds are concentrated in northern Iraq, eastern Turkey, and western Iran.

- **Moab** – The ancient Moabites lived in what is now southern Jordan. Today they've been inbred into most of the surrounding people groups. Their bloodline comes from the incestuous union between Lot and his daughters.

- **Hagrites** – The ancient Hagrites lived in the western parts of what is now Saudi Arabia and still live there today.

- **Gebal** – Modern-day Gebal includes the mountainous regions of the southern Dead Sea region. These people have inbred with other Arab groups living in the region today.

- **Ammon** – The Ammonites are another group of people who came from the union of Lot and his daughters, living today in Jordan. Their capital, Amman, is named after this ancient ancestor.

- **Amalek** – Amalek himself was one of Esau's progeny. Collectively, Amalek's descendants became know as the Amalekites. They were the ones who attacked the Israelites just after the Red Sea crossing. Four centuries later, Saul, the first king of Israel, was instructed by God to destroy these people. Instead, because of Saul's disobedience, God's people were almost destroyed by Haman, an Amalekite who descended from one of those whom Saul allowed to survive. These people have inbred with other Arab groups living in the region today. Originally, the Amalekites lived in the Sinai Peninsula, immediately to the south of Israel.

- **Tyre/Philistia** – The inhabitants of Tyre, including its sister city Sidon, were known by the Greeks as Phoenicians but known by the ancient Hebrews as the descendents of Canaan. Recall that Canaan was the cursed son of Ham, who was the son of Noah. These people lived to the immediate north of Israel, known to-day as Lebanon. They have also inbred into the local Arab tribes living today around Israel.

- **Assyria** – This nation, 2,700 years ago, was centered in the land we know today as Iran. Certainly Psalm 83:8 foretells that Assyria will play a supporting role in the second seal war, for just as the text predicts, Iran is already joining with the other enemies of Israel by supplying them with military materials and advisors.

Who Were Those Phoenicians?

Some historians have suggested that the Philistines and the inhabitants of Tyre came from the Phoenicians, the Greek name for the seafaring people who colonized the coastlands of the Mediterranean Sea. The Philistines lived in the area now known as Gaza, and they probably do share some bloodlines with the Phoenicians.

The cities of Tyre and Sidon were located in what is known as Lebanon today. However, their inhabitants, and those in the surrounding countryside, were not known as Phoenicians in the Bible. The Israelites recognized them as Canaanites, well known as those who were dwelling in the Promised Land when

---

the Hebrews arrived after escaping from Egypt around 1450 BC. According to Genesis 10, the Canaanites were the descendants of Ham. They were the ones whom God cursed when their father, Ham, sinned against his father, Noah. The Greeks knew them as the Phoenicians.

The Second Ring of Nations

The Bible contains multiple prophecies about the Edomites who will attack Israel. Indeed, taken together, Isaiah 34–35, Ezekiel 35, and the entire book of Obadiah (one chapter!) all foretell the same end-times war. They describe in great detail more of the events that surround the Psalm 83 war, and identify both the attackers and their allies.

Unfortunately for Israel, in these two end-times wars (first one attacked by Arabs; second one attacked by Russians and their allies) they get attacked two different times by two groups of people, which confirms the predictions found in our study of Revelation.

These two groups of attackers would form two rings around Israel. The first ring would be peoples from lands that are mostly contiguous with the borders of Israel. The second group of allies that attack Israel, led by Gog and Magog, form a ring that surrounds Israel but doesn't physically touch its borders.

The Gog Pictograph

The Hebrew letters that spell the word *Gog* are *gimel/vav/gimel*. The pictographic understanding of these letters is to "lift up the covenant of pride."

This is an extremely fitting description of Russia and its leaders. As dogmatic atheists, the Russian leaders have been opposed to religion of any sort, but especially to Christianity and Judaism. They have opposed any representation of God, the church, or any other organizations that would spread any ideas about the Christian and/or Jewish Bible in the nations they have ruled over.

They have killed and persecuted millions of people during the last 100 years, destroying their places of worship by turning them into museums or using them in any way other than the original purposes intended by their builders.

The Hebrew letters that spell the word *Magog* are *mem/gimel/vav/gimel*. The pictographic meaning here is to "lift up the covenant of pride *and chaos*." The word Magog can also refer to the location where the people of Gog live, which is "the land of Gog."

Certainly the history of Russia illustrates what happens when you manage your life and country without including God and His core values. Abuse, death camps, utter disregard for human life and freedom, and management by fear are all the results of a prideful, chaotic, godless society.

However, fortunately for Israel, in both of these first two wars God steps forward to defend and defeat their foes, just as He has done in sometimes miraculous ways since the founding of Israel as a separate nation in 1948. Gog and Magog's destruction (i.e., that of Russia) is foretold in the following passage:

> [18]"It will come about on that day, when Gog comes against the land of Israel," declares the Lord GOD, "that My fury will mount up in My anger. [19]In My zeal and in My blazing wrath I declare that on that day there will surely be a great earthquake in the land of Israel. [20]The fish of the sea, the birds of the heavens, the beasts of the field, all the creeping things that creep on the earth, and all the men who are on the face of the earth will shake at My presence; the mountains also will be thrown down, the steep pathways will collapse and every wall will fall to the ground.
>
> [21]"I will call for a sword against him on all My mountains," declares the Lord GOD. "Every man's sword will be against his brother. [22]With pestilence and with blood I will enter into judgment with him; and I will rain on

> him and on his troops, and on the many peoples who
> are with him, a torrential rain, with hailstones, fire and
> brimstone. [23]I will magnify Myself, sanctify Myself, and
> make Myself known in the sight of many nations; and
> they will know that I am the LORD." (Ezekiel 38:18–23)

At the end of Volume 2 in this series we noted that, at the conclusion of this sixth trumpet war between Israel and Russia (Magog), the Revelation text reveals that only seven years remain before the arrival of the true King, coming on a white horse to set up His millennial kingdom. Remember that what follows the sixth-trumpet war in Revelation will be the 3½ years of the two witnesses and the 3½ years of the beast's kingdom. This amounts to a total of seven years, at the end of which we have Armageddon.

Ezekiel 39 contains an interesting reference to the destruction of Gog and Magog. It says that, in the land of Israel, the Israelites will be picking up Gog's weapons and using them for fuel for seven years. We don't know whether they will run out of weapons to burn at the end of that time, but we do believe that that's when God will come back and set up His kingdom.

This also suggests a vastly devolved economic state of the world during these last seven years. Why else would someone with access to today's technology opt to burn weapons, probably wooden, for heating?

The Third Ring of Nations

In the third war, which virtually all biblical scholars refer to as *Armageddon*, the allies who attack Israel come from lands that form a ring even farther out. However, rather than identifying those allies at this point, we will discuss this war in far greater detail in chapter 7 of this volume.

What About Those Rings?

With respect to the nations and people groups that make up Israel's end-times attackers, there's one more set of what some might call "coincidences" that tie the members of each group together.

Most of the attackers in the first ring descended from brothers, representing the inheritance covenant. Most of the attackers in the second ring, which would represent the friendship covenant, come from lands that used to be friendly with Israel. The attackers in the third ring have all had relatively little direct contact with Israel over the years, but nonetheless they have allied themselves together to destroy Israel and commandeer all her resources, both natural and developed.

Question: Will there be some sort of counter-covenant going on here, whereby Satan will rally those who will help him oppose Israel? For example, is it just coincidental that the first ring includes brothers of Israel? Is it accidental that the second ring includes groups that were once mostly friendly toward Israel?

To continue the covenant concept, the third group would include those with the most distant relationships with Israel, both now and in the ancient past.

Meanwhile, keep in mind that, as we arrived at the end of chapter 11 in the book of Revelation in Volume 2 in this series, we also arrived at the beginning of the last seven years before the return of the King. These last seven years begin with the appearance of the two witnesses. The witnesses will be given authority for 1,260 days (approximately 3½ years), at the end of which they will be killed and then resurrected. The beginning of the last 42 months (also 3½ years) will be identified by the blowing of the seventh and last trumpet (I Corinthians 15:51–54).

Upon the death of the two witnesses at the hand of Abaddon, the False Prophet, the False Messiah establishes his godhead by announcing to the world that he "is God," at which point he sits on God's throne in the Temple in Jerusalem.

On the master menorah the midpoint was reached by the blowing of the seventh trumpet. However, God in His great wisdom sees fit to digress here and give us more historical background. Starting in Revelation 12, the text takes us back in time and gives us more information about our Adversary.

His identity, description, purpose, and plan are all revealed here, making it plain to anyone who will listen that he is not worthy of our attention, love, obedience, and adoration. However, most of us will somehow miss these clear warnings.

It's important for mankind to understand that God really does have a plan for each one who chooses Him. But God also has an overall plan, extending from the beginning of creation to its final conclusion, which He's revealing here in the book of Revelation. We get to choose whether to be part of His grand plan . . . or not.

However, from the beginning of time until now, Satan has also had a substitute plan, and his endgame is described in the next few chapters of this volume. He's all about stealing our identity and our authority, and in the end he will attempt to steal God's identity and authority as well. In fact, for a while he will rule and reign with what will appear to be most of God's own authority, and he will thereby claim to be God Himself. Much of mankind will be deceived by that claim, and by the false evidence of Satan's power and authority. The key for each of us lies in how we apply the word "self" to our own lives. Are we *selfish* or *selfless*?

In Summary . . .

As we close this chapter and move into our discussion of the seven evil kingdoms, let's recall what will happen just before the last of the seven evil kingdoms comes into focus.

Psalm 83 and Ezekiel 38–39 both prophesy two great wars in the last days, between Israel and the Arabs and between Israel and Magog. Both of these foes bring many allies to each of the conflicts. However, Ezekiel and the author of Psalm 83 each identify different groups of attackers.

- Psalm 83 lists a group of end-times attackers who surround Israel but are also in immediate contact with her borders. These include the Edomites (Arabs, descended mostly from Esau), the

Ishmaelites (Bedouins and Kurds), the Moabites (in southern Jordan, descended from Lot and his daughters), the Hagrites (Arabs in western Saudi Arabia), the Gebalites (from the mountain regions around the southern Red Sea), and the Ammonites (descendents of Lot and his daughters, now living in Jordan). These also include (1) the descendants of Canaan, concentrated today in Lebanon, and (2), in a supporting role, the Assyrians who are known today as the Iranians.

- Ezekiel 38–39 identifies Magog as the leader of the second group of Israel's end-times attackers. The descendants of Magog, who was one of the sons of Japheth as recorded in Genesis 10:2, migrated north and settled in Russia.

- Ezekiel 38–39 also identifies a number of Magog's allies. Together this group surrounds Israel, but none are in immediate contact with Israel's borders. These include Persia (Iran, now directly involved in attacking Israel whereas, in the previous war, they acted only in a supporting role), Cush (Sudan and Ethiopia), Put (Libya), Gomer (Ukraine and Russia), and Togarmah (Armenians, Georgians, and Turks).

What Does Daniel Have to Say?

Here's one of the more familiar passages from Daniel:

> [24]"Seventy weeks have been decreed for your people and your holy city, to finish the transgression, to make an end of sin, to make atonement for iniquity, to bring in everlasting righteousness, to seal up vision and prophecy and to anoint the most holy place. [25]So you are to know and discern that from the issuing of a decree to restore and rebuild Jerusalem until Messiah the Prince there will be seven weeks and sixty-two weeks; it will be built again, with plaza and moat, even in times of distress.
> [26]"Then after the sixty-two weeks the Messiah will be cut off and have nothing, and the people of the

> prince who is to come will destroy the city and the
> sanctuary And its end will come with a flood; even
> to the end there will be war; desolations are deter-
> mined. [27]And he will make a firm covenant with the
> many for one week, but in the middle of the week
> he will put a stop to sacrifice and grain offering; and
> on the wing of abominations will come one who
> makes desolate, even until a complete destruction,
> one that is decreed, is poured out on the one who
> makes desolate." (Daniel 9:24–27)

Many prognosticators mistakenly assume that this passage from Daniel refers to the Great Tribulation, and that it lasts only seven years.

However, the seven years Daniel referred to in verse 27 constitute the final seven years, which are actually just a portion of the total tribulation period prophesied in the book of Revelation. The tribulation in Revelation starts in chapter 6 and is defined all the way through chapter 19.

Meanwhile, the Ezekiel prophecy contains an especially interesting passage with respect to Magog:

> "Then those who inhabit the cities of Israel will
> go out and make fires with the weapons and burn
> them, both shields and bucklers, bows and arrows,
> war clubs and spears, and for seven years they will
> make fires of them." (Ezekiel 39:9)

This verse describes events that will occur in the immediate aftermath of the miraculous destruction of the army of Gog. For seven years the weapons of Gog will be used to fuel fires in the land of Israel. Why only seven years? Does the supply run out at the end of seven years, or is something else happening here?

We believe that the time period is seven years because only seven years are left before the coming of the King! When the Messiah comes there will be no need to make such collections in the land of Israel, for the land will be cleansed of such things when He sets up His kingdom. This confirms the text of Revelation and the understanding of the sixth trumpet representing the Magog attack on Israel, as described in Ezekiel 38 and 39.

This seven years, in which the inhabitants of Israel collect weapons and burn them, is the same seven-year time period in the book of Revelation, in which the first half features the time of the two witnesses while the second half features the ruling and reigning of the False Messiah. All of this constitutes a period of seven years that occur after the second-seal war and all the other seal disasters, and all of the catastrophic events described in the first 5½ trumpets, including the world war that Gog and Magog will initiate. These events, which fall outside the last seven years, certainly sound like a tribulation period as well.

Chapter 2
Shamash of the Seven
Evil Kingdoms

IN VOLUME 2 IN THIS SERIES WE BRIEFLY DISCUSSED AN EXTREMELY IMPORTANT yet rarely recognized aspect of the text of Revelation. Just as most modern movies contain a main plot, often called a main thread or storyline, the book of Revelation contains a main storyline as well. But just as many modern movies also contain parallel storylines introducing subplots that enrich and embellish the main one, Revelation also contains one major subplot.

Unfortunately, that subplot often gets confused with the main plot, which can lead to a lot more confusion.

The Real Subplot – Multiple Disasters

The more obvious storyline of Revelation, considered by most scholars to be the *main* storyline but which our research indicates is actually the *subplot*, consists of end-times disasters, plagues, wars, and judgments of God on the earth and the people who dwell there. In Volume 2 in this series we demonstrated that these events formed a clear timeline that could be organized – and thereby better understood – by viewing it as a series of mini-menorah events arranged on a large master menorah (see Figure I-1). We then started with the extreme right side of the master menorah and covered the first four mini-menorahs, the first three of which featured seven major end-times events (or "lights") discussed in considerable detail.

Those three mini-menorahs, in order, were the letter, seal, and trumpet mini-menorahs. Together they included a total of twenty-one separate and distinct events, all arranged in a strict chronological sequence, based on the Scriptures. This visual layout allows us to identify where we are, at any given time, in relation to other events that are either about to happen or have already transpired.

Even more important, knowing where we are in the overall sequence lets us know exactly where we are in relation to the conclusion of the 6,000-year time period that God has given to mankind. We will complete our discussion of this overall chronology in this third volume when we cover the seven bowls, which are a continuation of the letter-seal-trumpet chronology.

The other three mini-menorahs, one of which we covered in Volume 2 (thunders), all describe events that occur *concurrently* with the four chronological mini-menorahs, whose events occur *sequentially*. The two mini-menorahs that contain the concurrent events, which we will talk about in this volume, are the evil kingdoms and the angelic proclamations mini-menorahs.

The 6,000-year time period that we mentioned above will be followed immediately by the one-thousand-year reign. These two time periods are separated by the greatest event in human history, looked forward to by literally millions (and probably billions) of people who have dedicated their lives to the Lord. Of course we are referring to the coming of the King on His white horse, at which point He will put an end to rebellion and set up His kingdom and His government. Unfortunately for many, His second coming will also put an end to the span of time during which all of us have the opportunity to prepare ourselves for eternity.

Remember, He has already come once, in the flesh, as a man whom much of the world now knows as *Jesus Christ* even though *Yeshua* was his actual Hebrew name.

The Real Main Plot – Two Brides, Two Destinies

As we indicated a few paragraphs earlier, the *main plot* in Revelation, focusing on the events that lead directly to the Wedding of the Lamb, often gets confused with the subplot. The main plot literally details the greatest expectations of the people of God and explains "one more time" how mankind can be restored to a right relationship with Him.

The sections of the Revelation text that we called shamash chapters[1] talk about this great *plan* of God. These sections are usually placed just ahead of the portions of Revelation that inform us about the events that reveal the *judgments* of God. This mirrors the format of Torah, God's foundational text, in which He details the blessings for obedience first and the curses for disobedience second. He's following the same pattern here in Revelation.

Figure 2-1 gives us a complete picture of the portions of Revelation text that describe the mini-menorah events (the judgments, which are denoted by the passages *below* each mini menorah), coupled with the shamash text (the blessings, which are denoted by the passages *above* each mini menorah) that details the preparations for the wedding. Again, these two stories actually represent the fulfillment of the blessings (for the wheat) and the curses (for the weeds) that God promised mankind through the Israelites way back in the first five books of the Bible, as detailed in Deuteronomy 27–28.

In other words, to clarify the difference one more time, here in Revelation the *curses* constitute the subplot while the *blessings* constitute the main plot. After all, in the first chapter at the very beginning of the book of Revelation (which is the first shamash chapter), Yeshua comes to John, identifies Himself, and begins to reveal the story of the marriage, which is – without question – the main plot.

43

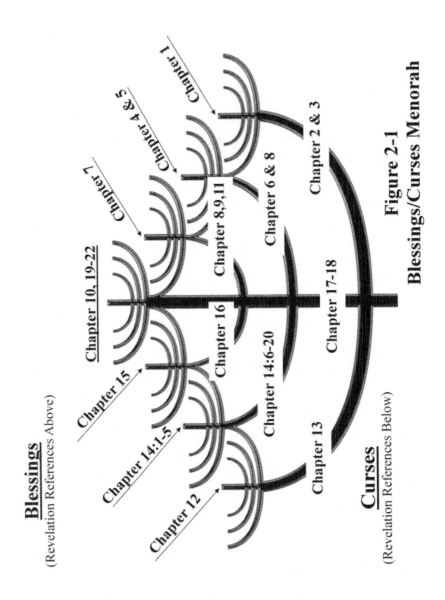

Blessings
(Revelation References Above)

Curses
(Revelation References Below)

Figure 2-1
Blessings/Curses Menorah

Chapter 1

Chapter 4 & 5

Chapter 7

Chapter 10, 19-22

Chapter 15

Chapter 14:1-5

Chapter 12

Chapter 2 & 3

Chapter 6 & 8

Chapter 8,9,11

Chapter 16

Chapter 14:6-20

Chapter 13

Chapter 17-18

Thus mankind has been informed of these things since the very beginning of time, and God has reinforced the same message over and over again during the 6,000 years that He has given us. Our destiny is in our own hands. Our choices about God and His offering of a free gift of eternal life, if we choose to cooperate with His will, will someday be measured and judged. Our relationships and obedience to Him will determine whether we partake of the curses or the blessings.

In Revelation 1, God described Himself as the First and the Last, the Creator. But He also identified Himself as the Messiah who died but lives again. Chapters 4 and 5, also shamash chapters, then focused on the throne of God and the Messiah, who was the only one able to open the mysterious scroll.

This scroll is actually a ketubah, a Hebrew wedding contract.[2] It was the Hebrew custom to allow only the groom (in this case, the Messiah) to open the wedding contract. One of the five sections of each ketubah includes the obligations of the groom and the bride. The groom reads these agreed-upon contractual obligations – joint commitments, if you will – to determine if his bride is ready.

In this case, those who are part of the Bride can never be truly ready without His ransom of our sins on the cross. It is incumbent upon us to accept His ransom, but God's Bride has done something additional as well. By accepting the covenant relationship and the responsibilities that go with it she has integrated those holy and godly principles into her life. However, this holiness does not bring her salvation; only the blood of Yeshua can do that.

In Revelation 7, which is organized into two portions, we are then introduced to the next shamash/main plot section. God's groomsmen, the 144,000, receive a special mark signifying their identity. They will also be protected from the coming judgments that are about to be poured out upon the earth in the form of the seven trumpet judgments. In the second part of this shamash chapter, the Apostle John saw a great multitude of people before the throne of God in heaven. They were holding palm branches in their hands, and it seems obvious that they were waiting for some special event to start.

Of course! They are the guests at the soon-to-begin wedding of the Lamb. We know they are guests because they are *before* the throne, not *under the chuppah* that covers the throne of God. And they have palm branches in their hands.

In ancient times the bride and groom would be honored as kings and queens on their wedding day. This was signified by the laying down of palm branches in their path for them to walk on. In that era the people would honor the real king of their country in the same way. Thus the guests in Revelation 7 are preparing to honor their king and queen in an identical manner.

At this point in John's vision, prior shamash chapters have introduced us to the Father of the Groom, the Groom Himself, and His grooms-men. They have also detailed the preparations at the site of the wedding and the gathering of the guests.

In Volume 2, when we discussed the seven thunders of Revelation 10 we indicated that for the first time Revelation included no introductory or shamash section of text introducing the next set of seven mini-menorah judgments. It appears that the shamash/mini-menorah pattern was broken, but in actuality the two were synonymous. This happened because this particular mini-menorah occupied the shamash position itself at the very top of the master menorah. The shamash and the thunder mini-menorah itself were one and the same, as seen in Figure I-1.

At this climax, when He read the ketubah (i.e., "thundered forth"), God revealed to us His principles for holy living, which were also the marriage obligations. The Bride was identified even more clearly when the ketubah described the kind of works she had been doing. These are also the very same principles by which God will judge mankind.

The Fifth Shamash

Instead of being on the fifth mini-menorah (the next one in chronological time), chapter 12 is located on the seventh mini-menorah on the master menorah, the one to the far *left*. Just as the first mini-menorah

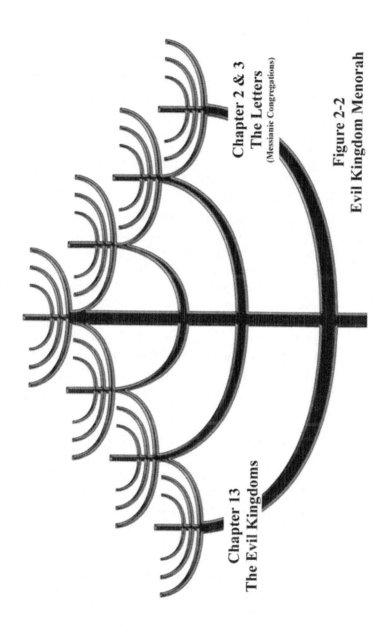

Chapter 2 & 3
The Letters
(Messianic Congregations)

Figure 2-2
Evil Kingdom Menorah

Chapter 13
The Evil Kingdoms

revealed God's original plan of covenant with mankind, which He has pursued for the last 6,000 years, the seventh mini-menorah and the shamash on the lower left reveal the workings of Satan as well.

The shamash of the seventh mini-menorah tells of events that occur just before the snatching of the Bride. Those events also detail the thinking and planning of our Adversary. This shamash reveals the Bride, but also her Adversary, the Dragon/Satan. The events in this shamash chapter are described in Revelation 12:

> [1]A great and wondrous sign appeared in heaven: a woman clothed with the sun, with the moon under her feet and a crown of twelve stars on her head. [2]She was pregnant and cried out in pain as she was about to give birth. [3]Then another sign appeared in heaven: an enormous red dragon with seven heads and ten horns and seven crowns on his heads. [4]His tail swept a third of the stars out of the sky and flung them to the earth. The dragon stood in front of the woman who was about to give birth, so that he might devour her child the moment it was born. [5]She gave birth to a son, a male child, who will rule all the nations with an iron scepter. And her child was snatched up to God and to his throne. [6]The woman fled into the desert to a place prepared for her by God, where she might be taken care of for 1,260 days.
>
> [7]And there was war in heaven. Michael and his angels fought against the dragon, and the dragon and his angels fought back. [8]But he was not strong enough, and they lost their place in heaven. [9]The great dragon was hurled down – that ancient serpent called the devil, or Satan, who leads the whole world astray. He was hurled to the earth, and his angels with him. (Revelation 12:1–9, NIV)

Keep in mind that we are studying a shamash chapter, and we are anxious to have the Bride revealed. Thus it's especially intriguing that this chapter starts out by describing a woman. There has been much speculation on whom this woman is and what the above text is all about, so let's take a closer look.

First, we see her standing with the moon under her feet. Ancient Hebrew writings reveal that, among other things, the moon symbolized Israel. It was thought to represent God's people because we are a reflection of His light, not the source, just as the moon reflects the light from the sun. All this is confirmed by the twelve-stars-on-her-head description that follows. Clearly, the twelve stars represent the twelve tribes of Israel.

The Hebrew word for crown is *nazar*, which is the root word for *Nazarite*. This word means *to take a vow, to consecrate oneself, to separate oneself, to abstain*. In Torah a Nazarite was a person who took a special vow of obedience to God. God's instructions to the Nazarite included not cutting one's hair, not touching dead bodies, and setting oneself apart in actions, deeds, and motives. This is the vow that Samson made with God in the book of Judges.

More Than One Meaning

The word *nazar* also means *crown*. One who wears a crown is set apart from others and is recognized as being different. In the case of this woman, the crown tells us that she, too, is set apart. Therefore her actions, thoughts, and motives have to be worthy of this royal designation.

Beginning when Israel received the Torah and extending into the B'rit Hadashah (i.e., the New Testament), Israel was referred to many times in the text as God's Bride:

> "Lift up your eyes and look around; All of them gather together, they come to you. As I live," declares the LORD, "You will surely put on all of them as jewels and bind them on as a bride." (Isaiah 49:18)

> I will rejoice greatly in the LORD, My soul will exult in my God; For He has clothed me with garments of salvation, He has wrapped me with a robe of righteousness, As a bridegroom decks himself with a garland, And as a bride adorns herself with her jewels. (Isaiah 61:10)

"Can a virgin forget her ornaments, or a bride her attire? Yet My people have forgotten Me days without number." (Jeremiah 2:32)

. . . the voice of joy and the voice of gladness, the voice of the bridegroom and the voice of the bride, the voice of those who say," Give thanks to the LORD of hosts, For the LORD is good, For His lovingkindness is everlasting"; and of those who bring a thank offering into the house of the LORD. For I will restore the fortunes of the land as they were at first,' says the LORD. (Jeremiah 33:11)

And Jesus said to them, "The attendants of the bridegroom cannot mourn as long as the bridegroom is with them, can they? But the days will come when the bridegroom is taken away from them, and then they will fast." (Matthew 9:15)

"He who has the bride is the bridegroom; but the friend of the bridegroom, who stands and hears him, rejoices greatly because of the bridegroom's voice. So this joy of mine has been made full." (John 3:29)

In ancient times, the bride and groom were recognized as king and queen and the bride was given a crown to wear. Is the Revelation text giving additional information about the Bride of Yeshua? Yes – this woman is Israel herself, representing the Bride.

Our Messiah Was a Jew

Yeshua was a Jew. We say this because many people don't seem to be aware of His true ancestry, as confirmed in many places in the Bible. The gospels give us his lineage. Many Old Testament prophecies inform us about His heritage. And they all agree that His human heritage was distinctly Jewish, Israelite, and Hebrew.

Chapter 12 in the book of Revelation takes us back 2,000 years to the time of Yeshua's birth. It reveals, from God's point of view, exactly what was taking place in the heavens while an Israelite woman was giving birth to the Messiah, who would someday take back His earthly throne. Revelation 9:15 tells us that "He will rule them [i.e., the nations] with a rod of iron," which clearly links Him to His messianic identification.

Here in chapter 12 it seems that someone was not especially happy about the birth of Yeshua and attempted to destroy the child as soon as He was born. This being is described as an enormous red dragon with seven heads, sprouting ten horns and seven crowns.

This dragon is Satan, who reappears in chapter 13. We will study him in detail then, to discover why God chose to describe Satan in this way. But for now, note the main parallel between the Adversary's attempts to destroy Yeshua as soon as He was born and those of Herod, the king of the Jews at the time. Remember that Herod ordered the killing of all male babies two years old and younger when he realized that the wise men were not coming back to tell him where the newborn child (the Messiah) was.

In Volume 1 of this series we explained the difference between devils and demons. The sad history of the fallen angels who chose to follow the Dragon's deceptions (and thereby became devils) is described here in chapter 12. They are the stars that are swept from the sky and thrown to the earth, which says a lot about the authority and the place of honor they once enjoyed. However, their destinies will be much worse than if they had only been condemned to live out their existence here on the earth.

In the Old Testament, these fallen angels have access to heaven and the throne of God as shown in this short extract from the book of Job:

> [6]Now there was a day when the sons of God came to present themselves before the LORD, and Satan also came among them. [7]The LORD said to Satan, "From where do you come?" Then Satan answered the LORD and said, "From roaming about on the earth and walking around on it." (Job 1:6–7)

After Yeshua's resurrection this access was denied, as prophesied in the book of Daniel:

> [39]"After you there will arise another kingdom inferior to you, then another third kingdom of bronze, which will rule over all the earth [Medo-Persia and Greece].
> [40]Then there will be a fourth kingdom [Rome] as strong as iron; inasmuch as iron crushes and shatters all things, so, like iron that breaks in pieces, it will crush and break all these in pieces. [41]In that you saw the feet and toes, partly of potter's clay and partly of iron, it will be a divided kingdom; but it will have in it the toughness of iron, inasmuch as you saw the iron mixed with common clay. [42]As the toes of the feet were partly of iron and partly of pottery, so some of the kingdom will be strong and part of it will be brittle. [43]And in that you saw the iron mixed with common clay, they will combine with one another in the seed of men; but they will not adhere to one another, even as iron does not combine with pottery." (Daniel 2:39–43)

The above passage describes Nebuchadnezzar's statue, which represents the last four world empires that will come. It had feet made of iron and clay, which represent the last empire before the second coming of Yeshua. The metaphorical Hebrew understanding of iron is "angelic activity on the earth." Satan and his devils are losing the war over control of God's creation, and one of the consequences and signs of their eventual judgment by God Himself is their loss of access to His throne.

Daniel's Seven Weeks

The above passage then introduces us to the last seven years before the coming of Yeshua on His white horse, as a conquering commander, with His army following Him. This seven-year period was originally revealed to God's people more than 2,500 years ago, through Daniel.

> [44]"In the days of those kings the God of heaven will set up a kingdom which will never be destroyed, and that kingdom will not be left for another people; it will crush and put an end to all these kingdoms, but it will itself endure forever. [45]Inasmuch as you saw that a stone

was cut out of the mountain without hands and that it crushed the iron, the bronze, the clay, the silver and the gold, the great God has made known to the king what will take place in the future; so the dream is true and its interpretation is trustworthy." (Daniel 2:44–45)

In Daniel 9, God outlines 490 years (70 "weeks," or 70 times 7) in which He will fulfill His plans for Israel by bringing in His rightful government and reestablishing His rulership throughout the world.

> [24]"Seventy weeks have been decreed for your people and your holy city, to finish the transgression, to make an end of sin, to make atonement for iniquity, to bring in everlasting righteousness, to seal up vision and prophecy and to anoint the most holy place. [25]So you are to know and discern that from the issuing of a decree to restore and rebuild Jerusalem until Messiah the Prince there will be seven weeks and sixty-two weeks; it will be built again, with plaza and moat, even in times of distress.
>
> [26]"Then after the sixty-two weeks the Messiah will be cut off and have nothing, and the people of the prince who is to come will destroy the city and the sanctuary. And its end will come with a flood; even to the end there will be war; desolations are determined. [27]And he will make a firm covenant with the many for one week, but in the middle of the week he will put a stop to sacrifice and grain offering; and on the wing of abominations will come one who makes desolate, even until a complete destruction, one that is decreed, is poured out on the one who makes desolate." (Daniel 9:24–27)

Most of this prophecy was fulfilled by the proclamations to restore Jerusalem in approximately 454 BC and 30 AD, the year of the death and resurrection of our Lord. The amount of time between these two events is 483 years (69 weeks) and was predicted by Daniel centuries before. This is one of the reasons for the common belief that Daniel was not written when it was claimed to be written – in the 6th century BC – but much later. By claiming a later date, anti-biblical students can ignore this prophecy and its miraculous fulfillment. However, they must also ignore the great volumes of textual, historical, and archeological evidence that support this passage as well as the rest of the Bible.

The Final Week

The final week, representing the seven remaining years, has often been the focus of end-times students of prophecy, including the authors of these three volumes. Unfortunately, the events both preceding and during the last seven years have often been greatly misunderstood, which has led to even more serious misunderstandings with respect to the clear meanings of other unfulfilled, end-times prophecies in the Bible.

One example is the teaching that the Apostle John's vision of Revelation will be completely fulfilled in seven years. This comes from the assumption that the last seven years Daniel wrote about would contain the great end-times Tribulation, which will then end at the coming of Yeshua to take over and destroy the beast.

Many in the Christian church are waiting for the last seven years to begin, because they have been taught that the so-called "Rapture of the Church" will happen at the start of the Tribulation period. Because they believe that most of the book of Revelation prophesies only about tribulation, they then assume that they will not have to endure any of its trials. After all, the Tribulation starts at the very beginning of Revelation. Everything after that point is therefore deemed irrelevant – "If you get to go you don't need to know."

However, the actual text of Revelation has embedded within it a definite timeline, and only certain events contained in that timeline are destined to occur within one specific seven-year period. *This does not include everything that is prophesied in Revelation.* This means that a number of end-times events will fall outside the seven-year framework that many commentators try to impose on the entire book of Revelation.

The actual last seven years spoken of by Daniel are also prophesied by him to be split into two groups of 3½ years each. Revelation also talks about two 3½-year periods, just before the end. In the Hebrew calendar, 1,260 days equals 3½ years. John refers to these two equal time periods and differentiates them from each other by describing the first half in terms of days, as 1,260 days, while describing the second half in terms of months (as "forty-two months," or "time, times, and half a time"). Starting in verse 6, Revelation 12 then describes the first half of these last seven years.

Also, keep in mind that chapter 12, a shamash chapter, describes some events that happen concurrently with the sixth trumpet. Right here on the timeline God is telling us that the last seven years are about to start. The ancient prophecy of Daniel is about to be completed. As shown on our master menorah, the last seven years begin at the middle of the sixth trumpet, then include the seventh trumpet and all of the seven bowls.

Recall that the sixth trumpet is divided into two sections. The first section describes a great war between Israel and Russia that results in Russia's demise. The second section describes the 1,260 days during which the two witnesses have authority on the earth. At the end of this period of time they are killed by Abaddon and resurrected by God. The time of the two witnesses, and the 1,260 days given to the woman, are actually the same time period.

To repeat our main point here, *these 8½ lights on our 49-light master menorah (see Figure 2-3) have a duration of seven years.* Obviously, the book of Revelation foretells events that last significantly longer than that. Meanwhile, the 1,260-day period introduced in Revelation 12:6 describes the protection God provides to this woman, for the first half of the seven-year period.

Another War in Heaven

The next section of verses in chapter 12, describing Michael and his angels battling Satan and his angels and casting them from heaven, is a description of events that happened in the past, not here in the timeline in Revelation. This war is not to be confused with God's casting Satan from heaven, back in the beginning, for his original rebellion.

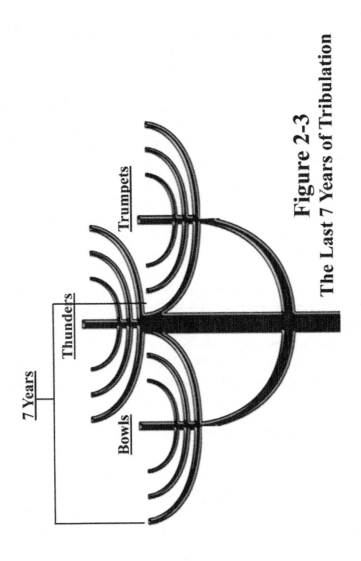

Figure 2-3
The Last 7 Years of Tribulation

This battle, described in Revelation 12, took place at the death and resurrection of Yeshua, as described in the following quote from Volume 2 in this series:

> Chapter 12 of Revelation talks about a male child who was born with a dragon (Satan) waiting to consume Him. But the dragon wasn't able to consume Him; that is, he wasn't able to cause Him to sin during any part of His life on earth, as ultimately proved by Yeshua's victory over sin on the cross.
>
> This brought on a war between Ha Satan and the archangel Michael, because Yeshua didn't succumb to Satan's temptations. Michael thus powered the righteous angelic hosts over the rebellious angelic horde, which meant that Satan lost his place in the second heaven and fell to earth (Revelation 12:7–9).
>
> To help understand all this, remember that – prior to Yeshua's triumph over sin –Satan was still able to come before the throne of God, as he did back in the book of Job. However, in a post-resurrection world Satan has been able to function only upon the earth and within its atmosphere.[3]

A Brief Aside . . . .

If you want to be the Bride of Yeshua you should be about doing the will of the Father and not forgetting what you look like. James speaks about this very issue:

> [21]Therefore, get rid of all moral filth and the evil that is so prevalent and humbly accept the word planted in you, which can save you. [22]Do not merely listen to the word, and so deceive yourselves. Do what it says. [23]Anyone who listens to the word but does not do what it says is like a man who looks at his face in a mirror [24]and, after looking at himself, goes away and immediately forgets what he looks like. [25]But the man who looks intently into the perfect law that gives freedom, and continues to do this, not

> forgetting what he has heard, but doing it – he will be blessed in what he does. (James 1:21–25, NIV)
>
> The Hebrew term for *word* in the passage above is *Torah*. This passage suggests that we should integrate Torah into our very soul so it becomes the standard that governs our every action. Our behavior, our works, and our thoughts should all mirror holiness. Yeshua said that we should look like Him. He also said in John 1:1 that He was *the Word,* which is Torah. And John was referring to the Old Testament at this point because the New Testament did not yet exist.

This fall from heaven occurred 2,000 years ago, at the resurrection of Yeshua. In Revelation 12:9 we saw the defeat of Satan and his fallen angels – their punishment is the loss of access to God's throne. Michael, whose name means "Warrior of God," led the forces of heaven against the Dragon and threw his evil horde out of the presence of God. Unfortunately for the earth, the Adversary is now confined within its borders.

> [10]Then I heard a loud voice in heaven, saying, "Now the salvation, and the power, and the kingdom of our God and the authority of His Christ have come, for the accuser of our brethren has been thrown down, he who accuses them before our God day and night. [11]And they overcame him because of the blood of the Lamb and because of the word of their testimony, and they did not love their life even when faced with death. [12]For this reason, rejoice, O heavens and you who dwell in them. Woe to the earth and the sea, because the devil has come down to you, having great wrath, knowing that he has only a short time." (Revelation 12:10–12)

The woman (i.e., Israel) who bore the child (i.e., Yeshua) now flees into the desert where she is protected during the next 3½ years. As God protected Israel from the Edomites (Arabs), and Gog and Magog (Russia and all her allies), He now steps forward again to protect Israel – and those who are grafted in – from the Dragon (Satan) who hates her.

Sometimes the next passage, about the believers overcoming the Dragon, is also misunderstood. Some commentators believe that verse 11 is a promise that God will keep all believers safe. The only problem is that the last half of the verse negates that hope. Here's what we mean.

Truly, believers can overcome the wiles of Satan. Their protection comes from their identity. Believers are sealed by God at salvation and identified as His, as the verse above tells us, "because of the blood of the Lamb." Additional protection from the deception of the Dragon is revealed via "because of the word of their testimony."

Yada! Yada! Doesn't always Mean Keep Talking!

The Hebrew root word for testimony is *yada*, which means *to know.* So, this word can mean *to be informed and knowledgeable,* but it also includes a more intimate understanding as well. This same word was used in Genesis to tell us that Adam *knew* Eve and begat children, thereby imparting the idea of *knowing a person intimately* as a husband would know his wife. Protection comes through being able to hear God's voice, to know what He is thinking and doing, plus knowing His ways and doing them. The people this passage is describing have an intimate relationship with God and thereby the ultimate guard around them.

In Proverbs 1 and 2, *wisdom* and *knowledge* are the keys to an out-pouring of the Holy Spirit. In I Corinthians 2, the Holy Spirit is the one who brings comprehension and direction from God. These directions, if we hear them, can save us from physical harm, but more important they can also save us from spiritual harm. And, they can be especially valuable to new believers who would otherwise be easily detoured from the paths of God because they either were not familiar with them or chose not to listen.

However, mature believers, the wise ones, stand firm. Their God-given wisdom helps them see through the fog. God's people need the protections that come from both *salvation* and *intimacy* if they want to survive during this time – or during any time, for that matter. But does this survival include being saved from persecution and death?

Not always, as shown throughout the entire Bible. Mature believers throughout time have faced persecution for their beliefs, including Noah, Daniel, most of the prophets, and even the whole nation of Israel itself.

Despite all that, the last half of verse 11 explains that this protection *extends to* and *guards* their relationship and the covenant they have with God even in the face of death.

> [11]And they overcame him because of the blood of the Lamb and because of the word of their testimony, and they did not love their life even when faced with death. [12]For this reason, rejoice, O heavens and you who dwell in them. Woe to the earth and the sea, because the devil has come down to you, having great wrath, knowing that he has only a short time.
>
> [13]And when the dragon saw that he was thrown down to the earth, he persecuted the woman who gave birth to the male child. [14]But the two wings of the great eagle were given to the woman, so that she could fly into the wilderness to her place, where she was nourished for a time and times and half a time, from the presence of the serpent.
>
> [15]And the serpent poured water like a river out of his mouth after the woman, so that he might cause her to be swept away with the flood. [16]But the earth helped the woman, and the earth opened its mouth and drank up the river which the dragon poured out of his mouth. [17]So the dragon was enraged with the woman, and went off to make war with the rest of her children, who keep the commandments of God and hold to the testimony of Jesus. (Revelation 12:11–17)

What's being said in the passage above is that end-times believers overcome Satan by Yeshua's sacrifice and resurrection, and the relationships that they have established in their lives with God. These relationships are a reflection of their testimony and commitment to Him even unto death. This promise saves their souls but not necessarily their physical, fallen bodies.

Get Mad and Get Even!

The Dragon does not appear to give up easily. He is now all about revenge for his increasing loss of authority and dominion. He knows who the woman is and what she represents. Killing her, Yeshua's own Bride, would be the most satisfying way to get back at the Creator whom he refuses to recognize or acknowledge.

The pharaoh of Egypt had similar ideas about Israel, the Bride of God. After setting God's people free, 3,500 years ago, this pagan leader responded in exactly the same way as the Dragon by trying to recapture them to put them back into bondage – or to kill them.

Standing Up for Good!

Satan is perfectly happy with believers who do nothing, stand for nothing, and say nothing in the face of evil. As the well-known quote by Edmund Burke says, "All that is necessary for the triumph of evil is for good men to do nothing."[4]

Do our lives stand for something when we're faced with the temptations of the Adversary? Do we melt and find excuses? Or, are we confused ourselves whenever we're confronted? His temptations bring only bondage but they never look like that when they're first offered. Meanwhile, God Himself knows every single plan Satan can dredge up and is never caught off guard. He anticipates every one of Satan's attempts at revenge and will provide protection.

The two passages below use the same metaphor to describe God as an eagle, delivering protection and a way of escape into the wilderness for his people.

> You yourselves have seen what I did to the Egyptians,
> and how I bore you on eagles' wings, and brought you
> to Myself. (Exodus 19:4)

> Like an eagle that stirs up its nest,
> That hovers over its young,
> He spread His wings and caught them,
> He carried them on His pinions. (Deuteronomy 32:11)

The eagle metaphor in the Exodus passage suggests that it was God who saved Israel from the tyranny and bondage of Egypt, just as God also saves us from sin's grip of death and frees us of the bondage of our worldly ways. The Deuteronomy passage uses this same metaphor in a prophetic way. The combined messages forewarned Israel about falling away from God.

The Apple of His Eye

In Proverbs 7:2, God indicates that He wants us to cherish His teachings as "the apple of your [our] eye." Also, in Psalm 17:8 and Zechariah 2:8, He used very intimate language to describe the relationship that He wants to have with His people by calling them "the apple of His [my] eye."

In addition, just a few verses beyond the above passage from Deuteronomy, God refers to Israel as *Yeshurun* even as He informs them of their great falling away from Himself that will occur in the future. The author of *Gesenius* defines this word as "*a tender and loving appellation of the people of Israel.*"[5] He suggests that the meaning comes from the Hebrew root *yashar*, which means *to be righteous, straight, upright, and with integrity.*

Always a Loving, Intimate God

In other words, in spite of their lack of love for Himself – and also despite knowing what they will eventually do – God still refers to His people using the same loving, intimate name, Yeshurun. At the end of this prophecy, which culminates with the coming of the Messiah to set up His righteous kingdom, God promises to take vengeance on those who are His foes. As we explained in detail in the first two volumes in this series, within the Hebrew betrothal process the groom defends his bride against all accusers.

The prophecy ends with Deuteronomy 32:43:

> Rejoice, you nations, with his people,
> for he will avenge the blood of his servants;

> he will take vengeance on his enemies
> and make atonement for his land and people.

Even though God's people are far from perfect, He will again protect them from the hateful vengeance poured out by the Dragon. Satan's intent is for destruction; the Eagle's intent is for protection and salvation.

This protection lasts for 3½ years, the first half of the last seven years that end with the coming of the Messiah to set up His kingdom forever. From Revelation 12 we can see that these years just before His coming will be filled with persecution and suffering, but ultimately God's protective covering will prevail.

What's the Deal With "Grace"?

Revelation 4:8 pronounces that the Lord God Almighty is holy when it proclaims:

> Each of the four living creatures had six wings and was covered with eyes all around, even under his wings. Day and night they never stop saying: "Holy, holy, holy is the Lord God Almighty, who was, and is, and is to come." (NIV)

In other words, God thinks righteous thoughts, He does righteous deeds, and He has righteous motives. In Hebrew, the word for holy is *kadosh* and is spelled *koof/vav/dalet/shin*. The underlying pictography says to "put in the past the covenant pathway that consumes you." Thus, when we disobey God and reject His holiness we actually enter into a destructive counter-covenant with the Adversary. This counter-covenant is negated and replaced with a better covenant, with God, when we repent, conforming our ways to His will. I Peter 1:13–15 says:

> [13]Therefore, prepare your minds for action; be self-controlled; set your hope fully on the grace to be given you when Jesus Christ is revealed. [14]As obedient children, do not conform to the evil desires you had when you lived in ignorance. [15]But just as

---

> he who called you is holy, so be holy in all you do;
> [16]for it is written: "Be holy, because I am holy." (NIV)

So what, then, is God's standard for holiness? We are admonished also to be holy in several passages in Torah, including the following:

> "For I am the LORD your God. Consecrate yourselves therefore, and be holy, for I am holy. And you shall not make yourselves unclean with any of the swarming things that swarm on the earth." (Leviticus 11:44)

> "Speak to all the congregation of the sons of Israel and say to them, 'You shall be holy, for I the LORD your God am holy.'" (Leviticus 19:2)

> "Thus you are to be holy to Me, for I the LORD am holy; and I have set you apart from the peoples to be Mine." (Leviticus 20:26)

These texts were among the original instructions about being holy and tell us what holiness is all about. Nonetheless, some commentators suggest that the Old Testament principles have been abolished because we now live under grace.

Actually, we do live under grace. But in truth, God's people have always lived under grace, because the sacrificial system was nothing more nor less than a forward-looking memorial to the time when Yeshua Himself would literally become the sacrificial Lamb for all of mankind. He didn't save just those who arrived on earth after His death – He saved ALL believers, since the beginning of time, who put their faith in God and lived their lives accordingly.

Messianic Believers?

Revelation 12:17 could be more clearly interpreted as, "and he (i.e., the Dragon) went away to make war on the remainder of her descendents, the watchmen or leaders who know Yeshua's principles and are guardians of God's mitzvot (commandments)." This passage specifically refers to the remaining believers who accept the responsibility to walk out the commandments of the Old Testament. And, who recognize Yeshua as Messiah.

To get control of a group or a population, the typical response of most tyrants is to go after the opposing leaders. Hitler copied Satan's way and did exactly that when he killed or put away all those who opposed him, whether they were in the political, business, religious, or ethnic arenas. Sadly, the Dragon/beast will do the same. And the general population, dulled by their lack of perspective and knowledge, will once again turn a blind eye to these machinations.

The woman who appears in heaven (Revelation 12) represents the Israelites during the days of Yeshua. The woman who appears on earth represents Israel, comprising both Jewish and Gentile believers. They believed in His messianic identity and helped to facilitate the spreading of the biblical message to the nations. Those who came to believe in Him because of that work are represented here as her descendants and become targets of the Dragon.

This understanding is complemented by the prophecy in Isaiah 56. Isaiah proposed that there will be Gentile believers who will be enfolded into Israel during the last days. He then went on to say that their honoring of the Shabbat, and their holding fast to God's covenant, will make their sacrifices and offerings acceptable on the altar of God.

In the process of inspiring Isaiah God also makes a clear allusion to His Old Testament identification of two very ancient godly concepts. The first concept models the creation week in which the seventh day has always been recognized as beginning at sundown on Friday and ending at sundown on Saturday. The second concept is a reference to ancient covenant, which we covered extensively in Volumes 1 and 2 of this series. It specifically refers to the increasing level of intimacy, authority, and responsibility that the believer is asked to walk in within his relationship with God.

That's what these descendants of the woman are seen doing. And the price they're paying for this obedience to God is "becoming the new target" of the Dragon. They are represented in Revelation 14:18–20 as the grapes that are harvested. These grapes, in contrast to those of the other harvests that preceded this one, are not taken to be with God but are thrown into the winepress of God's wrath, which is a reference to the seven bowls of judgment.

At this point one could certainly ask: With the Dragon at the heels of the woman, why does he now change his focus and pursue her descendants? Why not continue to try to kill her? After all, she is the target of the Dragon's hate.

Keep in mind that the Dragon has been pursuing her for 3½ years. What happens at the end of this time? The text does not tell us here but we learned in Volume 2 of this series that, in the middle of this last seven-year period, God will come for His Bride in the clouds.

> In Revelation 11:15, after the death and resurrection of the two witnesses, the seventh trumpet sounds. Yeshua then comes as a Groom, paralleling Hebrew wedding customs, to snatch away His Bride.[6]

Why Is the Dragon So Mad?

We propose that the Dragon is furious enough to change his target from the woman, Israel (comprising believers from all nations, including both Jews and Gentiles), because they are now gone. God has taken His Bride to be with Himself. The only ones left who still hold to the Truth and the Way are those who will become the guests at the wedding. These believers, whom we talked about above, are the "grapes" and will suffer through the last 3½ years of the seven bowl judgments that lead to Yeshua's arrival on His white horse as the conquering King.

As we said in Volume 2 in this series:

> However, here in Revelation 11, the seventh trumpet is more of a major announcement than anything else. Via this trumpet

call to the faithful, God is now proclaiming the coming marriage between Himself and His Bride.

Indeed, I Corinthians 15:51–52 . . . tells us that the arrival of Messiah (i.e., Yeshua) for His Bride will occur at the sounding of the last or seventh trumpet. The Groom will come for His Bride just after the seventh trumpet and just before the first bowl of judgment is poured out on the remaining earthly inhabitants.[7]

Also, keep in mind that this event represents the seventh and last trumpet. The preceding trumpet, number six, described two witnesses of God who had authority to judge mankind for 1,260 days. Those 1,260 days are the same 1,260 days referenced here in chapter 12 when the woman flees into the desert. So the time of the two witnesses in the sixth trumpet occurs at the same time when Satan pours out his persecution on the woman for 1,260 days.

It's obvious that God's means of protection for the woman during this time is via the two witnesses (Elijah and Enoch, as we explained in Volume 2). With all the above in mind it becomes clear that there's a war going on. Satan is destroying and killing God's people (or trying to, anyway) and the two witnesses are pouring out the chastisement of God, so it's like one kingdom warring against another – lightning bolts from the heavens versus counterpunches from an ant.

Yet despite all the evidence, the typical Christian church view is that Satan is persecuting only the 144,000 and their converts. They believe these are end-times witnesses for the Lord rather than the groomsmen for the wedding of the Lamb, who (as we will learn later on) are the first to get harvested ("raptured").

Are We Righteous or Holy – or Both?

Those who propose that we cannot become holy through the blood of Yeshua are technically correct if they mean that salvation per se, which is what we attain by accepting the blood sacrifice of Yeshua as remediation for our sins, is not automatically *holiness*.

Unfortunately, many who assert the above also make no distinction between (1) *righteousness* – which is what we attain through salvation – and (2) *holiness*, which is what we can attain by making an active choice to do so. Righteousness is a *result of salvation*, whereas holiness results from our choice to *redefine the essence of ourselves.*

Here's how James, Yeshua's own brother, put it:

> [14]"What use is it, my brethren, if someone says he has faith but he has no works? Can that faith save him? [15]If a brother or sister is without clothing and in need of daily food, [16]and one of you says to them, "Go in peace, be warmed and be filled," and yet you do not give them what is necessary for their body, what use is that? [17]Even so faith, if it has no works, is dead, being by itself. (James 2:14–17)

As one Bible study guide explains:

> [James] never claimed that works can substitute or "stand in" for faith. . . . we cannot have a saving relationship with the Lord [i.e., we cannot become righteous] by doing good deeds and relying on those . . . Since sin first entered our world God has made it very clear that salvation, meaning *our ability to have a meaningful relationship with God and eventually to spend eternity in His presence,* requires (1) confession of our sins and (2) acceptance of His pardon for those sins, made possible by the sacrifice of His Son.

> However, once we have confessed and accepted forgiveness, through faith in God's willingness to forgive us, as we build a 'working relationship' with Him He begins to 'link up' with us spiritually so that we desire, more and more, to be as much like Him as possible. At that point we begin to show love, compassion, and a desire to help others exactly as He shows those things to us.[8]

And that is the essence of holiness. In other words, only as we begin to yearn for and eventually achieve holiness will our good works have any lasting, eternal value.

So . . . does any of the above suggest that we can live our lives any way we want? Have the actual words of God, defining what holiness is, been done away with? Remember, these ideals are the very principles that define God's own holiness. If the principles for holy living explained in the Old Testament really have been abolished, would that also abolish the holiness of God?

In Summary . . .

Later in this volume we will more thoroughly identify and describe the different harvests and their timing, as we began doing in Volume 2. But for now the text seems to support the idea that God rewards His Bride in a different way than He rewards His servants. This is paralleled in the ancient Hebrew marriage as well.

The bride is picked up by the groom, coming at midnight with his groomsmen blowing trumpets all the way to her house. She is then swept off her feet and is taken to a place that has been prepared for a midnight celebration, featuring the bride and groom but also including the groomsmen and the bridesmaids. This occurs the night before the public wedding ceremony as described in Matthew 26, in which the guests (or servants) are gathered and included with the groom as well. But again – more on that later!

This shamash chapter gives us a very quick review of the past, taking us back to the time when Satan had the authority to be in heaven. He lost that authority at the resurrection of the Messiah. Just when he thought he had won, via the death of Yeshua, he then realized that he had actually lost. For the "dead" Yeshua did not *stay* dead but rose again. With the loss of access to God's throne, Satan now realizes that his time is short. His only option now is to destroy the Bride of the King and play his last card.

That card both *constitutes* and *fulfills* his plans from the beginning when, in Eden, he offered godhood to Eve. Satan's goal has always been to regain what he lost (i.e., his identity and his authority) when he rejected God and rebelled. Remember, Satan is not a name – it is a description. Satan once had a name like all the other righteous angels.

All of those had names that ended with *el*, such as Michael, Gabriel, and Uriel. *El* is one of the Hebrew words for God. The name God gave each angel described their authority and identity, such as *warrior of God* or *light of God*. Satan is after the authority God gave to man, which is to manage His creation.

But Satan also wants God's identity as well. Remember, God made man in His image. Therefore, Satan proposes to steal man's identity too. Then he will proclaim to be the God of creation and heaven and lord it over those who have fallen asleep – those who cared more for the things of this world than the things of God.

This chapter gives us the context in which we can then see this satanic endgame being played out. The next mini-menorah of seven events details what might seem – to him alone – Satan's victory. However, Satan will be running his victory laps for only 3½ years, and he certainly won't feel like he won anything during the last half of the last seven years.

But more on that later.

Chapter 3

The Seven Evil Kingdoms

CONSIDER THIS STORY OF TWO FAMILIES. ONE LIVED IN A FINE STONE mansion on a hill overlooking a small village. They dressed like royalty, drank from golden goblets, and looked with disdain on their poorer neighbors. They preyed on those weaker than themselves and gained their riches by intimidation, thievery, and violence. And no one dared challenge the lord of the manor nor his two brutish sons, who scoured the countryside by night, breaking into homes and carrying away anything they could get their greedy hands on, assuming it had some value.

Directly below the mansion, in a tumbledown shack, another family lived. They were poor but they were blessed with an abundance of good-natured camaraderie and love for each other. They worked hard, yet whenever they managed to save up any extra money, grain, or produce, the thieving sons of the wealthy family would come and steal their increase away. This happened year after year, with no end in sight.

One day the wife of the wealthy man put on some self-righteous airs and sent down a basket of unwanted scraps to the poor family, expecting groveling and slavish gratitude in return. When the poor family offered no word of thanks – and no offer to pay for the scraps – she became enraged. How dare they snub her generosity!

The poor family knew, of course, that they were receiving only the dregs of what had been stolen from them, but none of this mattered to the rich lady of the manor in the stone mansion above. So she complained to her husband of their neighbors' ingratitude and pointed out that their ramshackle house was an eyesore and a blight to the village.

Together the couple devised a plan. They would bake a loaf of bread laced with poison. With this they would eliminate the entire family, then seize their house, level it, and be rid of any trace of them forever. The wife brought down the poisoned bread the next evening and left it on the doorstep. Before the poor family could discover it, however, the eldest son of the wealthy family, passing by, stole the loaf and took it home. The wealthy family then ate the bread intended for their neighbors, and died from their own poison.[1]

The above story illustrates the Adversary's kingdom, filled with pride, hatred, strife, envy, and selfish ambition. It's also tyrannical and murderous and is filled with jealousy over the joy and peace that are the hallmarks of the kingdom of God.

Satan's Desire to Rule

Whether we know it or not, thieves and murderers are wandering about, seeking whom they may devour. These are the powerful kingdoms of this world referred to in Revelation 17:9–11. Seven kingdoms are mentioned. John the Apostle also sees an eighth, which is led by the False Messiah and is a continuation of the seventh, Rome. It is called "a mystery, 'BABYLON THE GREAT, THE MOTHER OF HARLOTS AND OF THE ABOMINATIONS OF THE EARTH.'" (Revelation 17:5).

Satan desires to rule over all mankind, but since he lacks the attributes necessary to do this, such as omnipotence and omniscience, he must employ other methods. He uses key individuals to wield great power on his behalf. These human leaders, in league with evil, create hierarchial systems and form alliances in the hope that Satan will fulfill his promise to make them gods, having authority and power.

These hierarchies are the kingdoms (governments and cultures) that become the status quo and basically control the lives of humanity. For example, the father-son duo of Hafez and Bashar Al-Assad has controlled Syria, even as Moammar Gaddafi once controlled Libya, for more than forty years. Despots like these have been with us since the Tower of Babel.

In reality all these kingdoms are reincarnations of the original Babylon of King Nimrod. Reading between the lines in Genesis 11:1–9, what was the Tower of Babel really about? It was far more than a physical building. In truth it was a visual symbol of a major covenant with evil. Part of this covenant involved an effort to storm heaven and make God subject to the will of man.

The arrogance of this first Babylon (Sumer) has manifested itself in all subsequent kingdoms. Nimrod ruled the first Babylon, which existed from approximately 2250 BC to 1900 BC. Concurrent with Nimrod was Abraham, separated out from a pagan culture into a covenant of increased intimacy with the Most High. This was God's antidote to the strategies of evil.

Scripture identifies the powers of this world as part of a plan to steal our souls (i.e., our identity and authority). These kingdoms occupy positions on our master menorah and are referred to in Revelation 11:15, "The kingdom of the world has become the Kingdom of our Lord and his Messiah" (CJB). Before, during, and after Yeshua's time, prophets and rabbis alike were warning us not to trust the world systems of man. In Mishnah, Rabbi Shemaiah says, "Love work. Hate authority. Don't get friendly with the government."[2]

Considering that Rome had just conquered Israel (circa 90 BC) and installed a puppet government when the above quote from Rabbi Shemaiah was written, this would have been an understandable attitude. He was disturbed that, after years of war and much loss of life in the pursuit of justice and freedom, corruption and evil still managed to regain power with amazing ease. Rabbi Gamaliel, Paul's teacher, said: "Be wary of princes and governments; they get friendly only for their own gain."[3]

We can certainly see this truth being manifested today in governments around the globe. Yet conversely, Scripture admonishes us to "render to Caesar the things that are Caesar's" (Luke 20:25). The Jews were instructed during the captivity in Babylon to build homes and occupy the land (Jeremiah 29:4–7). We are called to a balancing act with the systems of the world of men. In order to achieve that balance we need some understanding, as revealed in Scripture, of who and what those systems are.

The Seven Kingdoms of the Dragon

Let's examine those seven kingdoms in a little more detail by looking at how the Creator divides history, as revealed through the prophet Daniel and John the Apostle in Revelation. In Daniel 2, God used a dream to show the seven kingdoms embodied in a statue, an idol.

This dream symbolizes the seven kingdoms of the Dragon (i.e., Satan) with an emphasis on the final four kingdoms. In this vision one kingdom is represented as the head. The other kingdoms are represented by branches (or limbs) on the left and right sides of a human body. Here's the text, doubtless familiar to all students of the Bible:

> [28]"However, there is a God in heaven who reveals mysteries, and He has made known to King Nebuchadnezzar what will take place in the latter days. This was your dream and the visions in your mind while on your bed. [29]As for you, O king, while on your bed your thoughts turned to what would take place in the future; and He who reveals mysteries has made known to you what will take place.
>
> [30]"But as for me, this mystery has not been revealed to me for any wisdom residing in me more than in any other living man, but for the purpose of making the interpretation known to the king, and that you may understand the

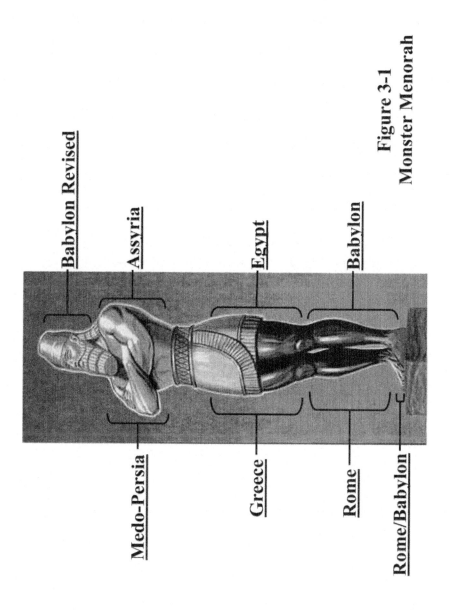

**Figure 3-1
Monster Menorah**

thoughts of your mind. [31]You, O king, were looking and behold, there was a single great statue; that statue, which was large and of extraordinary splendor, was standing in front of you, and its appearance was awesome.

[32]"The head of that statue was made of fine gold, its breast and its arms of silver, its belly and its thighs of bronze, [33]its legs of iron, its feet partly of iron and partly of clay. [34]You continued looking until a stone was cut out without hands, and it struck the statue on its feet of iron and clay and crushed them. [35]Then the iron, the clay, the bronze, the silver and the gold were crushed all at the same time and became like chaff from the summer threshing floors; and the wind carried them away so that not a trace of them was found. But the stone that struck the statue became a great mountain and filled the whole earth.

[36]"This was the dream; now we will tell its interpretation before the king. [37]You, O king, are the king of kings, to whom the God of heaven has given the kingdom, the power, the strength and the glory; [38]and wherever the sons of men dwell, or the beasts of the field, or the birds of the sky, He has given them into your hand and has caused you to rule over them all. You are the head of gold.

[39]"After you there will arise another kingdom inferior to you, then another third kingdom of bronze, which will rule over all the earth. [40]Then there will be a fourth kingdom as strong as iron; inasmuch as iron crushes and shatters all things, so, like iron that breaks in pieces, it will crush and break all these in pieces. [41]In that you saw the feet and toes, partly of potter's clay and partly of iron, it will be a divided kingdom; but it will have in it the toughness of iron, inasmuch as you saw the iron mixed with common clay.

[42]"As the toes of the feet were partly of iron and partly of pottery, so some of the kingdom will be strong and part of it will be brittle. [43]And in that you saw the iron mixed with common clay, they will combine with one another in the seed of men; but they will not adhere to

one another, even as iron does not combine with pottery.⁴⁴ In the days of those kings the God of heaven will set up a kingdom which will never be destroyed, and that kingdom will not be left for another people; it will crush and put an end to all these kingdoms, but it will itself endure forever.

⁴⁵"Inasmuch as you saw that a stone was cut out of the mountain without hands and that it crushed the iron, the bronze, the clay, the silver and the gold, the great God has made known to the king what will take place in the future; so the dream is true and its interpretation is trustworthy." (Daniel 2:28–45)

We believe that these seven parts form an evil kingdoms menorah, an idol/monster menorah of seven lights representing seven kingdoms that have become world powers throughout history. They are the seven kingdoms, or kings, referred to in the passage below and are under the control of the Dragon, Satan:

⁹"Here is the mind which has wisdom. The seven heads are seven mountains on which the woman sits, ¹⁰and they are seven kings; five have fallen, one is, the other has not yet come; and when he comes, he must remain a little while." (Revelation 17:9–10)

However, unlike a biblical menorah whose lights and branches point upward, the limbs of the idol menorah point downward even as the arms and legs of this statue point downward.

- Based on Hebrew anatomical understanding, the right foot and lower leg is the first branch, symbolizing the first evil kingdom, Babylon.

- The right upper leg and thigh correspond to the second evil kingdom, Egypt, which supplanted Babylon as the ruling world empire during the time of Joseph, around 1850 BC. They did so using a combination of military force and economic resources. During a worldwide famine Egypt took full advantage of the reserves created by Joseph, enslaving the Middle East in exchange for food (Genesis 47:14–20).

- The third menorah branch, or the right arm and chest, is the kingdom of Assyria. The Assyrians exploited Egypt's weakness wrought by God's plagues prior to the exodus and began to rise in power around 1200 BC. Over the next six hundred years, Assyria became the new ruling power in the world. The Assyrians invaded the land of Israel in 722 BC and conquered the ten northern tribes. A couple decades later they confronted King Hezekiah and made Judah into a vassal state. Recall the confrontation between Sennacherib and God, when God destroyed Sennacherib's entire army (II Kings 19:35). This was probably the turning point in Assyria's supremacy, and from that moment on their power diminished. Ninety years later they were confronted by the new rising authority, revised Babylon, which destroyed them once and for all.

- The fourth kingdom is revised Babylon under the leadership of Nebuchadnezzar. He was the son of Nabopolassar, a Chaldean chief who in 626 BC led a revolt against Assyrian rule, proclaimed himself king of Babylon and, in alliance with the Medes and Scythians, succeeded in overthrowing the vast Assyrian Empire and destroying Nineveh, its capital, in 612 BC.

Nebuchadnezzar, as crown prince, was given command of the Babylonian army, which he used to harry the remainder of the Assyrians in northern Syria. Nebuchadnezzar thus became head over the fourth evil kingdom, a renewed Babylon. The vision in Daniel pictures this king as the head of the statue, made of gold, putting him in the *shamash* or fourth position of the evil kingdoms menorah, around 600 BC. Like Nimrod before him, Nebuchadnezzar attempted to subjugate God to man by assimilating Him into the world system.

Although Daniel 3:28–29 reads as though the king is paying homage to God as the one true God, Nebuchadnezzar actually lowered Him to the position of just another bloodthirsty tyrant by ruling that anyone not worshiping the God of Daniel should be torn limb from limb.

- The fifth kingdom, the empire of Medo-Persia as represented by the arms and chest of silver on the left side of the monster menorah, was led by Cyrus, followed by Darius who took over the kingdom of Babylon, killing Nebuchadnezzar's descendant, Belshazzar, after the Lord predicted the king's demise via the handwriting on the wall (Daniel 5; circa 538 BC).

- The sixth kingdom, Greece, rose to power under Alexander the Great, who as general and king swept through Egypt, Asia Minor, Syria, and Mesopotamia, conquering the Medo-Persian empire and seizing control of the known world, around 332 BC. Greece is represented in the statue by the thighs and belly of brass, placing it sixth on the monster menorah.

- Rome, the seventh kingdom, replaced Greece as the ruling power near the middle of the second century BC, and is represented first by the iron thighs and later by the iron and clay mixed together in the feet of the statue.

Romulus and Remus

Some commentators suggest that the tribe of Dan was excluded from the 144,000 in Revelation 7 because their tribe got deeply involved in paganism. In particular, the 17th and 18th chapters of the book of Judges tell the story of the tribe of Dan's involvement with a pagan priest named Micah, whom they installed as their own priest over their own tribe in direct contradiction to all that God had required of them.

It has also been suggested, by ancient historians, that the origins of Troy and the Trojans find their roots in the tribe of Dan. The original peoples who made up Troy were called "Danaans."

According to ancient legend, Romulus and Remus were twin brothers descended from Troy. One of them founded the city of

Rome in 753 BC and named it after himself. Remus, on the other hand, vied with his brother to found a different city on a different hill, but lost the pagan augury (divination) contest by which they decided whose site would be chosen. Remus was not happy with the result; he was killed when he violated the sanctity of his brother's city by leaping over its wall.

It's interesting to note that every single tyrant mentioned above thought of himself as descended from divinity, and therefore as if he *were* a god. In their mythologies, their belief that they were descended from gods (i.e., via gods mating with human women) strikes a parallel chord with the Bible, which describes fallen angels as mating with human women and producing nephilim, or "men of renown."

So . . . were these men descended from gods or fallen angels? Were they nephilim? If so, then it would be appropriate that these tyrants were rulers themselves . . . but only in Satan's kingdom. These kings represent the personification and the unfolding plan of Satan to conquer and rule over God's creation. That authority was given to man by God, not to Satan.

Where Will All This Lead?

Satan's strategy to rule the kingdoms of this world began as it will end, with a one-world government. Ancient Babylon was the unified world system under the evil king Nimrod (Genesis 10:8–12; 11:1–9). It is also known as *Shinar* in Genesis 10:10 and as *Sumeria* or *Assyro-Babylonia* in archeological circles. This kingdom is the first of seven mentioned in Scripture and is the master pattern for all the systems of evil men that follow.

God divided Nimrod's kingdom into people groups by giving them different languages at the Tower of Babel, forcing them to scatter and spread out over the earth as the Lord had originally directed. Mankind, through the authority and power manifested in these kingdoms, has invested many lives and much blood attempting to restore the supremacy and power of the original kingdom of Nimrod.

To subjugate the known world was the desire of every major kingdom in history and was, for the most part, accomplished by each of these evil empires . . . but only for a time. Again today we hear about renewed efforts to bring all the nations under the rule of a one-world system. The Bible prophesies that the Antichrist, the False Messiah, empowered by the Dragon, will reign over a restored one-world government, a kingdom called Babylon in the Bible (Revelation 17:5, Daniel 11:36–45, Revelation 13:7–17).

Nimrod (also known as *Amraphel* in Genesis 14:1), or possibly one of his successors, codified a set of laws that became the standard for civic and moral conduct. Historians applaud the attempt at ethical accountability yet fail to recognize its basic flaws, namely that its author was none other than the infamous Nimrod, giving property a higher value than human life.

Some biblical archeologists suggest that Nimrod, Amraphel, and Hammurabi could have been the same person. What is generally agreed upon is that all of these tyrranical individuals, whether one person or three, ruled over Babylon.

Every student of history is familiar with the Code of Hammurabi. It was created to control people and maintain the existing authority. Some suggest that this code was the source out of which Torah instruction grew. Nothing could be further from the truth. Efforts to denigrate the uniqueness of Torah and its teachings are rooted in a uniformitarian cosmology that denies the existence of a God who opposes the flawed principles that Nimrod's Code tried to establish.

An in-depth study of the precepts contained in the Code of Hammurabi reveals a shocking display of cruelty and injustice in marked contrast to the Hebrew Scriptures. For example, a slave who expresses a desire for freedom should have his ear cut off.[4] Slave hunting was legal sport, which was also encouraged by both Greece and Rome in extreme contrast to God's way of legislating, which protects all life, rich or poor, free or slave. In Torah, a runaway slave is protected by law and set free automatically (Deuteronomy 23:15–16).

Punishment for a crime is to be exactly equal to the crime, not exceeding the dictates of true justice as exemplified in Numbers 35:31. God speaks a very different kingdom message: "He has told you, O man, what is good; and what does the LORD require of you but to do justice, to love kindness, and to walk humbly with your God?" (Micah 6:8).

What Has the Highest Value?

In God's system, human life has the highest value – it is beyond measure. In contrast, in man's system, everything is reduced to property and human life is rarely the most valued commodity. This value system is the legacy of Nimrod's Babylon and all evil kingdoms that came after it, yet it was the first of the seven evil kingdoms instituted by Satan.

The second kingdom of evil is Egypt, called *Mitzraim* in Hebrew (Genesis 10:6, 13). Like Babylon before it, Egypt was built on the concept of ownership, property values, and the exercise of power (i.e., the strong over the weak), whereas God is the strong protector of the weak.

Isn't that also the direction in which the world – including America – is moving today, with increased centrality of power, with control (and individual rights as well) being moved from local governments into a centralized governmental authority, which is contrary to Scripture? The basic biblical construct for government includes extreme personal freedom and responsibility. The reason is that God wants man to be responsible, directly, to his neighbor – not indirectly, which is what centralized governments desire, and which is also what they use to control and manipulate the population.

Egypt was built on the idea that human life is a form of property. Slavery was then considered common and desirable. Man was not valued as the apex of creation. Life was something to bargain with, as evidenced by Pharaoh's attitude in Exodus 1:14–22. So, when you're tempted to admire the splendor of ancient Egypt, remember that most of it was built on the backs of slaves. While it is true that the great pyramids were constructed by paid laborers, these were rare exceptions to Egypt's general practice. And even in this case, the stones for the great monuments were quarried by slaves doomed to a premature death by this dangerous, tedious, grueling labor.

As the Egyptians began to fade from world power, a third kingdom arose – Assyria (sometimes called Macedonia by archeologists). This powerful merchant-nation waged war and built a navy unmatched in its time. The Assyrians, however, added economic warfare to their repertoire. In fact, military control over commerce throughout the eastern Mediterranean region was their primary mode of controlling territory and wielding vast power. If you were favored by the Assyrians, you prospered. They used both enticement and punishment to convince people to comply.

Eventually greed, corruption, and hunger for power led to the rise of a new military force. Revised Babylon, under the leadership of King Nebuchadnezzar, envied the wealth and power of Assyria. They conquered and consolidated the Mediterranean peoples into one massive kingdom. In Nebuchadnezzar's dream, he is the head of gold as interpreted by Daniel (Daniel 2:36–38). For seven years Nebuchadnezzar became like a beast. In Daniel 4:16, Nebuchadnezzar had his soul changed from that of a man to that of an animal. His kingdom, Babylon, was symbolized by a lion with eagle wings (Daniel 7:4). We believe it is scripturally and historically significant that this beast-man is in the shamash position.

The kingdom of Medo-Persia (539 BC to about 332 BC) was described in Daniel 7:5 as a rampaging bear. Indeed, from our vantage point, the Medo-Persians were just as brutal. This kingdom as a world power didn't seem to have much focus, nor any wondrous accomplishments to commend it. Medo-Persia ravaged the world in an attempt to feed its voracious appetite without even pretending to benefit humanity. Like the four preceding evil kingdoms, Medo-Persia was not only destructive but was self-destructive as well. The appetites that men sought to satisfy ultimately destroyed them.

God Has Always Restored His People

In contrast, in the midst of these chaotic circumstances wrought by evil men, God refined and restored His people. He even used the designs of the evil kingdoms themselves to bring blessings to the people of His kingdom. For example, the Medo-Persians returned the Israelites to the land of Israel and were instrumental in the building of the second Temple (Ezra 5:13–6:5).

After the inevitable fall of the Medes a "leopard" arose (Daniel 7:6). This prophecy foretold the rise of Greece, the sixth branch of our monster menorah, represented by bronze in the statue described in Daniel 2:39. From 322 BC to 160 BC, Greece ruled the world in more ways than one. Alexander the Great conquered the known physical world, but in a more profound way, Greece conquered humanity. The attractive sophistication and refinement of this beastly kingdom influenced the face of civilization, and all of western culture is now built on the foundation of Greek philosophy and mythology. And by the way, Greek mythology is based on Babylonian mythology.

Within twenty years, by 300 BC, Greek culture had begun to pre-dominate. It was during this Hellenistic period that various warlike city-states banded together to fight for "civic honor." Their true cause, however, was economic greed, for they sought to seize food and other resources from neighboring lands. Whole populations were reduced to poverty and slavery in the process. Meanwhile, while Greece was justifying theft, murder, and slavery as noble causes, part of the Code of Draco (from which we get the term "draconian") made taking a single cabbage from a Greek punishable by death. As we pointed out in some detail in Volumes 1 and 2 in this series, most current western interpretations of God's Scripture are still mistakenly based on a Greek system of hermeneutics.

A Pattern Emerges

At this point a pattern in these evil kingdoms should be apparent. They were all self-destructive, operating in the manner of the evil family at the beginning of this chapter.

Encouraging the worst attributes in those who were loyal to them, the evil kingdoms destroyed themselves from the inside out. It is appropriate that Greece should be the sixth kingdom – six being the number of man – since the Greek empire is generally considered the apex of human cultural achievement. The Greeks were the ultimate humanists. They believed they were the greatest of all humankind, intrinsically noble and good.

Greek art was based on the worship of humanity and the human form. Physical perfection was so valued that a new father would examine his newborn for the first ten days of its life, and if he found the child to be flawed he left it in a public place to die of exposure. The Greek system applauded suicide as well, considering it a noble way to exit one's life.

Homosexuality was also accepted as the norm and was often admired. Likewise, the word "lesbian" once meant a native of Lesbos, an island in the Aegean Sea predominantly inhabited by women. Greek poetry and literature glorified immorality, making a hero of Oedipus who tragically murdered his father then married his own mother.

And yet, how often do we look upon the dazzling accomplishments of ancient Greece with awe? We admire the kingdom that gave the world the Olympics, classical art and poetry, gleaming marble statues and temples, even as we overlook the underlying foundation of corruption and immorality on which ancient Greece was built.

By Yeshua's time, the Greeks had disappeared as a military world power, but they had left behind their cultural influence. Rome, the seventh evil kingdom, had risen in Greece's place. Rome incorporated Greece into its own empire, yet despite Rome's confidence in their superior government the Romans knew they could never match the Greeks in science, philosophy, art, or literature. Rome's strength lay in its ability to assimilate other peoples through military conquest.

In Matthew 4:8–10, Satan tempted Yeshua with all the kingdoms of the earth. This was consistent with the Roman approach to life: assimilate or die. Once again, evil offered what it didn't rightfully own to bring men into allegiance to its agenda.

A Kingdom Divided

Creation is the domain of the Creator despite the machinations of men. Rome, of course, disagreed with this because its people shared the same values as the six evil kingdoms preceding it. In the year AD 327, under Emperor Constantine, Rome took control of Christianity by assimilating it into the Roman Empire. Just as Nebuchadnezzar proclaimed death to all who opposed Daniel's God, Rome forced Christianity on its citizens, mandating the same penalty for all Jewish expressions of faith.

The Mettle of the Metals

Recall that Daniel's interpretation of Nebuchadnezzar's dream came directly from God, who used specific metals to represent specific kingdoms, starting with the most valuable. As we work our way down the list, the metals become mixtures, even as the kingdoms themselves become mixtures as well – of different people groups.

Even though Nebuchadnezzar was a tyranical despot, in comparison to the other kingdoms, from God's perspective he was the best. Each kingdom beneath him, as represented by the sections of the statue in his dream, became more and more degraded as represented by the decreasing value of the metals.

The initial attempts of Nimrod and Nebuchadnezzar resulted in Rome's efforts to absorb and incorporate God's covenant relationship with man. This was designed to bring God into submission to the kingdom of man. Its goal was to bring the very form of religion that represents God's people under its own authority and power. That's why Christianity – especially the Catholic form – includes so many practices and beliefs that are taken right out of pagan Babylonian, Egyptian, and Greek cultures.

While the Roman Empire and its Greek predecessor no longer exist, together they formed the foundation for all western culture and politics. Throughout history, these kingdoms have fought over the authority to rule. Because the kingdoms were established on greed and lust for power, they ruled by controlling others for personal gain. No wonder that their power could not be maintained. As Yeshua said, "Any kingdom divided against itself is laid waste; and a house divided against itself falls" (Luke 11:17). In the end, all evil kingdoms amount to new clothing on the same old Babylon.

The Last Evil Kingdom

Ancient Rome represented the calves of iron on the statue in Nebuchadnezzar's dream. But what about the feet of iron and clay and the ten toes? This kingdom is yet to come and represents the second phase of the ancient Roman Empire. We know that the world will be divided into ten sections and the leaders of each will give their authority to the beast, or False Messiah. One identifying feature of this last kingdom is described by its components of iron and clay.

In Hebrew understanding, iron can represent angelic activity on the earth. One of the Hebrew words for man is *adam*, and one of the Hebrew words for ground (clay), is *adamah*. In other words, Hebrew thought teaches that men are made of clay. Daniel 2:43 teaches that man (clay) and angels (iron) will once again intermingle. As in the days of Noah, mankind will be sexually interacting with fallen angels (Genesis 6:1–4). We know that these angels were also the same ones who were locked in the abyss during Noah's era, by God, and who will also be released by Abaddon (Revelation 9) as we explained in Volume 2.

These seven evil kingdoms have many things in common, including what brought on their downfalls. When each of these kingdoms grew powerful enough they would confront God's people. God has always risen up to protect His people, while Satan's plans have always included subjugation, destruction, or deportation.

The confrontation between Abraham and Amraphel (Nimrod) in Genesis 14 occurred at the pinnacle of Nimrod's kingdom. From that point on, Babylon became weaker while Egypt grew more powerful. However, Egypt, the next evil kingdom, never recovered from the ten plagues brought on by God's judgment on Pharaoh.

Assyria, after destroying and exiling the northern ten tribes to Nineveh in 722 BC, tried to do the same to Judah. Hezekiah, the Judean king ruling from Jerusalem, saved his land and his people from the Assyrians by worshiping the one true God. As a result of the confrontation between Hezekiah and King Senacharib, 185,000 soldiers of the Assyrian army were found dead in their camps the next day. The Assyrians never recovered, and ninety years later they lost what was left of their kingdom to the Babylonians.

In 539 BC, the end of the Babylonian empire occurred when Belshazzar, a descendant of Nebuchadnezzar, defied God by slandering Israel and Israel's authority in public. The finger of God literally wrote Belshazzar's judgment. That night his kingdom fell to the Medo-Persians.

The movie *300* depicted a battle between Greeks and the Medo-Persians, which took place soon after Haman, one of the highest officials of the Medo-Persian kingdom, tried to destroy all the Jews in the land. His efforts were thwarted and God's judgments were revealed in the results of the battle with Greece. From this time onward the Medo-Persians became weaker while the Greeks grew more powerful.

Alexander the Great, the leader of the united Greek city states, conquered the known world in 332 BC, but died ten years later. His kingdom was split into four parts and ruled by his four generals. One of the last ones to rule was Antiochus Epiphanes, whose death, due to what historians believe was syphilis, occurred shortly after his confrontation with the Jews in Israel, where he desecrated the Temple and defied God. His army, huge as it was, was embarrassed and defeated by an untrained band of Jewish farmers and priests, known to history as the Maccabees.

This vacuum allowed the Roman beast to rise to power in 69 BC. The Romans, through military force and political intrigue, controlled, manipulated, and slaughtered the Jews, and exiled the survivors from their own land. In the Bar Kokhba rebellion in 132 AD, Rome confronted the Jews one last time and destroyed the Jewish nation, dispersing the people all over the world and eliminating most of the Jewish population in Israel. The nation of Israel wasn't reestablished until 1948.

During the intervening 1,800 years, various world governments continued to pursue the Jews throughout the world, wherever they could find them. We've seen the same thing in pogroms such as the Spanish Inquisition and the slaughter of the Jews in Russia, France, England, and other countries, culminating in the rise of Adolf Hitler. Unfortunately, the last manifestation of the Roman Empire, the one made of iron and clay, will again attempt to attack Israel and exterminate the Jews once and for all, as prophesied several times in the Bible.

It's also interesting to note that, with respect to all of these evil empires, most of the kings, rulers, or founders themselves were said to be the offspring of a human woman and a "god." Unfortunately, the same will be true of the ruler of the last evil kingdom. It will have a leader known as the Antichrist, or False Messiah, who will be part man and part devil, impersonated by Satan himself proclaiming to be the God of the Bible.

Losing Our Way

Look at what Rome accomplished by yanking Christianty under its wing. It essentially stripped out most of the Torah-based ideas that were widespread and prevalent before Rome messed with it. Sadly, in the centuries that followed, Satan has further attempted to subvert the true worship of God, in ways that have resulted in forms of religious expression that have very few connections to the Bible. Thus we have the *form* of religion but not the *power*.

Unfortunately, the former emperor of Rome, Constantine, the leader of the last evil kingdom, is portrayed today as a great Christian leader who incorporated Christianity into his kingdom. Nothing could be further from the truth. He did it to control and pollute the kingdom of God. For him it was better not to feed the Christians to the lions but to water down their religion until it bore little resemblance to what Yeshua had taught. This also added to the rift between Christians and Jews.

Constantine's method was also much more effective. In Satan's kingdom there is no room for Jews even as he enfolded the religion of Christaintiy into his own empire in a perverted sense. Satan deluded the Jews until they missed their Messiah, and he deluded and corrupted the Christians until they lost the Torah-based roots of their beliefs.

Baptism and Communion

The modern Christian versions of baptism and communion, supposedly based on the standard practices established by the ancient Jews, have both been corrupted. The original *mikveh* (the forerunner of modern baptism) involved standing in a river, facing the current, and bowing forward, both literally and symbolically, toward the water's source. In contrast, modern full-body baptism typically involves being "saved from drowning in sin" by falling backwards into the literal "arms of the church" as wielded by a priest or a pastor. Some churches also teach that being baptized more than once is inappropriate – or downright wrong.

In contrast, the ancient Jews would mikveh frequently. The priests did so before they went into the inner court. Jewish women did so at the end of every menstrual period, as a way of ritually purifying themselves. Like any other legitimate rabbi, Yeshua Himself also did so just prior to beginning his active ministry.

What the modern church now calls "communion" is based on the original Passover/Last Supper meal at which (1) Yeshua washed the disciples feet then shared (2) bread and (3) wine with them. All three of these were based on the three covenants leading up to betrothal. Washing his disciples' feet mirrored the sandal (inheritance) covenant; eating the bread together mirrored the salt (friendship) covenant; drinking the wine mirrored blood (servant) covenant, which Yeshua reinforced by noting that this was the last cup of wine He would share with His people before coming back for His Bride. In other words, it was the third cup in the sequence of four, which would culminate in the sharing of the wine by the bride and groom at the wedding itself.

The False Prophet and the False Messiah Revealed

Ultimately, Satan's kingdom is divided against itself and will cause its own demise. Chapters 12 and 13 of the book of Revelation give us insight into the Adversary's kingdom and the schemes he will foist upon all of creation.

However, before we continue with the coming events, let's pinpoint our position in time. The seventh trumpet has blown and the Bride of Messiah has been snatched away, which will be described in greater detail in Revelation 14. We have also received more information about the Adversary – his being cast down from heaven, his attempt to murder the true Messiah and destroy Israel, and his efforts to pursue Israel's offspring who keep the commandments of God and observe the customs of Yeshua.

The time of the two witnesses is now done. The first 3½ years of the last 7 years of Revelation are complete, and we are now in the last 42 months of the Great Tribulation. Here and now, Abaddon and Satan will be revealed to the world and will rise to power, but the world won't recognize who they really are and will believe one of the most horrendous lies ever perpetrated on mankind. The people of the world should have known better, but because of their lack of a relationship with God they were deceived.

Let's review Revelation 13:1–10 to see what comes next:

> ¹[AS] I stood on the sandy beach, I saw a beast coming up out of the sea with ten horns and seven heads. On his horns he had ten royal crowns (diadems) and blasphemous titles (names) on his heads. ²And the beast that I saw resembled a leopard, but his feet were like those of a bear and his mouth was like that of a lion. And to him the dragon gave his [own] might and power and his [own] throne and great dominion.
>
> ³And one of his heads seemed to have a deadly wound. But his death stroke was healed; and the whole earth went after the beast in amazement and admiration. ⁴They fell down and paid homage to the dragon, because he had

bestowed on the beast all his dominion and authority; they also praised and worshiped the beast, exclaiming, Who is a match for the beast, and, Who can make war against him?

⁵And the beast was given the power of speech, uttering boastful and blasphemous words, and he was given freedom to exert his authority and to exercise his will during forty-two months (three and a half years). ⁶And he opened his mouth to speak slanders against God, blaspheming His name and His abode, [even vilifying] those who live in heaven. ⁷He was further permitted to wage war on God's holy people (the saints) and to overcome them. And power was given him to extend his authority over every tribe and people and tongue and nation,

⁸And all the inhabitants of the earth will fall down in adoration and pay him homage, everyone whose name has not been recorded in the Book of Life of the Lamb that was slain [in sacrifice] from the foundation of the world. ⁹If anyone is able to hear, let him listen:

¹⁰Whoever leads into captivity will himself go into captivity; if anyone slays with the sword, with the sword must he be slain. Herein is [the call for] the patience and the faith and fidelity of the saints (God's people).
(Revelation 13:1–10, AMP)

The beast that comes from the sea is a nephal that we know as the Antichrist, or the False Messiah. It is hideous in every respect – ten horns, seven heads, and ten crowns, each with a name that reviles and curses God. As we explained in Volume 2, in Hebraic understanding the sea can signify mankind.

The implication is that this beast has his genetic source in man. But as we will see, the spirit of the Adversary, Satan, will dwell in him. Both of these entities combined will create the final "being" that Satan has intended to become since the beginning of time. Satan will provide this being with the evil spirit and the rebellious nature that identifies the Adversary to mankind. This beast will provide the human body that Satan has long desired to possess and operate from.

The Pinnacle of Evil

The above is further substantiated by the detailed description of the beast. It's clear that this beast has his origin in mankind. The Dragon in Revelation 12 has his origin in heaven but loses his place and is thrown down to the earth. This Dragon, and the beast that comes out of the sea, combine to produce the Antichrist.

The beast that rises up out of the sea resembles a leopard. He has the feet of a bear, the mouth of a lion, and the authority of the Dragon. This same description was introduced before in Daniel 7. Daniel has a vision in which the four winds are churning up the sea (mankind), and four beasts arise *from* the sea.

> [4]"The first was like a lion, and it had the wings of an eagle. I watched until its wings were torn off and it was lifted from the ground so that it stood on two feet like a man, and the heart of a man was given to it.
>
> [5]"And there before me was a second beast, which looked like a bear. It was raised up on one of its sides, and it had three ribs in its mouth between its teeth. It was told, 'Get up and eat your fill of flesh!'
>
> [6]"After that, I looked, and there before me was another beast, one that looked like a leopard. And on its back it had four wings like those of a bird. This beast had four heads, and it was given authority to rule.
>
> [7]"After that, in my vision at night I looked, and there before me was a fourth beast – terrifying and frightening and very powerful. It had large iron teeth; it crushed and devoured its victims and trampled underfoot whatever was left. It was different from all the former beasts, and it had ten horns." (Daniel 7:4–7, NIV)

Beast	Description	Classification	Scripture
Lion with eagle's wings	Wings torn off, stood on two feet, given man's heart	Pre-Flood nephilim	Daniel 7:4
Bear raised on one side with three ribs in its mouth	Told to consume flesh	Post-Flood nephilim (Giants: Goliath, King Og)	Daniel 7:5
Leopard with four wings and four heads	Given authority to rule	Giants intermingling with humanity (Jezebel)	Daniel 7:6
Beast/Dragon has iron teeth, seven heads, ten horns, and is powerful and terrifying	In Revelation 13 it has the mouth of a lion, feet of a bear, resembles a leopard, but is a beast/dragon	The end-times nephilim (False Messiah, False Prophet)	Daniel 7:7, Revelation 13:1-2

Figure 3-2: Four Types of Nephilim

Figure 3-2: The Four Types of Nephilim

These beasts represent different evil kingdoms that have existed throughout history. They also represent the different types of nephilim that have existed at different periods of time on the earth, as follows:

- **Verse 4:** This beast is a lion with the wings of an eagle. The wings are torn off and the lion is set on two feet, like a man. It is given the heart of a man. This represents the pre-Flood nephilim, described in Genesis 6 and also in the book of Enoch.[5]

- **Verse 5:** This beast is a bear, raised on one side and with three ribs in its mouth. Clearly it eats flesh. This represents the post-Flood nephilim, including giants such as Goliath and King Og.

- **Verse 6:** This beast is a leopard with four wings and four heads, which is given authority to rule. This represents what resulted when the post-Flood nephilim intermingled with mankind. These types resemble humanity in size and form, but like leopards they are camouflaged and blend in with their surroundings. Their "authority to rule" is also unique. Jezebel was this type of nephal, having descended from nephilim tribes. At one point she also ruled over Israel, bringing it to the brink of physical and spiritual destruction.

- **Verse 7:** This last beast, "terrifying and frightening," has iron teeth. It tramples and destroys everything it sees. It has ten horns and seven heads, and was personified by the entity we know as Satan. In Revelation 13:2, this beast, indwelled and powered by Satan, is characterized as having the mouth of a lion and the feet of a bear, and is like a leopard but is a dragon. This indwelled beast we know as the Antichrist, or the False Messiah. This is the final type of nephilim, the ones that arise during the end times, with attributes from all the other types. They are the worst of their kind – *pinnacles of evil* – true abominations.

The horrifying implication is that Satan has been perfecting his evil offspring so they will possess the necessary skills to bring death and destruction to all of God's creation. An abomination indeed – this is what the False Messiah and the False Prophet embody. They are the last type of nephilim, arising during the catastrophic judgments that will fall on the earth. The fallen teraphim are released from their bondage in the abyss in Revelation 9, and at the direction of Abaddon, the devil of death, they begin again the horrific atrocity of producing nephilim so they can bring forth their messiah.

Where Did Jezebel Come From?

Genesis 6 gives us a few details about the origin of the nephilim (*nephal* in the singular). *The Book of Enoch*, quoted in Volume 1 in this series, tells quite a bit more of the story. According to Enoch . . .

> "A group of 200 of Satan's fallen angels (teraphim), led by one named *Samyaza*, made a pact whereby they took on human form, seduced the daughters of men, and produced giant offspring, a hybrid of devils and humans called *nephilim*. . . . Remember, as indicated in Genesis 6:2, teraphim can take on fleshly form for extended periods of time. And yes, to put it bluntly one more time, they *did* have sexual relations with human woman . . . and they *did* produce *offspring* that were *not* created by God.

> "Many students of the Bible believe that angelic beings can't reproduce. Didn't Yeshua say so Himself, in Matthew 22:30? Not exactly; in context, Yeshua was referring to the state of humanity and angels in heaven. Fallen teraphim, on the other hand, are cited in Scripture . . . as *interbreeding with mankind* on earth (Genesis 6:1–4, II Peter 2:4–14, Jude 7). The Bible describes an order of angels that take on human form – those that we sometimes 'entertain unawares' (Genesis 18 and 19, Hebrews 13:2)."[6]

It is our opinion, based on extensive research into both the character and the apparent physical characteristics of the "woman" herself, that Jezebel was also a nephal.

Heads and Horns

The seven heads and the ten horns of both the beast and the Dragon are extremely symbolic. Hebraically, heads are signs of authority while horns are symbols of strength. We don't know what the blasphemous names are, but a name in Hebrew is a symbol of identity, so each head has a blasphemous nature. As to what these ten horns are, the answer can be found once again in Daniel 7:24–27.

> [24]"As for the ten horns, out of this kingdom ten kings will arise; and another will arise after them, and he will be different from the previous ones and will subdue three kings. [25]He will speak out against the Most High and wear down the saints of the Highest One, and he will intend to make alterations in times and in law; and they will be given into his hand for a time, times, and half a time. [26]But the court will sit for judgment, and his dominion will be taken away, annihilated and destroyed forever. [27]Then the sovereignty, the dominion and the greatness of all the kingdoms under the whole heaven will be given to the people of the saints of the Highest One; His kingdom will be an everlasting kingdom, and all the dominions will serve and obey Him."

The fourth beast, Satan, is the ruler of this final kingdom. This beast – or this evil kingdom – is the seventh and last kingdom prophesied in Nebuchadnezzar's vision. The ten horns are ten kings that represent this last worldwide kingdom.

A Burning Question . . .

Most readers will remember the account in the third chapter of Daniel in which Nebuchadnezzar, the king of Babylon, tried to intimidate Shadrach, Meshach, and Abednego into bowing down to his own golden image. Here's how they responded:

> [16]Shadrach, Meshach and Abednego replied to the king, "O Nebuchadnezzar, we do not need to give you an answer concerning this matter. [17]If it be so, our God whom we serve is able to deliver us from

> the furnace of blazing fire; and He will deliver us out of your hand, O king. [18]But even if He does not, let it be known to you, O king, that we are not going to serve your gods or worship the golden image that you have set up." (Daniel 3:16–18)

Everyone knows what happened next. The fire in Nebuchadnezzar's furnace was so hot it killed the men who threw the three Hebrew youths into it. But none of the three were harmed; not even a single hair on their heads was singed. Indeed, the incredulous king then saw them walking around with a fourth man, of whom he said, "the appearance of the fourth is like a son of the gods!" (Daniel 3:25)

And so it was. The statue represented Nebuchadnezzar himself, glorifying all the false, temporary power he maintained over the kingdom of Babylon during his lifetime, all of which passed on to his descendant, Belshazzar (Daniel 5:2), when Nebuchadnezzar went to his grave.

This "time, times, and half a time" in Daniel is an Hebraic expression that means 3½ years. Thus for 3½ years the False Messiah will reign, persecuting and murdering God's people. This is the same amount of time alloted to the beast to rule the earth in Daniel 7:25. At the end of this time period (also known as forty-two months), God will come back and the beast will be judged and thrown into the lake of fire.

As described in Revelation 12, the Dragon, infuriated over losing the woman (Israel), pursues and fights the rest of her children, especially those who obey God's commands and observe the customs of Yeshua.

On one level, the seven heads of the Dragon represent the seven evil kingdoms that have dominated the earth since the Tower of Babel. In Revelation 13:3, one of those heads appeared to have a fatal wound but that wound is now healed. Again, the Hebrew perspective regarding the head is that it is a symbol of authority.

Another Metaphor

So, metaphorically, if the head of the beast is wounded its *authority* is wounded. We know that Satan was stripped of identity and authority when he was cast from heaven.[7] When he deceived Adam and Eve at the Tree of Knowledge he stole their authority – and continues to steal mankind's authority today. We also know that, at the crucifixion and resurrection, Yeshua the Messiah fulfilled the prophecy in Genesis 3 that states:

> "Because you have done this,
> Cursed are you more than all cattle,
> And more than every beast of the field;
> On your belly you will go,
> And dust you will eat
> All the days of your life;
> [15]And I will put enmity
> Between you and the woman,
> And between your seed and her seed;
> *He shall bruise you on the head,*
> *And you shall bruise him on the heel."*
> (Genesis 3:14–15, italics added)

The head wound from which the beast is healed, combined with the Revelation text that we will talk about in greater detail momentarily, implies a resurrection. This is also another attempt, by Satan, to emulate the death and resurrection of the real Messiah.

Yeshua's death and resurrection caused the head wound inflicted on the beast in the book of Revelation. This is a sign of the Messiah's power, authority, and judgment. He wounded the Adversary's stolen authority. Appropriately, the Hebrew words used in the Genesis passage can actually give us insight into what is taking place in the 13th chapter of Revelation.

The Hebrew word for head in this passage is *rosh* (*resh/aleph/shin*). It means *a head, highest, supreme, a prince, or chief.* Idiomatically, to strike one on the head or to *give upon one's head* is to repay them for their evil deeds.[8]

The word for heel is *akev* (*ayin/koof/beit*). It means *the heel, to come from behind, to supplant, to circumvent, to defraud.*[9] Both of these words help to describe the motivations and interactions that Yeshua and Satan have with one another. Yeshua the Messiah has struck the Adversary's head – literally, he smashed Satan's authority. Hebraically, he has "given upon his head to repay him for his evil deeds."

Satan, the serpent and the Dragon, strikes Yeshua upon the heel, the place where the sandal resides. The sandal is a symbol of inheritance. So, the Adversary seeks to *supplant, circumvent, and defraud* Yeshua from His inheritance, which is the authority to rule over all creation at the right hand of God.

Satan first did this to Adam and Eve, the father and mother of mankind. Now he seeks to do the same to the Messiah and ultimately to God. He does so with the symbols of his strength and authority – seven heads and ten horns. That is, seven kingdoms, or nations, and ten kings. It's not accidental that Satan is representing his kingdom by a beast with ten heads representing ten kings. Hebraically, the number ten means *righteous government*. This is exactly how Satan will attempt to portray his end-times kingdom, as being righteous. Of course, that is the last thing Satan's kingdom will *ever* be. But, as a deceiver he will attempt to *look* righteous to fool as many people as possible.

The words "seven kingdoms" also have numerical meaning embedded within them. The number seven represents perfection and completion, which amounts to another ruse by the enemy to copy God and fool mankind in the process. So Satan is trying to appear holy, righteous, and perfect. What a farce!

A Parallel of Comparisons

As we explained in Volume 2, the seven letters of the book of Revelation were addressed to seven actual Messianic congregations in the time of John the Apostle. They also represent the seven patriarchs of covenant and the congregations that have served God throughout all of history.

The seven evil kingdoms are the exact counterparts of these congregations. Notice the parallel but opposite locations that the evil kingdoms mini-menorah occupies on the left side of the master menorah (see Figure 2-2), versus the right side position of the letter mini-menorah that represents the seven congregations. The seven evil kingdoms and the seven congregations resemble mirror images of each other. One is a reflection of God's people; the other a reflection of Satan's minions.

These evil kingdoms are seven actual kingdoms of the world that have served the Adversary throughout all of history. In other words, they existed at the same time as God's congregations. Here is the list:[10]

- **1 – Babylon:** Ruled by Nimrod, also known as Amraphel. Nimrod attempted to enslave Lot, Abraham's nephew.

- **2 – Egypt:** Ruled by Pharaoh. The Egyptians enslaved the Hebrews.

- **3 – Assyria:** Sennacharib, the Assyrian king, enslaved most of the people of the known world, including the ten northern tribes of the Israelites.

- **4 – Revised Babylon:** Nebuchanezzer enslaved the remaining Judeans comprising the southern tribes, including Daniel the prophet.

- **5 – Medo-Persia:** King Ahasuerus presided over the drama involving Esther and Haman, in which Haman almost destroyed the Jews.

- **6 – Greece:** Alexander the Great, who also conquered the known world, put the Israelites back into bondage and introduced moral and spiritual corruption into the Jewish people, through what became known as *Hellenization*.

- **7a – Rome:** Ruled by Casear, the Romans destroyed the Temple, oppressed the Jews, and scattered them throughout the world.

- **7b – Rome/Babylon:** This is the one remaining kingdom that has yet to manifest. This kingdom will be identified by a king whom our text describes as a beast/dragon. This king will be

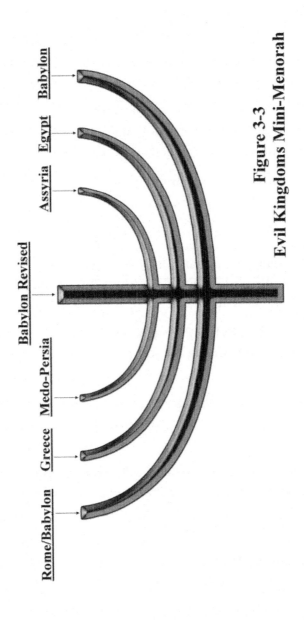

Figure 3-3
Evil Kingdoms Mini-Menorah

assisted by the False Prophet and the whore of Babylon. These beings will once again attempt to corrupt and destroy all of God's own people.

These are the tyrannical, despotic, evil kingdoms of Satan that have risen and fallen throughout time. Again and again the Adversary has attempted the same scheme, in repeated endeavors to usurp God and destroy His people. Here in the book of Revelation he is making one final, concerted effort, knowing that his own judgment is due.

A Fatal Head Wound

Let's continue with our examination of the verses in Revelation 13.

> . . . but its fatal wound was healed and the whole world followed after the beast in amazement. They worshipped the dragon, because he had given his authority to the beast; and they worshipped the beast saying, "Who is like the beast? Who can fight against it?"
> (Revelation 13:3–4, CJB)

This fatal head wound is the very wound prophesied back in Genesis 3:15, which we quoted a few pages back. God promised mankind that he would take care of both the corruption and the corrupter. The authority to accomplish this was gained at the resurrection of the Messiah 2,000 years ago.

At the same time, for reasons that only He fully understands, God now allows Satan to appear as though he and his authority have not been destroyed. And one last time He allows Satan to attempt to deceive mankind into thinking that the Adversary has at least *something* under control. He is therefore allowed to rule temporarily over a false kingdom with himself on its throne, governing it and claiming to be God.

Popular interpretation of this passage of Scripture claims that the False Messiah will recover from a fatal head wound, possibly being resurrected from the dead. We concur with this understanding. The verbiage from the Hebraic background of Revelation 13:1–10 implies that the False Prophet and the False Messiah are the same type of beasts. Daniel describes this fourth beast as a composite of the previous three. The False Prophet is none other than death personified, Abaddon. Remember, this is the star that fell out of heaven back in the fifth trumpet, the same one that unlocks the abyss and releases the teraphim.

The terrifying implication that some derive from this passage is that Abaddon causes breath to enter the False Messiah, raising him from the dead. In reality this is a warped and perverse image of Elijah the Prophet and Yeshua the Messiah. Let's look at the corresponding passage in Matthew 24:

> [15]"Therefore when you see the ABOMINATION OF DESOLATION which was spoken of through Daniel the prophet, standing in the holy place (let the reader understand), [16]then those who are in Judea must flee to the mountains. [17]Whoever is on the housetop must not go down to get the things out that are in his house. [18]Whoever is in the field must not turn back to get his cloak. [19]But woe to those who are pregnant and to those who are nursing babies in those days!

> [20]"But pray that your flight will not be in the winter, or on a Sabbath. [21]For then there will be a great tribulation, such as has not occurred since the beginning of the world until now, nor ever will. [22]Unless those days had been cut short, no life would have been saved; but for the sake of the elect those days will be cut short.

> [23]"Then if anyone says to you, 'Behold, here is the Christ' [Messiah], or 'There He is,' do not believe him. [24]For false Christs [Messiahs] and false prophets will arise and will show great signs and wonders, so as to mislead, if possible, even the elect." (Matthew 24:15–24)

A Perfect Match

This passage is a direct corrolation to Revelation 13. The Hebrew in Matthew is especially intriguing. It reads *Meshichei sheker u'neviei kazav*, which equates to *lying, deceiving False Messiahs and deceiving*

False Prophets,[11] which matches up perfectly with these verses from Revelation 13:

> [5]There was given to him a mouth speaking arrogant words and blasphemies, and authority to act for forty-two months was given to him. [6]And he opened his mouth in blasphemies against God, to blaspheme His name and His tabernacle, that is, those who dwell in heaven. [7]It was also given to him to make war with the saints and to overcome them, and authority over every tribe and people and tongue and nation was given to him. [8]All who dwell on the earth will worship him, everyone whose name has not been written from the foundation of the world in the book of life of the Lamb who has been slain. (Revelation 13:5–8)

The False Messiah in Matthew 24:5, 23–26 is the same as the beast in Revelation 13. This is describing the fulfillment of Yeshua's prophesy in Matthew 24. Meanwhile, here are some additional comments about Matthew 24 from Volume 2 in this series:

> Most believers in Yeshua are familiar with the 24th chapter of the book of Matthew, in which He answers the question below, from His disciples:
>
> > "Tell us, when will these things happen, and what will be the sign of Your coming, and of the end of the age?" (Matthew 24:3)
>
> This particular chapter is one of the most fascinating in all of Scripture and contains a whole series of very definite, very specific clues to the end times, some of which are completely missed and/or misunderstood by Western/Greek-oriented commentators. Some of these "failures to apprehend" we will discuss later, but right here we want to point out something that we find especially interesting.
>
> When Yeshua responded to His disciples He spoke in a very ordered, very linear way about what was coming in the end times. In fact, in terms of their order of presentation, His own

comments correspond exactly to the sequence of the seven seals. For example:

- Matthew 24:4–5 talks about being careful and letting no one mislead you, even those who come in His name and claim to be the Messiah, for they will lead many astray. All of this, incidentally, reminds us of what Paul said in his second letter to the believers at Thessalonica:

> ¹BUT RELATIVE to the coming of our Lord Jesus Christ (the Messiah) and our gathering together to [meet] Him, we beg you, brethren, ²Not to allow your minds to be quickly unsettled or disturbed or kept excited or alarmed, whether it be by some [pretended] revelation of [the] Spirit or by word or by letter [alleged to be] from us, to the effect that the day of the Lord has [already] arrived and is here. ³Let no one deceive or beguile you in any way, for that day will not come except the apostasy comes first [unless the predicted great falling away of those who have professed to be Christians has come], and the man of lawlessness (sin) is revealed, who is the son of doom (of perdition), ⁴Who opposes and exalts himself so proudly and insolently against and over all that is called God or that is worshiped, [even to his actually] taking his seat in the Temple of God, proclaiming that he himself is God. (II Thessalonians 2:1–4, AMP)

Thus we have Yeshua's prophecy about many who come and falsely claim to be the Messiah, thereby causing much deception and leading people into error. All of this precisely corresponds to what the first rider on the white horse is all about.

- In Matthew 24:6, Yeshua talks about wars and rumors of wars. These refer to the second horse rider, who comes to take peace from the earth.

- Matthew 24:7 says that "nation will rise against nation, and kingdom against kingdom, and . . . there will be famines and earthquakes," which overlays the third horse rider.

- Matthew 24:8 reminds us that the death and disease brought by the fourth horse rider are "merely the beginning of birth pangs."

- Matthew 24:9 talks about tribulation, hatred, and death for God's people, which correspond to the fifth seal.

- Matthew 24:10–16 speaks of increasing lawlessness, False Prophets, and the Abomination of Desolation prophesied in the book of Daniel, all of which relate to the 6th and 7th seals, and to some prophetic material in the trumpets.

  Thus the confrontations we see in the seals, and in Matthew 24 (which embellishes that material), indicate that this is just the beginning of end-times difficulties. God is not through offering salvation yet, but the road is going to get tougher.[12]

In other words, in Matthew 24 Yeshua was describing – or *previewing* – the basic outline of the book of Revelation, in brief. He highlighted the key events: the seals, the trumpets, the rise of the False Prophet and the False Messiah, the persecution of God's people, and His own return in power and glory.

So, we can see that the False Prophet and the False Messiah appear as the leaders of the seventh, or final, evil kingdom that will culminate the plans of Satan.

Now let's continue with the Revelation text.

The False Prophet

For many years, most explanations and/or discussions of the following passage from Revelation 13 have lacked the most vital Hebraic insights.

> [11]Then I saw another beast coming up out of the earth; and he had two horns like a lamb and he spoke as a dragon. [12]He exercises all the authority of the first beast in his presence. And he makes the earth and those who dwell in it to worship the first beast, whose fatal wound was healed. [13]He performs great signs, so that he even makes fire come down out of heaven to the earth in the

presence of men. [14]And he deceives those who dwell on the earth because of the signs which it was given him to perform in the presence of the beast, telling those who dwell on the earth to make an image to the beast who had the wound of the sword and has come to life. [15]And it was given to him to give breath to the image of the beast, so that the image of the beast would even speak and cause as many as do not worship the image of the beast to be killed. (Revelation 13:11–15)

This beast is different from the first beast (the False Messiah) that rose from the sea, in that it comes up out of the earth. The earth can also be symbolic of mankind, since Adam was formed from the *adamah*, the clay, the dirt, the earth itself. It can sometimes be symbolic of the grave, too, which is in the earth.

This beast is similar to the first one in that it is the fourth type of beast introduced in Daniel 7. It is a nephal, exhibiting characteristics of all the previous types of nephilim. It is not a giant per se, but it possesses certain attributes of the giants.

Why Didn't Adam and Eve Die?

Lots of people claim that the Genesis text is wrong, because obviously Adam and Eve did not die when they ate the forbidden fruit. But being separated from God encompassed the concept of death from an Hebraic perspective, not what physical death involved from a western perspective. Here, once sin entered the world it separated man from God, and therefore they literally "died" on the day they sinned *because they were separated from Him*.

What comes next is very intriguing. The beast has two horns like a lamb but speaks like a dragon. Again, horns signify strength and authority. This beast's strength is twofold. The beast comes in the guise of innocence, like a lamb. However, the Hebrew in this passage reveals something different.

"Speaking like a dragon" can be interpreted as something other than the literal meaning. The Hebrew word commonly translated as *dragon* is *tanin* (*tav/noon/yood/nun-sofit*). However, the root word for dragon is *taan*, which can also mean a *jackel, a wild dog, or a wolf*. So, this beast could actually be a wolf in sheep's clothing. Either way, it comes disguised as something innocent but speaks like a wolf, or a devourer. This beast is most definitely the False Prophet.

This description of the False Prophet, as a wolf, reminds us of a passage from II Peter:

> [1]But false prophets also arose among the people, just as there will also be false teachers among you, who will secretly introduce destructive heresies, even denying the Master who bought them, bringing swift destruction upon themselves. [2]Many will follow their sensuality, and because of them the way of the truth will be maligned. (II Peter 2:1–2)

Further along in II Peter 2, in verses 15–18:

> [15] . . . forsaking the right way, they have gone astray, having followed the way of Balaam, the son of Beor, who loved the wages of unrighteousness; [16]but he received a rebuke for his own transgression, for a mute donkey, speaking with a voice of a man, restrained the madness of the prophet. [17]These are springs without water and mists driven by a storm, for whom the black darkness has been reserved. [18]For speaking out arrogant words of vanity they entice by fleshly desires, by sensuality, those who barely escape from the ones who live in error.

As Yeshua Himself said, "Beware of the false prophets, who come to you in sheep's clothing, but inwardly are ravenous wolves" (Mathew 7:15).

More than ever we should be on guard, because this jackal will claim to be Elijah the Prophet, who precedes the coming of the Messiah. But in this case Abaddon, the False Prophet, will be preceding the coming of the *False* Messiah. Now the False Prophet will even be able to summon fire from the sky to prove his authenticity.

Remember, in Elijah's day he confronted the false prophets of Ba'al and they had a contest to see who could call down fire from heaven to burn up the sacrifice on the altar. But the prophets of Ba'al failed and were destroyed. This *false* Elijah will try to establish his identity as the *real* Elijah by doing the same thing. But remember, he is also the one who killed the prophet Elijah (one of the two witnesses) at the end of the sixth trumpet.

Beware of False Prophets – Again!

The passage in Revelation describes the False Prophet performing great miracles to deceive mankind. This is a reminder to us even now to guard our hearts and ears. The performance of miracles is not proof of one's being approved and sent by God. As in the book of Matthew, we are admonished to "judge a tree by its fruit." No good fruit comes from any false prophet.

We're also told in the Revelation passage that the False Prophet makes an image of the first beast, the False Messiah, Satan. He is allowed to put breath (in Hebrew *ruach*, or *spirit*) into the image. The Hebrew word used in these verses for image is *tzelem (tsadik/lamed/mem-sofit)*. It means *a shadow, an image, a likeness, an idol.*[13]

This is reminesent of the time of the Maccabees in ancient Israel, when the Assyrian dictator, Antiochous Epiphenes, ordered the murder of the Jewish people who refused to bow to an idol of Zeus that he'd erected in the Temple. Likewise, the False Prophet has those who do not worship the image of the False Messiah put to death.

In addition to the erection of an idol in the newly rebuilt Temple, as in the time of Antiochus, from an Hebraic perspective the imagery conveyed here is also connected to the False Prophet's resurrection of the False Messiah. Remember, the creation of the nephilim is an attempt by the Adversary to replace mankind in his own image. *A nephal is an image, a shadow of a man.*

In a perverse, copycat version of God's giving life to Adam, the first man, what's also being conveyed in the Revelation passage is a description of the False Prophet supposedly breathing life and spirit into the nephal body of the False Messiah. The "making" of the False Messiah itself is nothing more than the creating of an image for mankind to worship.

Indeed, he's not just a statue; the "image" is the *False Messiah himself* – the False Messiah *in the flesh*. Thus the False Prophet appears to create a "god" in his own image just as God created man in His image. The False Prophet is seen here pretending to fulfill the prophecies about the real Messiah, having power over death and being able to resurrect himself from the dead.

This image is described as a shadow, which is created via the absence of light. Again we see confirmation that this particular image of the False Messiah is, indeed, a shadow of the true Messiah. We can learn things from the shadow about the original. In this case the shadow, the False Messiah, is indeed copying and attempting to look like the real one. But in actuality he's a poor would-be substitute, the absence of light rather than the source.

This leads us to a classic old, familiar story by a nineteenth century writer named Mary Shelly, that beautifully illustrates all the above.

Frankenstein's Monster

Dr. Victor Frankenstein is an up-and-coming scientist with a passion for discovery and an obsession to create life. Using body parts from corpses and conducting experiments that spit in the face of morality, he creates a grotesque image of life, of man. Suddenly awakening to the horror of what he has literally "constructed," he flees in terror without taking responsibility for his actions, and for the life that he's created, however perverse it might be.

The creature, confused and tormented by its lack of fatherly care, begins its own discovery of mankind. Seeing the good that man can convey, yet tormented by mankind's great selfishness and evil, the creature begins a quest to discover his maker. When he finds the man who brought him into life he is overcome by rage and jealousy at the wonderful and happy life Dr. Frankenstein has wrought for himself, all the while seeming to have no regard – or even fond remembrance – for the thing he created.

So the creature embarks on a mission to destroy his master's life by stalking and murdering those who are dear to him in an effort to transfer some of the pain and suffering it has endured onto its creator. Finally, the creature meets Victor himself in a cave. There he has a dialogue with him.

The creature knows that it is an abomination. Even so, it desperately covets the love and family relationships of its creator and won't let anything stand in the way of its satisfaction, even as it continues to bring suffering and destruction on all that Dr. Frankenstein holds dear. The creator and his creation thus develop a mutual relationship of hatred and desired destruction, each for the other. In the story's finale, Dr. Frankenstein pursues his monster to the frozen Arctic to both of their deaths.

This familiar story offers some interesting parallels into the creation of the nephilim, and into Satan's kingdom. Like the False Prophet and the False Messiah, Dr. Frankenstein does not adhere to godly principles and therefore creates a grotesque image of life rather than something wonderful and creative – a fiend, a monster, and an abomination. And, of course, that "creation" then brings about his own destruction.

The Frankenstein story is also not the first of its kind. It has its roots in a story even more ancient, with direct connections to the Jewish people.

The Golem

In Jewish folklore, a golem is an animated, anthropomorphic being created entirely from inanimate matter. The word *golem* (*gimel/lamed/ mem-sofit*, meaning *embryo* or *fetus*) is also used in the Bible to refer to an embryonic or incomplete substance.

> Your eyes have seen my *unformed substance* [Ed.
> Note: *golem*];
> And in Your book were all written

> The days that were ordained for me,
> When as yet there was not one of them. (Psalm 139:16)

The above passage uses the word golem to mean *my unformed substance*. The same word passed into Yiddish as *goylem*. In modern Hebrew the word golem means *dumb* or *helpless*.

The same word is often used today as a metaphor for brainless lunks or entities who serve man under controlled conditions but are hostile to him at other times. It is also a Yiddish slang insult for someone who is clumsy or slow.

The original story of the golem had its beginnings in Nimrod's Babylon, more than 4,000 years ago. The concept of the golem originated within Babylonian mysticism, where it referred to a creation made in the likeness of man, usually from clay or stone. It was made to be an archetype of a deliverer, but from a biblical perspective it was always a *false* deliverer.

The ancient Babylonian legends speak of a golem who sat at the gates of Babel to protect it from enemies. It was created by Ishtar, the queen of Babylon who was also worshipped as the queen of heaven. The golem was made in the likeness of her son and husband, Nimrod.

The meaning of 666

Kabbalah, the body of Jewish mysticism that came from the combining of Babylonian mysticism with Judaism, says that two Hebrew letters were engraved on the golem's forehead and that these letters carried power and gave the golem life. We disagree with the foundational teachings of Kabbalah, but it does "steal" from many biblical, Hebraic concepts.

In contrast, remember that Hebrew letters have numerical value. The letters on the head of the golem, combined with their numerical value, give an amazing insight into Revelation 13:16–18.

> [16]And he causes all, the small and the great, and the rich
> and the poor, and the free men and the slaves, to be given

> a mark on their right hand or on their forehead, [17]and he provides that no one will be able to buy or to sell, except the one who has the mark, either the name of the beast or the number of his name. [18]Here is wisdom. Let him who has understanding calculate the number of the beast, for the number is that of a man; and his number is six hundred and sixty-six.

In a fascinating parallel to all the above, the Hebrew letters that were carved into the head of the golem were *chet/yud*. These letters form the Hebrew word for life – *chai*. The numerical value of this word is 18 (*chet* = 8, *yud* = 10). The numerical value of 18 corresponds to the combination (or "adding together") of three digits – 6, 6, and 6.

However, according to the book of Genesis we're made in the image and likeness of God:

> [26]Then God said, "Let Us make man in Our image, according to Our likeness; and let them rule over the fish of the sea and over the birds of the sky and over the cattle and over all the earth, and over every creeping thing that creeps on the earth." [27]God created man in His own image, in the image of God He created him; male and female He created them. [28]God blessed them; and God said to them, "Be fruitful and multiply, and fill the earth, and subdue it; and rule over the fish of the sea and over the birds of the sky and over every living thing that moves on the earth." (Genesis 1:26–28)

We also know that man has three parts, just like God: a body, a soul, and a spirit. In Hebrew thought, numbers are associated with certain principles, or aspects of life and creation. The number seven is associated with God – in Hebrew that number means *perfection, completion*. These concepts are directly associated with God, for He is both perfect and complete.

Thus God, perfect and complete in body, soul, and spirit, is a 777. Man and woman, made in the image and likeness of God prior to the Fall, were also 777 in body, soul, and spirit.

But when Adam and Eve disobeyed and ate the fruit from the Tree of Knowledge they became one less than perfection in all three aspects, or 666. This is what the book of Revelation alludes to in chapter 13. Six is the number of man; one less than God. Thus the number 666 refers to *fallen* man in all three aspects of his existence.

As we explain below, this fulfills God's warning that "in the day that you eat from it [the forbidden fruit] you will surely die." However, we need to remember why God drove man from the Garden of Eden and the Tree of Life. It wasn't because God hated man; it wasn't even because He was angry. On the contrary, He expelled Adam and Eve because he *loved* them and didn't want them to stay trapped in their fallen state forever.

This state would have been likened to the concept that we sometimes refer to as "the walking dead." Like Frankenstein or the golem, Adam and Eve would have been alive yet dead. However, this "dead" concept has to be identified from an Hebraic perspective. In Hebrew, *dead* means being separated from God; having no relationship with Him. In that condition a person can be alive physically but the Bible still refers to that state as death from a spiritual perspective.

> [22]Then the LORD God said, "Behold, the man has become like one of Us, knowing good and evil; and now, he might stretch out his hand, and take also from the tree of life, and eat, and live forever" – [23]therefore the LORD God sent him out from the garden of Eden, to cultivate the ground from which he was taken. [24]So He drove the man out; and at the east of the garden of Eden He stationed the cherubim and the flaming sword which turned every direction to guard the way to the tree of life. (Genesis 3:22–24)

Covenant Means Restoration[14]

God is in the process of restoring man back to what he was before the Fall in the Garden of Eden. Man's body, soul, and spirit fell from a perfect 777 to a 666 (the number of man, Revelation 13:18).

In this process of restoration, man's spirit is restored first, occurring when Yeshua died on the cross. The restoration of the spirit was available for anyone who wanted to accept God's free gift and enter into relationship with Him. Many have accepted that relationship over the past 2,000 years and have been restored to a position of 7-6-6 (and even quite a few who lived in the BC era to whom Yeshua proclaimed freedom after He died to those in prison, as described in I Peter 3:19.)

Man's soul is being mended and restored through covenant. When man dies or Yeshua returns man is restored to a 7-7-6. The restoration of the body occurs last "in the twinkling of an eye" and will once again render man as a 7-7-7, the same as he was before the Fall. We will be given new bodies that cannot suffer pain. This will occur starting at the last trumpet during the Second Coming and will be completed at the Great White Throne Judgment that comes at the end of the thousand-year reign.

Restoration is a process – and it all involves covenant. We have much to look forward to.

An Act of Mercy

What God did was an act of mercy. If mankind had stayed in the Garden and continued to eat of the Tree of Life he would have lived forever but would have remained a 666, in an eternal, corrupted, irredeemable state – separated from God . . . and dead! Never again could he have been restored to a complete and perfect state so that he could be reunited with God. God had Adam and Eve driven from the Garden to give them a hope and a chance to make the choice – the choice that would lead to restoration.

As a direct result, instead of being permanently dead to God, mankind now became the beneficiary of God's redemptive plan, already interwoven into creation. This plan was (and still is) a *process* and not just a *one-time event*. It started when God killed an animal and clothed Adam and Eve. At that point, mankind became a 766, via a renewed covenant with God whereby mankind's spirit (i.e., one-third of mankind's identity) could become perfect again through its unity with Him.

By accepting and wearing the skin of the animal, Adam and Eve made a covenant with God to be obedient to His redemptive plan, thereby starting the process of restoring their relationship with Him. As we enter into all three levels of covenant, we also continue that process of restoration/redemption.

As we explained in Volume 1 in this series, *blood* covenant restores your spirit, *salt* covenant restores your soul, and *sandal* covenant restores your body. Recall the concept of light. Light comprises three primary and three secondary colors, which correspond to the three levels of covenant as explained above. As these colors of light are recombined, they produce perfect white light, and that is the color of the Bride of Messiah. This Bride will be perfect and complete in body, soul, and spirit – in every way a true 777.

God's redemptive plan was pictured in His slaughtering of the lamb to make a covering for Adam and Eve. This act, by God, was also a prophecy about what His plan entailed. He would send His Son as an innocent lamb to die on the cross, thereby paying the price for our restoration from our fallen state into a renewed, perfected state of 777 in body, soul, and spirit . . . at the end of the age.

However, salvation is only the first step in a longer process as detailed in our discussion of covenants. For many of us (but not necessarily all of us), that process will eventually lead to becoming the Bride of Yeshua.

Satan Equals Impurity

The mark that the beast offers fallen man (Revelation 13:16) is something physical as well as spiritual. It identifies those who are part of his kingdom. This implies that those who are sealed will follow him into a permenant fallen state in which there will be no hope of redemption – an eternal 666. That is what 666 represents – a permanent fallen state and a permanent separation from God – death!

> . . . that is, the one whose coming is in accord with the activity of Satan, with all power and signs and false wonders, [10]and with all the deception of wickedness for those who perish, because they did not receive the love of the truth so as to be saved. [11]For this reason God will send upon them a deluding influence so that they will believe what is false, [12]in order that they all may be judged who did not believe the truth, but took pleasure in wickedness. (II Thessalonians 2:9–12)

The mark of Satan, which he will require his people to take, copies the special mark that God puts on His own people who love and accept Him. Remember, God specially marks His people as well.[15] God put a mark on the forehead and the hand of His people, which was His own sign of the covenant . . . a seal. The False Messiah is doing the same thing via a perverted copy of God's original way of identifying His own. Satan is "sealing" his flock, but for destruction instead of eternal life.

Satan's distorted and completely untrue version is also a sign of the futility of his plan. That plan, deceptive in every aspect, is the same plan that Satan started with in the beginning, to the effect that "You can become gods yourself, entirely on your own, with the authority to define all the principles that govern your existence. And you can do all this without being associated with God."

Certainly this is Satan's own endgame, for when his brief time comes he sits on God's throne in the Temple and claims to be the *real* God by offering the same forbidden fruit to everyone else. Yet what he is actually attempting to do, still part of his plan from the beginning, is to steal mankind's identity and authority. Remember, mankind's identity came from God, for we were created in God's image. And, mankind's authority was given to us by God, which gave us the right to manage His creation. Satan very much wants both of these, because God took away Satan's original identity and authority when Satan fell.

The completion of Satan's plan, based on owning what man has freely given to him (i.e., man's identity and authority), is to rule and reign in a fallen state while calling it "perfection." This is the very reason why God barred mankind from the Tree of Life, because He did not want man's fallen state to be his perpetual state – a state of permanent separation from God.

Missing the Mark

God's plan and order for His creation and its fulfillment does not depend on anything outside of His control. He does allow Satan authority for a time, but only in an effort to bring a disobedient Bride back to her first love. Satan's efforts do not change anything of God's master plan; they only help fulfill Yeshua's desire to draw His Bride to Himself.

God also allows these things to help "lock in" the mark of the beast concept. All in all, if we're even slightly willing to study what He has explained in the Bible we should be able to see what's happening. He has made sure that we'll have no trouble "hitting the mark" (as defined in Torah) if we're sincere in our efforts.

On the other hand, we also all need to remember what Paul said in his second letter to the Thessalonians:

> [1]Now we request you, brethren, with regard to the coming of our Lord Jesus Christ and our gathering together to Him, [2]that you not be quickly shaken from your composure or be disturbed either by a spirit or a message or a letter as if from us, to the effect that the day of the Lord has come. [3]Let no one in any way deceive you, for it will not come unless the apostasy comes first, and the man of lawlessness is revealed, the son of destruction, [4]who opposes and exalts himself above every so-called god or object of worship, so that he takes his seat in the temple of God, displaying himself as being God.
>
> [5]Do you not remember that while I was still with you, I was telling you these things? [6]And you know what restrains him now, so that in his time he will be revealed. [7]For the mystery of lawlessness is already at work; only he who now restrains will do so until he is taken out of the way. [8]Then that lawless one will be revealed whom the Lord will slay with the breath of His mouth and bring to an end by the appearance of His coming. [9]That

is, the one whose coming is in accord with the activity of Satan, with all power and signs and false wonders, [10]and with all the deception of wickedness for those who perish, because they did not receive the love of the truth so as to be saved.

[11]For this reason God will send upon them a deluding influence so that they will believe what is false, [12]in order that they all may be judged who did not believe the truth, but took pleasure in wickedness. [13]But we should always give thanks to God for you, brethren beloved by the Lord, because God has chosen you from the beginning for salvation through sanctification by the Spirit and faith in the truth. [14]It was for this He called you through our gospel, that you may gain the glory of our Lord Jesus Christ. [15]So then, brethren, stand firm and hold to the traditions which you were taught, whether by word of mouth or by letter from us. (II Thessalonians 2:1–15)

At a certain point, the above verses apply to all of us and we are effectively already judged. Someday this will be fulfilled in our own lives and will pertain to us. At that moment we will lose the ability to make other choices and will fall under God's judgment, for good or for bad.

The bowls, then, reflect God's judgment, at which point we lose the opportunity to chose to be with Him. All the judgments will include the concept of God's wanting us to repent – for example, as He said in Revelation 16:9 (NIV): " . . . but they refused to repent and glorify Him."

In Summary . . .

The letter mini-menorah represents God's involvement with mankind from creation until His Second Coming. The mini-menorah, in the opposite position on the left (see Figure 2-2), depicts the Adversary's kingdoms and his deceptive offer of counter-covenant with mankind. We call this mini-menorah the evil kingdoms menorah because the events represented there reflect Satan's efforts to deceive mankind throughout time.

The Bible makes it clear that we can serve either the kingdom of God or the kingdom of darkness. The Adversary has sought to convince us to covenant with him, proclaiming that he is the real God (Daniel 11:36). He comes with a myriad of names and clever disguises, providing various ways to receive his gifts. He even offers us the right to become gods ourselves if only we will pursue covenant with him. Adam and Eve actually fell for the same seductive offer, convinced that they could decide for themselves the difference between right and wrong. Unfortunately for them the result was death.

God wants us to live by His standard. He has provided a way for our sins to be forgiven – Yeshua's death on the cross. Although nothing more is needed for salvation, God still asks us to covenant with Him in order to grow into full maturity. The first covenant is service and obedience to His instructions as found in Torah and the B'rit Hadashah, putting our love for Him into action by keeping His commandments (John 14:15).

There is only one way to salvation – through Yeshua – described as a small gate and a narrow path in Matthew 7:14. As He Himself also said, "No one can serve two masters; for either he will hate the one and love the other, or he will be devoted to one and despise the other" (Matthew 6:24).

Meanwhile, Satan offers multiple pathways – anything that might tempt, distract, or deceive us into rejecting the narrow pathway that God offers. It is even possible that this False Messiah will present himself to the world as the Messiah/God of multiple religions, including Christianity, Judaism, and Islam. He could try to deceive people by emphasizing the idea that all religions can lead to God. The Temple Mount in Jerusalem is one of the major holy sites for all of these religions. Is this why the beast/Antichrist will set up his reign there?

Like God, Satan also wants us to become more intimate with him. After deceiving us into serving him, he demands ever greater commitment. He offers friendship and sonship, but only at a lethal price. What does Satan want? He is after the same thing he has coveted ever since man's failure in the Garden of Eden. He craves the identity and authority given to us by God.

Chapter 4

Shamash of the
Seven Angelic Proclamations

~~~~~~

REVELATION 14 IS UNIQUE BECAUSE IT INCLUDES BOTH THE DESCRIPTION OF the seven angelic proclamation events and their shamash. The shamash text includes verses 1–5, with the balance of the chapter describing the angelic proclamations themselves. Here are those first five verses:

> ¹Then I looked, and behold, the Lamb was standing on Mount Zion, and with Him one hundred and forty-four thousand, having His name and the name of His Father written on their foreheads. ²And I heard a voice from heaven, like the sound of many waters and like the sound of loud thunder, and the voice which I heard was like the sound of harpists playing on their harps. ³And they sang a new song before the throne and before the four living creatures and the elders; and no one could learn the song except the one hundred and forty-four thousand who had been purchased from the earth.

> ⁴These are the ones who have not been defiled with women, for they have kept themselves chaste. These are the ones who follow the Lamb wherever He goes. These have been purchased from among men as first fruits to

God and to the Lamb. [5]And no lie was found in their
mouth; they are blameless. (Revelation 14:1–5)

The story of the preparations for the coming marriage stand in marked
contrast to the storyline we've been examining until now. The mini-
menorah-event storyline has described disaster on disaster and judgment on judgment, all of it representing God's final attempt to get
unrepentant mankind's attention.

However, at the same time God is also revealing His plans for His
Bride. Instead of disasters and judgments He is planning something
completely different. He said in John 14:2–3 that He was going away
to prepare a place for His people. He also said that He would come
back and take us to be with Him.

So far we have been introduced to the Groom's father, the Groom, the
groomsmen, the preparations going on at the site of the wedding, and
the thundering forth of God's wedding agreement between Himself
and mankind. As in any good play, once the introductions are done
the action starts.

Immediately Mount Zion comes into view. This is the mount on which
the Temple of God resides, also known as Mount Moriah, and is the
location of the wedding and the gathering guests we were introduced
to back in Revelation 7. The Groom, referred to here as the Lamb, has
gathered the 144,000 groomsmen and is seen standing on the mount.

This is the second time these groomsmen have appeared in Revelation.
The first time, back in Revelation 7, they were being marked on their
foreheads to identify them as belonging to God. These men are now
identified as the same men by the statement above, "having His name
and the name of His Father written on their foreheads."

The 144,000 includes 12,000 from each of the listed tribes of Israel.
Here they are doing very groomsmen-like things, such as singing
and following the Lamb wherever He goes. They are called blameless and are defined as virgins, all of which would make for good
Hebrew groomsmen.

Remember that the groomsmen were from the same family as the groom in ancient times – in this case, Israel. They were unwed men, implying that they were virgins, and at the time of the snatching of the bride and on the wedding day they had the honor of protecting and doing the bidding of the groom and of following him wherever he went.

Presently the men gather at the Groom's side and follow Him to the throne of God, singing all the way. Now recall the ancient wedding ceremony itself. The night before the big event, the snatching of the bride would occur. The groom would first gather his previously selected groomsmen. As they shouted, sang, blew shofars and played other instruments, creating a ruckus that told the community that the groom was coming, these men made it clear that the wedding was imminent.

The groom's next stop was the bride's house. There he would sweep her off her feet and take her to a preselected location where the wedding party would have one last all-night celebration before the wedding ceremony itself.

This is the exact scene of this shamash section. The Groom has gathered His groomsmen. The men follow the Groom and are making merry. But where is the Bride? We will soon be introduced to her, but this shamash lets us see only the events just before the Groom makes His grand arrival at the place of her dwelling. The angelic proclamations reveal the long-awaited restoration of the Groom to His Bride.

Firstfruits in Person

In the above passage, these groomsmen are referred to as "firstfruits." To our western ears, that reference does not trigger any particular meaning. At most it might encompass the idea that these men were the first of a crop that was harvested.

However, the Hebraic meaning actually does provide an initial indication of who they are. *Firstfruits* was the name of the third feast, or holy day, mentioned in the Old Testament. This day occurred in the spring, following Passover and Unleavened Bread. Recall that Yeshua died on Passover. He was buried on Unleavened Bread and He was raised from the dead on Firstfruits. On this feast the Israelites were commanded to offer God some of the first fruits from the field. The barley harvest would have just been completed, so new stalks of barley would have been waved before the Lord and offered to Him. This offering was an expression of thanks for His blessings and bounty.

At this time of year the Israelites would bring in the tenth of their barley harvest – indeed, the best was always the first from the fields. In this way they would honor God by bringing to Him their tithe: their first and their best. Thus the 144,000 are a type of tithe to God; they're the first and best of the end-times barley harvest. However, the barley harvest is the second-best harvest – the best harvest is yet to come!

Why Some Do Not Tithe

Some people offer the excuse that they do not tithe because, by the end of the month, just before the next payday, they don't have enough money left to give Him His portion. There is just not enough available after paying all the bills and other important expenses.

Firstfruits models how we should give to God. We offer Him the first of our income, not the last. In other words, we make sure that our account with heaven is paid first. This obligation is the most important expense that we have. Then we pay our other obligations, trusting in Him to provide enough to get us to our next harvest, or paycheck.

As Malachi assures us, obedience to God guarantees His blessing and protection:

> "Bring the whole tithe into the storehouse, so that there may be food in My house, and test Me now in this," says the LORD of hosts, "if I will not open for you the windows of heaven and pour out for you a blessing until it overflows." (Malachi 3:10)

It is interesting that our Lord was also raised from the dead on First-fruits, and that He was called the firstfruits from among the dead (I Corinthians 15:20). He certainly is an example of the best harvest and fulfilled the spiritual understanding of this feast by rising from the dead on it. The implication is that these groomsmen are offerings of first fruits as well. Groomsmen represent the groom's best and most reliable, dependable, and trustworthy friends. It's our opinion that this scenario, as described here, actually takes place on a future feast of Firstfruits.

Of the seven feasts described in numerous places in the Old Testament, three of them recognize and celebrate times of harvest. They are called the barley harvest, the wheat harvest, and the wet harvest. The barley harvest was celebrated on feast of Firstfruits (early spring), the wheat harvest was celebrated on Shavout (called *Pentecost* in Greek, late spring), and the wet harvest was celebrated on feast of Trumpets (early autumn). The wet harvest represented the harvest of fruits such as grapes, citrus, and pomegranates.

Each one of these harvests metaphorically represents different members of a Hebrew wedding party. The barley harvest represents the groomsmen, who are being harvested first. This allows them to follow the Groom and help Him prepare for the wedding. The groomsmen also aid Him in the snatching of the Bride. The wheat harvest represents the Bride herself. The wet harvest represents the guests at the wedding.

This insight gives the student of the Bible clues about the timing of the harvest, commonly called the Rapture, of each one of these groups. Barley and fruit were important, but nothing was more important than having a good wheat harvest. Bountiful supplies of wheat would ensure that the Israelites had food to sustain life over the next year. The wheat harvest was always recognized as the best and the most important harvest.

Knowing that these harvests/raptures are correlated with the feasts, which occur at specific times in the year, will help us recognize these important events, including the timing of the Second Coming.

Where Do All These Events Fit In?

Where do the angelic proclamations and their shamash events fit in the chronology established on the right side of the master menorah? Remember that the left side events (evil kingdoms, angelic proclamations) up to this point occur simultaneously with the events on the right side (see Figure I-1).

The groomsmen (i.e., the 144,000) in Revelation 7, are introduced before the seven trumpets are sounded. Now, in Revelation 14, we see the 144,000 again, appearing just before the angelic proclamations. So the proclamations must occur somewhere within the seven trumpets. As we move forward it will become clear that all seven of the angelic proclamations occur within the same time period as the sixth and seventh trumpets.

We know that the seven angelic proclamations do not occur *within* the bowls, which come after the trumpets, because the events that follow the re-introduction of the 144,000 in the text of Revelation 14 *are the bowls themselves*. Thus, in chapter 14 the Apostle John assumes that you now know who the 144,000 are. He begins to reveal more information about them, especially what their purpose is and what they are now doing.

These seven bowl judgments are on the third mini-menorah from the left, just to the left of the master shamash (see Figure I-1). The implication is that the seven angelic proclamation events occur before these last bowl judgments begin toward the end of the trumpet events. In other words, the angelic proclamation events take place sometime between the very end of the sixth trumpet, the seventh trumpet, and the bowls of wrath.

In Revelation 14:9–11, the third angel warns mankind not to take the mark of the beast or give homage to it. We know that the beast, the False Messiah, presents himself to the world as the God of Israel and the Bible by sitting on God's throne in His Temple in Jerusalem right after the two witnesses are killed, just before the seventh trumpet is blown (which is the last trumpet, further proof, incidentally, that these events occur within the trumpet events).

Remember, we also now know that these two witnesses are given authority to govern and bring judgments to mankind for 3½ years, the first half of the last seven years prophesied in Daniel 9:27. These two witnesses are described in Revelation 11 and minister during the last half of the sixth trumpet.

This implies that the last trumpet and all the bowl judgments fulfill the last half of Daniel's seven-year prophecy. As both Daniel and the book of Revelation state, God's work will then be finished and the one-thousand-year reign will begin.

This strongly supports the idea that God will meet His groomsmen on Mt. Zion somewhere very close to the beginning of the seventh trumpet, just before the snatching of the Bride. This conclusion will be confirmed by the events of the angelic proclamations themselves. In the next chapter we will explore these seven events so we can firmly establish where they occur in our timeline.

In Summary . . .

As we indicated in the introduction to this volume, God allows the weeds to grow up and then lets them be cut down when the crop itself is harvested. But weeds are not the only plants that are left over and/or winnowed out when the main crop is harvested.

In biblical times, what the Bible calls "gleanings" were actually part of the main crop. They included the harvest in the corners and along the edges of the field, plus the grain that spilled onto the ground during the harvesting process. All these were to be left for the poor and the hungry to harvest for themselves.[1]

These gleanings, along with the wet harvest, will constitute the final harvest of God's people.

Chapter 5

The Seven Angelic Proclamations

THE SECOND MINI-MENORAH ON THE LEFT SIDE OF THE MASTER MENORAH
(see Figure I-1) is the angelic proclamations menorah. Seven angels
appear, one after the other, giving warnings and directions to those
who dwell on the earth and to other angels as revealed in the following verses:

> [6]And I saw another angel flying in midheaven, having
> an eternal gospel to preach to those who live on the
> earth, and to every nation and tribe and tongue and
> people; [7]and he said with a loud voice, "Fear God, and
> give Him glory, because the hour of His judgment has
> come; worship Him who made the heaven and the earth
> and sea and springs of waters." [8]And another angel, a
> second one, followed, saying, "Fallen, fallen is Babylon
> the great, she who has made all the nations drink of the
> wine of the passion of her immorality."
>
> [9]Then another angel, a third one, followed them, saying
> with a loud voice, "If anyone worships the beast and his
> image, and receives a mark on his forehead or on his
> hand, [10]he also will drink of the wine of the wrath of
> God, which is mixed in full strength in the cup of His

anger; and he will be tormented with fire and brimstone in the presence of the holy angels and in the presence of the Lamb. [11]And the smoke of their torment goes up forever and ever; they have no rest day and night, those who worship the beast and his image, and whoever receives the mark of his name." [12]Here is the perseverance of the saints who keep the commandments of God and their faith in Jesus. [13]And I heard a voice from heaven, saying, "Write, 'Blessed are the dead who die in the Lord from now on!'" "Yes," says the Spirit, "so that they may rest from their labors, for their deeds follow with them."

[14]Then I looked, and behold, a white cloud, and sitting on the cloud was one like a son of man, having a golden crown on His head and a sharp sickle in His hand. [15]And another angel came out of the temple, crying out with a loud voice to Him who sat on the cloud, "Put in your sickle and reap, for the hour to reap has come, because the harvest of the earth is ripe." [16]Then He who sat on the cloud swung His sickle over the earth, and the earth was reaped. [17]And another angel came out of the temple which is in heaven, and he also had a sharp sickle.

[18]Then another angel, the one who has power over fire, came out from the altar; and he called with a loud voice to him who had the sharp sickle, saying, "Put in your sharp sickle and gather the clusters from the vine of the earth, because her grapes are ripe." [19]So the angel swung his sickle to the earth and gathered the clusters from the vine of the earth, and threw them into the great wine press of the wrath of God. [20]And the wine press was trodden outside the city, and blood came out from the wine press, up to the horses' bridles, for a distance of two hundred miles. (Revelation 14:6–20)

The first warning is one directed to mankind. It tells man to understand that the time for decision making is running out. The heart of God is revealed, for He does not want anyone to be lost but for all to turn to Him. The angel's message is to worship the real God of creation, to pay Him honor, to give Him glory, and to accept His Messiah.

This gospel/good news is from Isaiah in ancient times, found throughout the Tanakh but especially in the book of Isaiah, which usually gets interpreted as "glad tidings." But it's the same Hebrew phrase that means "Don't worry! I'm coming back to save you!"

What is "Good News"?

Many people believe that the concept of "good news" is a new concept presented for the first time within the New Testament (i.e., the *B'rit Hadashah*). On the contrary, it's an ancient concept presented by God in the Tanakh, hundreds of years prior to the first century AD.

As within all the prophetic writings, the pattern here is the same. God is angry with His people for the evil they're embracing and the sins they're committing. He brings judgment, punishment, and hardship. Then He relents, has mercy, and says that He is going to return to His people and restore them. This is the good news!

And yes, mankind has a part to play in the restoration as well. God is coming for those who, in spite of their sin, have been attentive to His call.

One Last Attempt . . .

These angelic warnings represents one last attempt by God to reveal to mankind that He is the One who established and has the power to create (or destroy) all things. In the days to come the fulfillment of II Thessalonians 2 will occur.

> [1]Now we request you, brethren, with regard to the coming of our Lord Jesus Christ and our gathering together to Him, [2]that you not be quickly shaken from your composure or be disturbed either by a spirit or a message or a letter as if from us, to the effect that the day of the Lord has come. [3]Let no one in any way deceive you, for it will not come unless the apostasy comes first, and the man of lawlessness is revealed, the son of destruction,

[4]who opposes and exalts himself above every so-called god or object of worship, so that he takes his seat in the temple of God, displaying himself as being God.

[5]Do you not remember that while I was still with you, I was telling you these things? [6]And you know what restrains him now, so that in his time he will be revealed. [7]For the mystery of lawlessness is already at work; only he who now restrains will do so until he is taken out of the way. [8]Then that lawless one will be revealed whom the Lord will slay with the breath of His mouth and bring to an end by the appearance of His coming; [9]that is, the one whose coming is in accord with the activity of Satan, with all power and signs and false wonders, [10]and with all the deception of wickedness for those who perish, because they did not receive the love of the truth so as to be saved.

[11]For this reason God will send upon them a deluding influence so that they will believe what is false, [12]in order that they all may be judged who did not believe the truth, but took pleasure in wickedness. [13]But we should always give thanks to God for you, brethren beloved by the Lord, because God has chosen you from the beginning for salvation through sanctification by the Spirit and faith in the truth. [14]It was for this He called you through our gospel, that you may gain the glory of our Lord Jesus Christ. [15]So then, brethren, stand firm and hold to the traditions which you were taught, whether by word of mouth or by letter from us. (II Thessalonians 2:1–15)

This passage speaks of a great falling away and a great beguilement and seduction upon mankind. This will eventually result in God's honoring the choices all people have made. He is a gentleman and has given us a very valuable option – the right to make choices for ourselves.

He knows that we can choose to love Him or we can choose to reject Him. Without this right we would be nothing more than robots, preprogrammed to serve, love, and obey. He gave us true choice because, without it, we couldn't experience true love. When we serve and obey

Him via our own free will, it implies something about our character, our stewardship, and our priorities. This was what God has always wanted and intended for man.

Certainly the bowls also fulfill the words spoken in ancient times by God Himself, and recorded in Deuteronomy. They spoke about a coming curse and judgment on those who would reject God's relationship. For example, here are a few verses from Deuteronomy 28:

> [1]"Now it shall be, if you diligently obey the LORD your God, being careful to do all His commandments which I command you today, the LORD your God will set you high above all the nations of the earth. [2]All these blessings will come upon you and overtake you if you obey the LORD your God:

> [3]"Blessed *shall* you *be* in the city, and blessed *shall* you *be* in the country. Blessed *shall be* the offspring of your body and the produce of your ground and the offspring of your beasts, the increase of your herd and the young of your flock. [5]Blessed *shall be* your basket and your kneading bowl. [6]Blessed *shall* you *be* when you come in, and blessed *shall* you *be* when you go out.

> [15]"But it shall come about, if you do not obey the LORD your God, to observe to do all His commandments and His statutes with which I charge you today, that all these curses will come upon you and overtake you:

> [16]"Cursed *shall* you *be* in the city, and cursed *shall* you *be* in the country. [17]Cursed *shall be* your basket and your kneading bowl. [18]Cursed *shall be* the offspring of your body and the produce of your ground, the increase of your herd and the young of your flock. [19]Cursed *shall* you *be* when you come in, and cursed *shall* you *be* when you go out." (Deuteronomy 28:1–6; 15–19)

Unfortunately, many will choose to reject Him and align themselves with things and beings that are not God and do not have good intentions for them. However, in the end, II Thessalonians 2:10–12 will be fulfilled. Here God instructs us that He will honor our choices and our decisions about Him. Rejecting the truth, we learn, only separates us farther from God and leads us down a path to further delusion so that we will believe the lie of the Adversary, which is that he is God instead.

The Fall of Confusion

The second angel informs us that Babylon the Great has fallen, referring to Babylon as a "she." Babylon, as a harlot, is seen in a controlling position on the beast (Revelation 17:3), promoting and committing acts of immorality with those who dwell on the earth. This "woman," who will have authority over the nations of the world and symbolizes unregenerate mankind, will be hated and killed by the beast she rides (Revelation 17:15–16). In contrast, God so loved the world that He died for His Bride. Satan's desire can be clearly seen by his action toward his bride, the harlot. He doesn't choose a pure bride; he chooses the ultimate personification of impurity.

Plus, Satan enters into covenant relationship with her only to seize her identity and authority. Once these are stripped from her, he kills and discards her as described by the second angel, who calls the harlot "Babylon" (Revelation 17:5–18). The Hebrew word for Babylon means *to mix together or confuse*, and certainly that's what we see the enemy doing in our world today. He takes a little bit of truth and mixes it with lies and thereby cons and deceives mankind. This is exactly what Paul was prophesying in Thessalonians above.

In contrast, God uses the Word to help us understand and identify the spiritual state of corrupted mankind. For us to do that, however, we have to know the truth. And let's be clear: the truth is not subjective, situational, or whatever else we want it to be. In contrast, Satan's kingdom is built on the shaky foundation of confusion, deception, and delusion and plays off against our own selfish lusts.

It seems that this concept of a woman riding on a beast existed in ancient times as well. Archeological digs have uncovered many figurines that depict a nude woman riding on a bull. The woman was recognized and worshiped as the goddess Astarte, the goddess of fertility from whom we get the name for the Christian holiday we call "Easter" (Easter eggs, anyone?). Her origins go back to at least the time of Nimrod, the king of Babylon, or about 2000 BC. The bull represents the god Ba'al, who was considered the most powerful god by ancient pagan cultures.

About Those Gods and Goddesses[1]

[In ancient times], worship often took the form of sacrifices, which included the giving of fruit, animals, money and other valuables, devotion, and often even human children (Leviticus 20:2). The Egyptians sacrificed the Hebrew children to Nun, the fertility goddess of the Nile. Ishtar, the Babylonian earth-goddess, also required child sacrifice to gain her favor.

This same goddess . . . is the Ashtoreth, or Astarte, of Scripture (II Kings 23:13, I Samuel 7:3,4). We derive our modern word "Easter" from Ishtar, one of the biblical variants of the word Ashtoreth. Ashtoreth was the goddess of love and fortune, the Queen of Heaven. She was also the goddess of fertility. Thus we have our "innocent" Easter symbolism involving bunny rabbits (What's more fertile than a rabbit?), eggs, and baby chicks.

Ishtar, Nun, and other pagan entities were recognized as the gods of *life*, yet required the *destruction* of life to appease them. They also encouraged the use of hallucinogenic drugs to help the worshipper enter a more receptive state of consciousness.

Obviously, that bull (the god Ba'al) is Satan himself. He has a purpose for allowing this woman to ride in the position of authority on his back. He will seduce her into believing that she does have controlling authority, just long enough for him to accomplish his goal. At that point she will be discarded. Unfortunately for her, this destiny is similar to those who choose to live their lives without God. But more of that to come later.

The second angel is proclaiming the destruction (or fall) of this woman, this harlot, this city – Babylon. This city is portrayed as equal to this woman (Revelation 17 and 18), the false bride, who is called the whore. We will discuss the details of her fall later in this text.

For the moment, understand that the events of the second angelic proclamation, which will occur before we reach the time of the seven bowls, is when Babylon (which, as we'll explain later, is Rome), will be destroyed. We believe that this will be the moment in time when the Antichrist (the False Messiah) will move the focus and location of his reign from Europe to Jerusalem.

Those Who Worship the Beast

The third angel proclaims, "If anyone worships the beast and his image and receives his mark on the forehead or upon the hand, he also will drink of the wine of the wrath of God" – i.e., the bowls (Revelation 14:9–10). As detailed earlier in this text, we know that the "mark of the beast" is a sign taken by those who have entered into covenant with the Antichrist. It represents their inheritance as provided by their unholy "father." They readily want to be seen as allied with this powerful entity that falsely claims to be God Himself.

In the end, Satan and his followers will only earn an inheritance determined by God. The beast will be stripped of all his stolen authority, power, and identity, losing all the kingdoms of the earth. He will be given the bowls of wrath from God's heavenly Temple and will receive his just reward in the burning lake of fire.

Unfortunately, those who are deceived into serving Satan will also inherit God's wrath and judgment – that same lake of fire. The payment for sin made for them by Yeshua was rejected. Now a special blessing is reserved for those who endure and persevere through what's coming next, while a special curse is reserved for Satan's followers, mirroring the blessings and curses spelled out in Deuteronomy 27 and 28.

Revelation 14:12–13 also reminds us of the message to the congregation at Philadelphia:

> 7"And to the angel of the church in Philadelphia write: He who is holy, who is true, who has the key of David, who

opens and no one will shut, and who shuts and no one opens, says this: [8]I know your deeds. Behold, I have put before you an open door which no one can shut, because you have a little power, and have kept My word, and have not denied My name. [9]Behold, I will cause those of the synagogue of Satan, who say that they are Jews and are not, but lie – I will make them come and bow down at your feet, and make them know that I have loved you. [10]Because you have kept the word of My perseverance, I also will keep you from the hour of testing, that hour which is about to come upon the whole world, to test those who dwell on the earth." (Revelation 3:7–10)

As we explained in Volume 2 in this series, we believe that this congregation represents those living just before the second coming of Messiah. The message of the third angelic proclamation to God's people fits in perfectly with the above message to the congregation at Philadelphia, which includes a special blessing, encouragement to be patient, and confirmation that He does, indeed, see their perseverence and their works.

The Shamash Angel

The fourth angel is not an actual angel at all but is Yeshua Himself, coming with a sickle. This becomes evident when He is referred to as "one like a son of man" in Revelation 14:14. However, this description of the Messiah was originally found in Daniel 7:13.[2] This is not some casual set of words, as the phrase may appear to be in English. It was used after the exile, around 539 BC, to refer only to the true Messiah, who is Elohim in the flesh. This is why, when Yeshua used the phrase to refer to Himself numerous times in chapters 20, 24, 25, and 26 of the book of Matthew, people responded either by accusing him of blasphemy or acknowleding him as God.

The crown on His head and the sickle in His hand also support the understanding that this being is not an ordinary angel. This passage describes the fulfillment of the prophecy found in the book of Acts, in which the disciples observe the taking away of Yeshua in the clouds and are told by an angel that He will come back again in the same manner.

> [9]And after He had said these things, He was lifted up while they were looking on, and a cloud received Him out of their sight. [10]And as they were gazing intently into the sky while He was going, behold, two men in white clothing stood beside them. [11]They also said, "Men of Galilee, why do you stand looking into the sky? This Jesus, who has been taken up from you into heaven, will come in just the same way as you have watched Him go into heaven." (Acts 1:9–11)

Meanwhile, here in Revelation 14:14, the one bearing this sickle and coming to earth to harvest is arriving in the clouds. These two events are actually one and the same. Also, it is not accidental that the fourth "Angel," being in the shamash position in this mini-menorah, is none other than the Messiah Himself.

Remember that the fourth light on the menorah is called the shamash because it is the central light from which all the others are lit. It is the source of light for the other lights, just as God should be our source as we revolve around Him and mirror His life. The word "shamash" is also used to describe the sun, which was created on the fourth day. As the earth revolves around the sun so should our lives revolve around the ultimate Light.

This harvest by Yeshua occurred at the seventh trumpet and is also a reference to the parables in the book of Matthew that refer to the best harvest (the wheat harvest), which is celebrated on Shavuot. We believe it's very likely that this harvest, as described here, is going to occur on some future Shavuot, the fourth feast God instructed his people to observe (also in the shamash position on the festival mini-menorah).

Shavuot, the Feast of Weeks

Shavuot is a celebration of the wheat harvest, which in Hebrew thinking is the best harvest. Here the wheat, as in the parables of Matthew, represents people but not just any people. Three of the seven feasts that God commanded His people to celebrate are recognitions of three different literal harvest times that occurred throughout the year.

Earlier, at the beginning of Revelation 14, we saw the first harvest and referred to it as Firstfruits. God harvested a specific group of people at that time, who represented the barley harvest. We identified those as the 144,000, and as the groomsmen.

The seventh trumpet is the snatching of the Bride. And, of course, it's the next logical milestone in the natural course of events that reflects the typical ancient Hebraic social format that a Hebrew wedding would follow. This is the event we referred to in the following extract from Volume 2 in this series:

The seventh trumpet is introduced in the last half of Revelation 11, as follows:

> [15]Then the seventh angel sounded; and there were loud voices in heaven, saying, "The kingdom of the world has become the kingdom of our Lord and of His Christ; and He will reign forever and ever." [16]And the twenty-four elders, who sit on their thrones before God, fell on their faces and worshiped God, [17]saying, "We give You thanks, O Lord God, the Almighty, who are and who were, because You have taken Your great power and have begun to reign.
>
> [18]"And the nations were enraged, and Your wrath came, and the time came for the dead to be judged, and the time to reward Your bond-servants the prophets and the saints and those who fear Your name, the small and the great, and to destroy those who destroy the earth." [19]And the temple of God which is in heaven was opened; and the ark of His covenant appeared in His temple, and there were flashes of lightning and sounds and peals of thunder and an earthquake and a great hailstorm. (Revelation 11:15–19)

When the seventh angel blows the seventh trumpet he ushers in the events of the last woe, with these words from verse 15, as quoted above: "The kingdom of the world has become the kingdom of our Lord and of His Christ; and He will reign forever and ever."

Given that description – used so powerfully by George Frederic Handel in the great "Hallelujah Chorus" from *Messiah* – we might be tempted to believe that the end has finally arrived. However, seven more catastrophic events still remain, which the earth and those who still dwell on her will suffer.

In Revelation 11:19 the doors of the Temple are thrown open, revealing the ark of His covenant. Revelation 15:5 also describes the same phenomenon, thus allowing the seven bowls of the seven angels to pour out God's wrath upon the earth. . . . but meanwhile it's interesting to note that, as also recorded in Mishnah, the Temple veil was rent and its doors were thrown open in AD 30, just after the death of Yeshua. Predictably enough, Mishnah interpreted this opening of the doors to mean that the Temple had become an abomination through the corrupt leadership of the Sadducees.

In any case, at the last trumpet in Revelation the Temple doors are once again thrown open. The timing of this event comes at the exact point of the corrupting of the Temple through the abomination of desolation set up by the False Messiah. In the Temple he proclaims himself to be God (Daniel 9:27), which starts the last 3½ years of Daniel's prophecy.

However, here in Revelation 11, the seventh trumpet is more of a major announcement than anything else. Via this trumpet call to the faithful, God is now proclaiming the coming marriage between Himself and His Bride.

Indeed, I Corinthians 15:51–52 . . . tells us that the arrival of Messiah (i.e., Yeshua) for His Bride will occur at the sounding of the last or seventh trumpet. The Groom will come for His Bride just after the seventh trumpet and just before the first bowl of judgment is poured out on the remaining earthly inhabitants.

   . . . for centuries the feast of Shavuot has been recognized, exclusively, as the feast on which God gave the Torah on Mount

Sinai and made Israel His Bride, and it should also be recognized as the feast on which He will come back for His Bride.[3]

I Thessalonians 4:13–18 further describes the harvest (or snatching of the Bride) and adds the understanding that, of those who belong to God, the dead shall be resurrected first, then the living will be taken. I Corinthians 15:51–52 tells us that all of this will occur at the last trumpet. Or, in the Revelation context, trumpet seven.

Indeed, we have already learned that the events of Revelation 14 occur near the seventh trumpet. Certainly it is not accidental that there are seven trumpets. The seventh one brings the work of God to completion, and the number seven in Hebrew confirms this idea. It *means* completion and perfection.

Remember, in Volume 2 of this series we identified this seventh trumpet blast as probably occurring on the last of the seven daily trumpet blasts of the Temple service. Keep in mind that the day before Shavuot is a Shabbat, or Saturday. The sounding of the seventh trumpet, in Revelation 11:15–19, takes place fifty days after the time of the abomination of desolation. This is when the events in Daniel 9:27 will occur:

> And he will make a firm covenant with the many for one week, but in the middle of the week he will put a stop to sacrifice and grain offering; and on the wing of abominations *will come* one who makes desolate, even until a complete destruction, one that is decreed, is poured out on the one who makes desolate.

Satan will now set up his throne in God's Temple.

The Best Harvest of All

The fifth angelic proclamation is describing the Messiah, not riding on a white horse but riding on the clouds just as He's described in Acts 1. Note that Yeshua does not have a sword, but a sickle. A sword is used in battle but a sickle is used to harvest grain, and that is exactly what He is about to do. Revelation 14:16 represents the wheat harvest, which is the best harvest. Those harvested are taken to be with the Messiah. He is the harvester of His Bride.

The Israelites were an agrarian society, so God spoke to them using terms and perspectives they would understand. The word "Rapture" was not used because it would have been outside their cultural/social understanding. And, it would have meant nothing.

God used the same language he had used in more ancient times. He organized the seven festivals around His plans, goals, and purposes to bring about the consummation of His work on earth, which He then tied into the events occurring in the natural agrarian cycle of the year.

Also, keep in mind that the groomsmen, having just been harvested themselves, are now with their Groom assisting in the harvesting of the Bride.

In Your Face but in the Wrong Place!

Revelation 14:14–16 is a direct reference to the promise that the church has been anticipating for centuries – the long-anticipated, so-called "Rapture" is being described right here. Yet nowhere in our experience does the traditional Christian church reference this passage in describing this hoped-for event.

Why does the church miss this clear reference? One possible reason is that the Rapture doesn't happen at the beginning of Revelation; it happens toward the end, which means that believers will be going through years of worldwide tribulation. Plus, they're looking from a Greek mindset. They're not looking for an Hebraic cultural description of this event, so they miss it altogether even though God's Word itself is a Hebrew document in language, cultural references, and in every other significant way.

Unfortunately, the church has misidentified several other places in the Revelation text in which the Rapture supposedly happens. But in all of these descriptions the Rapture itself is never truly described. For example, it supposedly occurs in Revelation 4:1, where John is taken up to heaven. However, the text doesn't imply in any way at all that anyone else is taken up with him! It also supposedly occurs in Revelation 6:1, where we see a white horse rider with a bow. But again, that text describes no mass evacuation of earth.

There are a few other spots in which people speculate that the Rapture is occurring, but *never* is it actually described in the biblical text – other than in Revelation 14. Thus the argument for each of these speculations is always an argument from silence. We are told to blindly accept "prevailing wisdom" because someone else said so. Yet here it is "in your face but in the wrong place" . . . and so it consistently gets missed.

As shown in Figure I-1, it's not accidental, that the seventh trumpet, the first bowl, almost all the events of the angelic mini-menorah, plus the seven thunders are all occurring simultaneously. I Corinthians 15:51–54 and the fifth angelic proclamation also both prophesy that the harvesting of the Bride will occur during this seventh and last trumpet. Likewise, the harvesting of the Bride occurs almost simultaneously with the pouring out of the first bowl, which will be further described in chapter 7 of this volume.

The blessings and curses that differentiate the people who make up the Bride, versus the recipients of the bowl judgments, are defined (or differentiated) by the thunders located at the very pinnacle of our master menorah. Thus the harvesting of the Bride separates the sheep from the goats, the weeds from the wheat, and those on His left hand from those on His right hand – both metaphorically and in reality as well.

Obviously, the merging of so many of these events (represented by several mini-menorah lights) at the apex of our master menorah is a climactic fulfillment, by God, of the promises He made so many centuries ago.

Timing Is Everything

The timing of angelic proclamations four through six, on the left side of the master menorah, corresponds to the timing of trumpet seven and the first bowl on the right side of the bowl menorah. This is the transitional time between the seventh trumpet, the thunders, the angelic proclamations, and the first bowl. In other words, a very chaotic time.

Also, notice that way back in Revelation 11, in the description of the events of the seventh trumpet (I Corinthians, 15:51-52), the angel proclaims that the kingdoms of this earth have become the kingdoms of our Lord. And here, at the fifth angelic proclamation, He's coming and taking his Bride simultaneously with the blowing of the seventh trumpet.

The implication is that Satan is being allowed to rule for 3½ years, but it's a delusional reign because the nations and the kingdoms of the earth are still the Lord's. Yet God allows Satan his delusion. So, at the very moment Satan thinks he has actually won and proclaims himself to be god, the real God instead is proclaiming: It's mine!

Coming to Mt. Zion

In the shamash to the angelic proclamations we saw Yeshua coming to Mt. Zion (the mountain east of the Temple Mount). His groomsmen, the 144,000, met Him on Mt. Zion. They are described as following the Groom wherever He goes. These virgin men are also called the firstfruits. We have suggested that this meeting on Mt. Zion takes place on the festival of Firstfruits right after the two witnesses are killed and resurrected.

In Volume 2 in this series we explained why we believe these two prophets are killed on Passover, and why their resurrection occurs on Firstfruits, mirroring these same events in Yeshua's life. We have also learned that these events will occur in the middle of Daniel's last seven years of Tribulation (see Daniel 9:27) just before and at the blowing of the seventh and last trumpet.

The Messiah will come first for His groomsmen. They will follow Him to the Bride's dwelling place, blowing trumpets, singing, and carrying on as all ancient Hebrew groomsmen once did. From there they proceed to the location of the party before the wedding ceremony occurs on the next day.

The second harvest is the wheat harvest, which was the best and most important harvest of the year. It took place on the festival of Shavuot. At this time, Yeshua, with the 144,000, will come and sweep the Bride off her feet. This event is typically called the Rapture by the church.

Recall that Yeshua's arrival for the harvest of the Bride will occur in the shamash position on the angelic proclamations mini-menorah. The festival of Shavuot is in the shamash position among the seven festivals of God. The year begins with three spring festivals, followed by Shavuot just before the beginning of the summer, then three more festivals occur in the fall.

Yes, we are suggesting that the coming of Yeshua "on the clouds" will occur on the festival of Shavuot! It is described and celebrated as the festival of the best harvest (the wheat harvest). Also, keep in mind that the Second Coming is actually a trifurcated event. He returns in three stages.

- In the first stage, which occurs at the festival of Firstfruits, He comes for His groomsmen as described in the shamash verses introducing the angelic proclamations in Revelation 14:1–5.

- In the second stage he comes as a fulfillment of Acts 1, in which his disciples were told that he would return on the clouds, which we believe will occur at Shavuot as detailed above. As we said in Volume 2,[4] this second stage is also a fulfillment of I Corinthians 15:51–54.

- There is only one more harvest/stage left, which is celebrated at the Feast of Trumpets. This is also talked about in the angelic proclamations (Revelation 14:19–20). This time He comes back on His white horse and defeats the armies of Satan.

It should be clear that Yeshua is not coming at this point to set up His kingdom but to gather His Bride. That is the meaning of the festival of Shavuot, to celebrate the increase of holiness represented by the two loaves of leavened bread the Israelites were instructed by God to wave before the Lord, made from the newly harvested wheat.

During the Feast of Unleavened Bread, celebrated earlier in the spring, the leavening represented sin and the instruction to remove the leaven from our homes represented the choice to remove those things in our lives that stand in opposition to His ways. At Shavuot the leavened bread now represents the increase in righteousness and the fruit and works that result by aligning our lives with His purpose and plans. His Bride has made the difficult choice to incorporate holiness into her life, which her white garments symbolically represent (Revelation 19:8).

In the fall of each year, one more harvest festival occurs. This is known as the wet harvest and represents the harvesting of the wet fruits, such as grapes, citrus, and pomegranates. Notice that the groomsmen and the Bride have been taken/harvested during the previous feasts. Recall the parable in Matthew 22, of the wedding feast and its likeness to the kingdom of God. The focus is on the guests but the implication of any wedding feast is that it includes a groom, a bride, groomsmen, and guests. The first two harvests have included all the participants in the wedding except the guests. Let's see if we can find the last harvest in the text here in chapter 14.

> [17]And another angel came out of the temple which is in heaven, and he also had a sharp sickle. [18]Then another angel, the one who has power over fire, came out from the altar; and he called with a loud voice to him who had the sharp sickle, saying, "Put in your sharp sickle and gather the clusters from the vine of the earth, because her grapes are ripe."
>
> [19]So the angel swung his sickle to the earth and gathered the clusters from the vine of the earth, and threw them into the great wine press of the wrath of God. [20]And the wine press was trodden outside the city, and blood came out from the wine press, up to the horses' bridles, for a distance of two hundred miles. (Revelation 14:17–20)

Grapes of Wrath

The last two angelic proclamations now reveal the sixth angel, who carries a sickle, like the fourth angel. However, this angel is not the Messiah. The seventh angel instructs the sixth angel to harvest the fruit, proclaiming that the grapes are ripe and ready to be harvested.

Notice that the crop is not taken to be with God but is left on the earth and is thrown into a winepress. This winepress represents the indignation and wrath of God. Putting grapes in a winepress implies that they will be made into wine. This will require pressure and time. It appears that those represented by the grapes will be further tested, which will involve martyrdom. They were not included in the first two harvests. They are still on the earth. They were also not included in the late night bridal party the others were taken to.

As we begin Revelation 15, only three groups will be left on earth: the guests, the unbelievers, and the fallen angels with their offspring, the nephilim. The unbelievers were invited to the wedding but either came – yet were not wearing the proper covering – or chose not to attend. The fallen angels and nephilim have never had their names written in the Book of Life, nor were they ever invited. It seems clear that those referred to as the wet harvest are on earth during the time of the outpouring of the seven bowls. This concludes the events of the sixth mini-menorah and leads us to the last of the shamash chapters and the last events, the seven bowls of judgment.

In Summary . . .

The grapes mentioned in Revelation 14:17–20 represent a symbolic reference to the remaining believers who were not taken away at the harvest of the barley (the groomsmen) or the harvest of the wheat (the Bride). According to parallel texts from Joel, Daniel, and even previous chapters of the book of Revelation, these believers are going to be persecuted by the False Messiah. In fact, these verses imply a fulfillment of the 5th seal, mentioned back in Revelation 6 where it talks about those under the throne who are crying out and asking God when their blood will be avenged.

We believe that these "grapes" include believers who will be martyred. At the consummation of the seventh angelic proclamation, the seven bowls are about to be poured out upon the earth. During this time, which lasts 3½ years (or 42 months), these martyrs will suffer at the hand of the ruler of the earth, the False Messiah.

Chapter 6
Shamash of the Seven Bowls

REVELATION 15 IS THE SHAMASH TO THE BOWLS OF WRATH. To put the events of this chapter into chronological order, let's begin with its first eight verses.

> [1]I saw in heaven another great and marvelous sign: seven angels with the seven last plagues – last, because with them God's wrath is completed. [2]And I saw what looked like a sea of glass glowing with fire and, standing beside the sea, those who had been victorious over the beast and its image and over the number of its name. They held harps given them by God [3]and sang the song of God's servant Moses and of the Lamb:

> "Great and marvelous are your deeds,
> Lord God Almighty.
> Just and true are your ways,
> King of the nations.
> [4]Who will not fear you, Lord,
> and bring glory to your name?
> For you alone are holy.
> All nations will come

and worship before you,
for your righteous acts have been revealed."

[5]After this I looked, and I saw in heaven the temple –
that is, the tabernacle of the covenant law – and it was
opened. [6]Out of the temple came the seven angels with
the seven plagues. They were dressed in clean, shining
linen and wore golden sashes around their chests. [7]Then
one of the four living creatures gave to the seven angels
seven golden bowls filled with the wrath of God, who
lives forever and ever. [8]And the temple was filled with
smoke from the glory of God and from his power, and no
one could enter the temple until the seven plagues of the
seven angels were completed. (Revelation 15:1–8, NIV)

In our chronology of events, this chapter of the book of Revelation
comes directly after the seven angelic proclamations. In the Revelation
timeline, however, these next seven catastrophic events take place only
a few months after the sounding of the seventh trumpet.

This portion begins detailing for us, again, what is happening in the
spirit realm. We are bearing witness to the beginning of the end.
The last plagues of the Great Tribulation are about to be poured
out upon the earth, and they are the worst, most catastrophic judgments of all. Thankfully, there is a glimmer of hope. The passage
tells us that, with these last plagues, God's wrath against the earth,
and ultimately the Adversary's kingdom, will be complete because
it will have been destroyed.

Once more, continuing the pattern in which shamash text precedes
"plain" mini-menorah text, Revelation 15 is the shamash of the bowl
menorah. It provides the overview, or introduction, to the horrific
bowls of wrath. In the context of times and seasons, the events of
Revelation 15 will take place during the summer following the seventh
trumpet. This takes place at Shavuot, the Feast of Weeks, at the end
of spring and prior to the Feast of Trumpets in the autumn.

Song of Moses and Song of the Lamb

Before we continue, let's take a moment to consider the Song of Moses and the Song of the Lamb as described in the verses above. In heaven we see a group of people before the throne of God, worshipping and praising the King, their Deliverer. And they're singing two songs. What are those songs, anyway? Have we ever run across them before, or are they brand new songs being introduced to John for the first time?

Our Hebraic approach to the Scriptures again assists us in identifying these songs. Both can be found in the Old Testament; they were both songs that the Israelites sang to God, praising Him for delivering and redeeming them.

Many times, those who give the Bible a cursory reading completely miss the fact that one of these songs is actually found in Exodus 15. Our English translations insert the title of this passage as the "Song of Moses." However, no such title for this passage is included in the original Hebrew text. In contrast, we believe that it should be entitled the "Song of the Lamb."

> ¹Then Moses and the sons of Israel sang
> this song to the LORD, and said,
>
> "I will sing to the LORD, for He is highly exalted;
> The horse and its rider He has hurled into the sea.
> ²The LORD is my strength and song,
> And He has become my salvation;
> This is my God, and I will praise Him;
> My father's God, and I will extol Him.
> ³The LORD is a warrior;
> The LORD is His name."
> (Exodus 15:1–3)

This song is clearly a praise to God for delivering them from the oppression and the armies of Pharaoh, but it can also be viewed as a messianic prophecy of God as the Deliverer, with His name being Yeshua. Verse 2 could be read: The LORD is my strength and my defense; he has become my *Yeshua* (Hebrew for *salvation*).

In our opinion, verse 2 identifies this passage as the Song of the Lamb, because Yeshua is the Lamb of God. And, the *remez* level (i.e., the "hinting" level) of this text is identifying Yeshua the Messiah as the Lord and Deliverer; that is, the Lamb. Further, the passage in Exodus 15 and the song in Revelation 15 are similar in context. The ones singing the song in Revelation are "those who had been victorious over the beast and its image and over the number of its name" (Revelation 15:2). Like the Israelites at the parting of the Red Sea, those before the throne of God have been delivered from their oppressor in a dramatic and miraculous way. And, they are giving praise to the Most High for their salvation.[1]

In Revelation 15:2, these people – who are singing – are both the sea of glass glowing with fire and those standing beside it. Recall that, many times, in Hebraic terms, the sea can represent nations, mankind, and/ or different people groups. These people, at least in part, are those who have just been harvested at the seventh trumpet (I Corinthians 15:51–52), but they are also described in the fifth angelic proclamation in Revelation 14:15–16.

The actual Song of Moses, by our estimation, is revealed in Deuteronomy.

> [30]Then Moses spoke in the hearing of all the assembly
> of Israel the words of this song, until they were complete:
>
> [1] "Give ear, O heavens, and let me speak;
> And let the earth hear the words of my mouth.
> [2] Let my teaching drop as the rain,
> My speech distill as the dew,
> As the droplets on the fresh grass
> And as the showers on the herb.
> [3] For I proclaim the name of the LORD;
> Ascribe greatness to our God!
> [4] The Rock! His work is perfect,
> For all His ways are just;
> A God of faithfulness and without injustice,
> Righteous and upright is He."
> (Deuteronomy 31:30; 32:1–4)

Moses sings the entire song to Israel, as both a reminder and an admonition to recall all the Lord had done for them and to not turn from His ways. It also includes a prophecy detailing the punishment that will take place if they do turn away. The fulfillment of that punishment is what we have been reading about in graphic detail in Revelation. The song concludes with:

> Rejoice, O nations, *with* His people;
> For He will avenge the blood of His servants,
> And will render vengeance on His adversaries,
> And will atone for His land *and* His people.
> (Deuteronomy 32:43)

Yet, in Adonai's characteristic, ever-compassionate love He doesn't finish the prophecy in a negative way. The song ends with God forgiving Israel's sin and renewing His covenant relationship with them.

These two songs were extremely important in ancient Israelite history, especially in the practices at the Temple in Jerusalem. Both of these songs were sung by the people every Shabbat as they gave glory and praise and honor to Elohim. It's interesting that these songs were sung only on Shabbat, the day of rest. Recall that the coming of Yeshua for His Bride, which has already occurred in Revelation 14, heralds the beginning of the thousand-year reign.

In biblical history, this thousand-year reign would be the *seventh* thousand-year period. These thousand-year periods, in Hebrew thinking, parallel the seven days of creation. The first six represent the time that God gave mankind to either fish or cut bait. In other words, God has given mankind plenty of time to conform to His will by working out His salvation with "fear and trembling."

The parallels are obvious. God created the universe in the first six days and then rested. During the first six thousand years God will complete the fulfillment of His plan for the restoration of mankind. In the seventh and last thousand-year period, we see God resting after the completion of His work, ruling and reigning in peace over His creation.

155

The Temple in Heaven

The next portion in Revelation 15 describes the Temple in heaven, with the doors open. This verse connects us directly back to Revelation 11:19:

> Then God's temple in heaven was opened, and within his temple was seen the ark of his covenant. And there came flashes of lightning, rumblings, peals of thunder, an earthquake and a great hailstorm. (Revelation11:19, NIV)

Because the first bowl and the seventh trumpet are one and the same light on the master menorah (see Figure 2-3), the verse in chapter 11 that talks about the seventh trumpet is connecting that trumpet with the first bowl event, which is about ready to occur. Just as the Temple in heaven is opened in Revelation 11, Revelation 15 is referring to the same event and is picking up where the text left off in chapter 11.

In addition, the glory of God fills the Temple with the Shekinah cloud, and no one can enter into it. The details of this description are similar to the details of what customarily took place during Shavuot. In ancient times, at that same moment each year, as the counting up to Shavuot would be completed, the doors to the Temple would be thrown open at midnight to start preparations for the celebration of that festival.

As no one could enter the Temple in Revelation 15, so it was in ancient times as well. During the midnight preparation, no one was permitted to enter the Temple until everything was complete, at sunrise. This period of darkness is equivalent to the dark times of the next 3½ years (42 months); that is, the time of the False Messiah's kingdom. Therefore, at the end of his reign (i.e., the end of the preparation time at the Temple, and the seven bowls of judgment), the sun comes up, the Son returns, and the wedding of Yeshua occurs.

These verses also describe the cloud of glory, the Shekinah (the Holy Spirit), filling the Temple. This parallels all the principles of Shavuot, known to the church as the Greek word *Pentecost*. This is the time when God's Spirit descended upon Mount Sinai, back in the wilderness, and gave the Torah to His people, Israel. This was also the time when God's Spirit descended on His people at Pentecost. And now, in the end times, God's Spirit is filling the Temple to coordinate with all these events. Here we see God descending and filling His Temple in preparation for the final fulfillment of His plan, which is to reunite under the wedding chuppah with His Bride.

During the events at Sinai, God offered the wedding contract, the ketubah. In the events in the upper room in Acts 2, God sent His Spirit to intimately dwell with man. The Spirit's primary goal is to lead man into all the truth of Torah (I Corinthians 2). The Torah (the ketubah), which was the sealed book we were introduced to way back in Revelation 5, shows man how to become God's Bride by revealing to him the pathway that leads to God Himself.

As we have already indicated, we believe that the festival of Shavuot, which features leavened bread, is a celebration of the harvest (or "snatching up") of the Bride. Here we see the events that would occur at the Temple harmonizing with the concept of a bride ready for her groom.

The entire Bible, culminating in this portion of Revelation, is a picture of the preparation for the final leg of a 6,000-year journey that . . .

- Began in Genesis 1

- Came to a crescendo 2,000 years ago with the death and resurrection of Yeshua the Messiah

- Is now culminating in the destruction of the Adversary of God and man

- Includes the deliverance of God's people

Seven angels come from the Temple in heaven, are given the bowls of wrath from one of the cherubim, and are ready to fulfill their duty to bring the last judgments upon the earth.

The events represented by the bowl mini-menorah are about to begin.

In Summary . . .

Revelation 15 includes the last shamash of the last mini-menorah. Finally, after being introduced in the preceding mini-menorah shamashes to the Father of the Groom, the Groom Himself, and the groomsmen, we now see the Bride, united with her Groom in heaven. We see her expressing her thankfulness and celebrating her deliverance from the evil one, Satan the beast. Obviously, the wedding is about to take place.

Meanwhile, the wedding party is singing songs from the Torah that remind us of Old Testament passages in which Israel did the same thing. This is not accidental, for God is now about to pour out His wrath on the enemy's kingdom, in retaliation for Satan's and mankind's rejection of His principles.

This is the fulfillment of the curses God promised back in Deuteronomy, to all those who oppose Him – precisely the opposite of the blessings He promised to all those who obey Him. The same curses are further identified in the Song of Moses, and many other places in Torah.

Chapter 7

The Seven Bowls of Wrath

THIS NEXT PORTION OF THE BOOK OF REVELATION DEALS WITH ONE OF the most frightening displays of God's anger in the entire Bible. God's righteous anger is displayed and his judgment is delivered via the seven bowls of wrath that are poured out upon the earth.

> ¹Then I heard a loud voice from the temple, saying to the seven angels, "Go and pour out on the earth the seven bowls of the wrath of God." ²So the first *angel* went and poured out his bowl on the earth; and it became a loathsome and malignant sore on the people who had the mark of the beast and who worshiped his image. ³The second *angel* poured out his bowl into the sea, and it became blood like *that* of a dead man; and every living thing in the sea died. ⁴Then the third *angel* poured out his bowl into the rivers and the springs of waters; and they became blood.
>
> ⁵And I heard the angel of the waters saying, "Righteous are You, who are and who were, O Holy One, because You judged these things; ⁶for they poured out the blood of saints and prophets, and You have given them blood to drink. They deserve it." ⁷And I heard the altar saying,

"Yes, O Lord God, the Almighty, true and righteous are Your judgments."

[8]The fourth *angel* poured out his bowl upon the sun, and it was given to it to scorch men with fire. [9]Men were scorched with fierce heat; and they blasphemed the name of God who has the power over these plagues, and they did not repent so as to give Him glory.

[10]Then the fifth *angel* poured out his bowl on the throne of the beast, and his kingdom became darkened; and they gnawed their tongues because of pain, [11]and they blasphemed the God of heaven because of their pains and their sores; and they did not repent of their deeds.

[12]The sixth *angel* poured out his bowl on the great river, the Euphrates; and its water was dried up, so that the way would be prepared for the kings from the east. [13]And I saw *coming* out of the mouth of the dragon and out of the mouth of the beast and out of the mouth of the false prophet, three unclean spirits like frogs; [14]for they are spirits of demons, performing signs, which go out to the kings of the whole world, to gather them together for the war of the great day of God, the Almighty.

[15]("Behold, I am coming like a thief. Blessed is the one who stays awake and keeps his clothes, so that he will not walk about naked and men will not see his shame.") [16]And they gathered them together to the place which in Hebrew is called Har-Magedon.

[17]Then the seventh *angel* poured out his bowl upon the air, and a loud voice came out of the temple from the throne, saying, "It is done." [18]And there were flashes of lightning and sounds and peals of thunder; and there was a great earthquake, such as there had not been since man came to be upon the earth, so great an earthquake *was it, and* so mighty. [19]The great city was split into three parts, and the cities of the nations fell. Babylon the great was remembered before God, to give her the cup of the wine of His fierce wrath. [20]And every island

fled away, and the mountains were not found. [2] And huge hailstones, about one hundred pounds each, came down from heaven upon men; and men blasphemed God because of the plague of the hail, because its plague was extremely severe. (Revelation 16:1–21)

We Get What We Deserve!

It is important to understand that what God sends forth upon the earth with the seven bowls is in direct response to the atrocities committed by the whore of Babylon and the False Messiah – the beast in Revelation 13 and 17. The Holy One of Israel is enraged over the shed blood of His righteous saints. He will bring unparalleled judgment upon the beast, the whore, and any who have been in league with them.

As we said in our previous chapter on the seven angelic proclamations, in Revelation 14:17–20 the seventh and final proclamation describes an angel harvesting the earth. As we've stated, this coincides with the Hebrew Feast of Trumpets and is the time of the wet harvest, the early rain. At this season the ancient Hebrews harvested their fruit, including figs, dates, grapes, and several others.

Revelation 14:19–20 reads:

> The angel swung his sickle on the earth, gathered its grapes and threw them into the great winepress of God's wrath. They were trampled in the winepress outside the city, and blood flowed out of the press, rising as high as the horses' bridles for a distance of 1,600 stadia.

The wine described in this chapter is a picture of the wine that will be poured from the bowls of judgment in chapter 16. Let us now delve into some of the Hebraic insights that are clearly depicted in this crucial portion of Revelation.

The key to understanding what is found in this apocalyptic book is a knowledge of the ancient biblical sacrifices that are intimately interwoven with the appointed feasts and the concepts of covenant illustrated in Torah. As we've said, Revelation 15 and 16 chronologically follow the seventh trumpet of chapter 11. Seven angels are described as appearing with the seven last plagues – last because, with them, God's wrath is completed.

An amazing discovery begins to unfold as the plagues are revealed in Revelation 16. First, in Hebrew the "bowls" are actually drinking bowls, or cups. The cups of wrath represent outpourings of God's judgment. These bowls complete the judgments and curses that God promised to those who would disregard His principles and instructions as laid out way back in Deuteronomy. If one were to correlate the sins of the whore and the earth with those same judgments a terrifying understanding comes to light.

The Bowls Represent a Sexual Disease

The bowls of wrath came from the tabernacle, the Temple of God. They obviously signify judgment, but it's interesting to note that these bowls are filled with wine that represents the blood of sacrifices. This blood/wine came from the grapes (i.e., the guests) who were put into the winepress of God's wrath back in the seventh angelic proclamation in Revelation 14.

What's being conveyed here, by God, is that you can intentionally sacrifice your own will and desire or God will do it for you. One choice leads to salvation and purity; the other leads to judgment and death.

The whore and the inhabitants of the earth are being punished for their sexual immorality, idolatry, and the shedding of innocent blood. In fact, they are being judged for leading man into the three worst types of sin: idolatry, murder, and sexual immorality

In Hebrew thinking, these three represent the worst violations against God's laws. And, associated with these was the worst punishment, death. In Acts 15, these three are referred to as the starting place for Gentile believers wishing to come into the faith.

> [19]"It is my judgment, therefore, that we should not make it difficult for the Gentiles who are turning to God. [20]Instead we should write to them, telling them to abstain

from food polluted by idols, from sexual immorality, from the meat of strangled animals and from blood. [21]For the law of Moses has been preached in every city from the earliest times and is read in the synagogues on every Sabbath." (Acts 15:19–21, NIV)

These descriptions by James (*Ya'akov* in Hebrew, which actually translates as *Jacob*) are ancient metaphorical references to the three sins listed above, all deserving of death. Idolatry is a violation of our relationship with God. Murder is an obvious violation of our relationship with our fellow man. And sexual immorality, as Paul details in I Corinthians 5 and 6, is a violation of our own soul.

The Original Punishment Was Death

For each of these, God specifically directed, in Torah, that the punishment would be death. Certainly God can forgive these sins, but unlike the much less serious "sins of omission and commission" that we all commit on a regular basis, these are much more significant. Indeed, these are the very sins that the whore and the False Messiah have committed themselves, and have led mankind to commit as well.

We were surprised to discover – just as you will be – that the events and the corresponding symptoms that are spoken of in the bowls of wrath in Revelation 16 coincide, to an amazing degree, with a certain sexually transmitted disease called syphilis. Syphilis has been a scourge on mankind since ancient times. Whenever a culture's behavior has degraded to the point at which people committed this voluntary crime against themselves, again and again throughout the ages this disease has raised its ugly head.

In addition to what God Himself said in Deuteronomy, here's what the Apostle Paul said in one of his letters: "Flee from sexual immorality. All other sins that a man commits are outside his body, but he who sins sexually sins against his own body" (I Corinthians 6:18, NIV).

Syphilis absolutely devastates the health of anyone who contracts it. It causes terrible physical suffering and pain, ultimately ending in death. Perhaps it is not surprising, therefore, that God would choose this judgment as His finale, especially in light of the whore's success in tempting man to drop all of the morals about sexual propriety that have existed for so long.

In our own culture it's also not accidental that since the 1960s – when the morals of the western world began seriously deteriorating – we have seen a huge revival of this disease spreading all over the world. Given the dramatic increase in homosexuality, increased promiscuity, and prostitution, all things that God specifically forbids, we don't expect this unfortunate trend to decrease anytime soon.

Adolf Hitler, Alexander the Great, Antiochus Epiphanes, and numerous other tyrants throughout history – many of whom ruled various evil kingdoms within our mini-menorah – all suffered under this curse.

Here, then, is the order of events for the bowls of wrath and their comparison with the symptoms of syphilis.

- **First Bowl:** Poured out on the land; ugly and painful sores break out on the people who bear the mark of the beast and worship his image.
  First symptom of syphilis: Ugly and painful sores that break out upon the genitalia.

- **Second Bowl:** Poured out on the sea; it turns to blood like a dead man, and every living thing in the sea dies.
  Second symptom of syphilis: The disease retreats into the bloodstream.

- **Third Bowl:** Poured out on the rivers and springs of water; they become blood. Rivers and springs of water are symbols of the source of life.
  Third symptom of syphilis: The disease retreats even deeper into the body, hiding in the tissue and interstitial (between the cells) spaces. Random internal capillary bleeding occurs.

- **Fourth Bowl:** Poured out on the sun; the sun is given power to scorch people with fire. They are seared by intense heat and they curse God. Still they do not repent.

Fourth symptom of syphilis: Scorching fever and intense flu-like symptoms.

- **Fifth Bowl:** Poured out on the throne of the beast; his kingdom is plunged into darkness. Men gnaw their tongues in agony and curse the God of heaven because of their pains and sores. They still refuse to repent.
  Fifth symptom of syphilis: Blindness and blistering sores on the tongue, the roof of the mouth, and the soft tissues of the body.

- **Sixth Bowl:** Poured out on the river Euphrates; the water dries up to prepare the way for kings from the East. Three evil spirits, devils that look like frogs, come from the mouth of the beast and the False Prophet. They are spirits of devils that perform miraculous signs, gathering the kings of the whole world for battle on the great day of God Almighty. In other words they are spirits of power and deception.
  Sixth symptom of syphilis: Dehydration, insanity, and hallucination.

- **Seventh Bowl:** Poured out in the air; out of the Temple in heaven comes a loud voice from the throne, saying, "It is done!" Then come flashes of lightning, rumblings, peals of thunder, and a severe earthquake like no other the earth has ever seen. Whole cities are destroyed, islands disappear, and mountains collapse. Hundred-pound hailstones fall on men. God remembers Babylon the Great and gives her the cup/bowl filled with the fury of His wrath.
  Seventh symptom of syphilis: Death.

Deeper Insights from a Hebraic Perspective

Now let's take a closer look at each of these bowls.

- The contents of the first bowl are poured out on the earth. One of the words for earth, in Hebrew, is *adamah*. Its root word is *adam*, which is the word that God used to name the first man, but it's also used in a broader sense to define all mankind. So, in a sense, this word represents the flesh of mankind, which is exactly what we see these bowls attacking.

- The second bowl attacks the sea, causing it to turn to blood. This, again, is another allusion to the life-giving source that blood represents for mankind. The Hebrew word for blood is *dam*, which means blood or wine. It too derives from the word *adam* and is also used for bloodshed. Recall that these bowls are being poured out for mankind's murderous activity; this word also refers to the guilt resulting from slaughter, or murder.

- The third bowl affects the springs of fresh water. From an Hebraic perspective, these represent the source of life. This bowl is making it clear that, because of man's choices, God is cutting off the source of the life that mankind had enjoyed up to that time.

> . . . *that is*, the one whose coming is in accord with the activity of Satan, with all power and signs and false wonders, [10]and with all the deception of wickedness for those who perish, because they did not receive the love of the truth so as to be saved. [11]For this reason God will send upon them a deluding influence so that they will believe what is false, [12]in order that they all may be judged who did not believe the truth, but took pleasure in wickedness. (II Thessalonians 2:9–12)

This bowl reveals the ultimate heart of God, which is to allow man's choices to dictate his destiny. God is not a dictator.

- The important thing about the fourth bowl is that it affects the light-givers. The fourth light on this mini-menorah is, of course, the shamash, which represents the sun, the light-giver. The sun is supposed to be a blessing, but here we see God removing the light-generating power that He gave to mankind to sustain their lives.

Even at this late date, in bowl number four as well as number five, God is still desiring for mankind to return to Him. Unfortunately, when you've given your mind over to the deceiver, seeing the truth becomes very difficult. This is proven by the fact that most people who come to a belief in God come to that belief in their early years rather than their later ones.

Unfortunately, this will also not be the global warming that so many climate alarmists – including some of America's most prominent government officials – have worried about in books, speeches, and needless legislation. For decades.

- The fifth bowl is poured out on the enemy's kingdom now ruling the entire globe. This represents the idea that God is now attacking the authority that He gave mankind way back in Genesis 2 – the right (and responsibility) to manage God's creation. Because man has given that authority to Satan and the Dragon (the beast), God is seen here destroying that usurper and taking back His own authority.

- The sixth bowl is poured out on the River Euphrates. The Hebrew word for Euphrates, *Perath*, means *fruitfulness* and/or *sweet water*. So, this bowl is undermining and destroying the very ability of both the earth and the people who inhabit it to be fruitful, physically and spiritually. When that occurs, evil spirits now move in and produce deception, insanity, and false signs and wonders, which used to be identified with people who were possessed. (Can you produce good fruit when you're insane?). Ironically, this very deception causes the ultimate evil fruit by causing mankind to rise up against the Creator, thinking that they can actually defeat God. That is the ultimate deception.

We see three frogs coming out of the mouths of the beast, the False Prophet, and the Dragon. The Hebrew word for frog is *tsephardea*, which is an idiom for *temptation*. In other words, the idea being conveyed here is that Satan – and those in league with him – will continue to deceive mankind to further enable themselves to accomplish their goals. Could Satan also be continuing to use the three "master sins" referred to earlier – idolatry, murder, and sexual immorality – to tempt and deceive mankind one last time in an effort to save himself?

Now consider this passage:

> "Behold, I am coming like a thief. Blessed is the one who stays awake and keeps his clothes, so that he will not walk about naked and men will not see his shame." (Revelation 16:15)

The message of the above verse arrives before the very last bowl, just prior to the return of Messiah. And what is the message? It's a final warning that God is going to come like a thief when man least expects him. It also echoes the following passage:

> "Therefore be on the alert, for you do not know which day your Lord is coming. [43]But be sure of this, that if the head of the house had known at what time of the night the thief was coming, he would have been on the alert and would not have allowed his house to be broken into. [44]For this reason you also must be ready; for the Son of Man is coming at an hour when you do not think He will. (Matthew 24:42–44)

The verses from the two passages directly above are often used to promote the false idea that the Messiah will be coming back *before* the Tribulation. But clearly, considered in context, both passages refer to the very *end* of the Tribulation.

Stay Awake!

The warning to stay awake also includes the threat of losing your clothes and being naked. Obviously, John was familiar with the Temple rules and government. Guards serving at night at the Temple, if found asleep, would spend the rest of the night on duty but without their clothes.

There is also a deeper meaning here as well. Recall that immediately after Adam and Eve sinned, God clothed them and covered their nakedness. This was a graphic reminder – for us – of His promise to come someday and provide the blood covering that would take away the sin of mankind.

However, the people to whom God is talking, just before the pouring out of the seventh bowl, do not have that covering. God is imploring them, one last time, to serve Him. Indeed, that is the precise meaning of the very first covenant that God made with mankind, which is the blood (servant) covenant. Instead, these folks continue serving the kingdom of darkness and will pay the ultimate price.

The sixth bowl ends with all the forces that Satan can muster against the God of the universe, rallying at Armageddon where the final contest between these two will be played out. Many people speculate about where this valley might be. However, when we look at the Hebraic origin of the word *Armageddon* the answer becomes clear.

Armageddon takes place in the valley of Jezreel. In modern terms this is the valley of *Megiddo,* which lies just south of the Sea of Galilee, north of Jerusalem, and extends from east to west. It is a large, wide, flat valley, perfectly designed to accommodate multiple mechanized armies. If you ever wanted to have a massive tank battle, this would be the perfect place. General Patton would drool.[1]

- The seventh and final bowl tells us that God's work is done. Yeshua also said the same thing when He spoke His final words on the cross. In His first coming His work was limited to providing a means for mankind to be saved from their sins. This time His coming is just as important and every bit as momentous.

Both times He's referring to the reality that the Deuteronomic curses, resulting from mankind's sin, are complete. Messiah's first coming provided a pathway to forgiveness and a return to a covenant relationship with God. Right here, in Messiah's second coming, the bowls complete the curses against mankind and usher in a time when God will rule His creation.

This final bowl, and its judgments, also refer one last time to the city that has always represented rebellion and the kingdom of Satan . . . Babylon.

In Summary . . .

In conformity with the prophecies concerning the final curses in Deuteronomy 28, against those who oppose God, the bowls fulfill and complete those promised curses. Chapter 16 is the last chapter in Revelation that describes mini-menorah events. The rest of the book of Revelation further describes what happens to the kingdom of Satan.

In addition, it takes us into the future and describes how God's kingdom gets established and who He places in charge. It also details the final destiny of those who have opposed Him, including the beast, the Dragon, the False Prophet, and all the people who were in league with them.

In the end, God wins. In fact, the score is already rather lopsided at this point:

God – 777
Satan – 0

However, even though God absolutely wins that doesn't mean that you win, too. For you to be part of His victory you have to be found *clothed in His righteousness*, in active covenant with Him.

You have to be wheat, not a weed.

Chapter 8

The Whore/False Bride

A BEAUTIFUL BUT EVIL WOMAN ONCE LIVED IN A GREAT CITY. Unfortunately, to earn her living she had chosen a life of prostitution. However, her regular callers gradually stopped using her services when they realized that she was getting her customers drunk and robbing them as they slept. So, to avoid losing her income entirely she began luring travelers passing through from other lands.

The dark prince who ruled over the great city admired the prostitute's clever wiles and, realizing that she was as corrupt as he was, devised a way to put her talents to his own use. He began courting her, set her up in a magnificent mansion, and promised that if she gained a fortune for him he would marry her. Eager to be his bride and share his kingdom, the harlot complied.

The dark prince then sent his servants out to neighboring lands to spread the news of a beautiful woman who lived in a mansion on a hill and welcomed strangers, with extravagant hospitality. As rich travelers arrived at the harlot's home, she would seduce them then offer a golden goblet of wine. Her beauty and sensual talents distracted her customers from noticing that the fine wine she gave them was poisoned. After stripping them of their riches, the harlot would have the prince's slaves drag their bodies from her home, at night, and dump them on the garbage heap for burning.

After a few years the prostitute had amassed an enormous treasury for the prince. She sent a message, demanding that he keep his promise to make her his queen. Even though he had once promised to marry her the prince was unwilling to have a filthy whore share his throne as an equal. So he devised a plan. He dressed in wedding garments and appeared at her door, carrying a betrothal cup. Eager to seal their perverse covenant, the woman drank from it without realizing that – like the goblets she offered her customers – it contained deadly poison.

The body of the harlot was placed in a lead tomb that the prince had made especially for her – a replica of the mansion in which she had plied her trade. As promised, the dark prince shared his kingdom with her, making her a bride of death as she received her inheritance of destruction.

The above story perfectly illustrates Satan's plan, especially the destiny for his bride. In contrast, God literally offers up Himself to save His Bride. As the title of this volume anticipates, these two brides will definitely enjoy two distinct fates.

Back to the Top Again

Once again we have now reached the top of the master menorah. But this time we came up from the left side. Revelation 10 describes the seven thunders we find there, which we discussed in Volume 2 in this series. The thunders represent God's original instructions for holy living, as given to Moses way back on Mt. Sinai.

Now, as we approach these same thunders from the left side, other portions of Scripture come into sharper focus based on what they represent. For example, Matthew 13 describes a field ready for harvest, but tares have grown up with the wheat. The whore, and those aligned with her, represent the ultimate weeds, or tares, whereas God's Bride represents the best possible harvest – the wheat.

The master has given instructions to harvest the tares first and set them aside for burning. Likewise, in other parables, people are described not as wheat but as sheep and goats. In Matthew 25 these groups of people are separated, the sheep on the right and the goats on the left.

In other words, the net effect of God's rules for holy living (i.e., the seven thunders) was to separate people into two groups as in the following biblical analogies: (1) wheat and tares/weeds; (2) sheep and goats; (3) believers and unbelievers; (4) the righteous and the unrighteous (i.e., the wicked).

Recall God's message to the congregation at Laodicea – the hot and the cold versus the lukewarm. Both the hot and the cold pools offered health benefits. Only the lukewarm pool had no value. Which one are you?

Weeds Versus Wheat

Revelation 17–20 describes two groups: the believers and the unbelievers. Chapters 17 and 18 tell us about all those who will be put in the place of dishonor on the left side of the Creator. Matthew 25:41 tells us that He will say to them: "Be gone from Me, you cursed, into the eternal fire prepared for the devil and his angels."

Revelation 19–20 then describes those in the place of honor on the Creator's right hand. Matthew 25:34 tells us what the Father will say to them: "Come, you who are blessed of My Father, inherit the kingdom prepared for you from the foundation of the world."

Most shepherds know that sheep, because of their wool, don't tend to need any special protection from the lower temperatures at night, which is also why they're never sheared in winter. But goats, on the other hand, are not as prepared. This whole scenario is very similar to the believers vs. unbelievers dynamic we mentioned above.

God's people, the sheep, will be "wearing their wool coats" and will be prepared for the trials and tribulations that will come on the earth. But the unbelievers – the goats – will not be prepared, just as five of the bridesmaids were not prepared with sufficient oil in Matthew 25.

These two groups, whether called sheep and goats, believers and un-believers, righteous and unrighteous, or wheat and weeds, represent the Bride of God (the first group) versus the bride of Satan (the second group). Both God and Satan have brides, but each will experience two distinctly different destinies.

The focus of Revelation 17 and 18 is an alluring harlot. These chapters inform us that she has attracted all the nations of mankind to her, causing them to lust for money, power, and the dubious pleasures of immorality. These are the tares/weeds and the goats – those who have chosen to ignore God's principles for holy living and the shed blood that would save them from their sins. Let's take a look at the text.

> [1]Then one of the seven angels who had the seven bowls came and spoke with me, saying, "Come here, I will show you the judgment of the great harlot who sits on many waters, [2]with whom the kings of the earth committed acts of immorality, and those who dwell on the earth were made drunk with the wine of her immorality." [3]And he carried me away in the Spirit into a wilderness; and I saw a woman sitting on a scarlet beast, full of blasphemous names, having seven heads and ten horns.
>
> [4]The woman was clothed in purple and scarlet, and adorned with gold and precious stones and pearls, hav-ing in her hand a gold cup full of abominations and of the unclean things of her immorality, [5]and on her fore-head a name was written, a mystery, "BABYLON THE GREAT, THE MOTHER OF HARLOTS AND OF THE ABOMINATIONS OF THE EARTH."
>
> [6]And I saw the woman drunk with the blood of the saints, and with the blood of the witnesses of Jesus. When I saw her, I wondered greatly. [7]And the angel said to me, "Why do you wonder? I will tell you the mystery of the woman and of the beast that carries her, which has the seven heads and the ten horns. [8]The beast that you saw was, and is not, and is about to come up out of the abyss and go to destruction. And those who dwell on the earth, whose name has not been written in the book

of life from the foundation of the world, will wonder when they see the beast, that he was and is not and will come. [9]Here is the mind which has wisdom. The seven heads are seven mountains on which the woman sits." (Revelation 17:1–9)

Who Is This Harlot?

Through her lustful intoxications the false bride has deluded the earth. But who is this woman? Verse 1 describes her as "sitting on many waters." In Hebrew, that expression means *out of* mankind, or in a position *over* mankind. In other words, her responsibility is to deceive mankind by using all the temptations that would be lawless, or torah-less.

The Apostle John is then transported in the spirit to a wilderness place. Here he witnesses the harlot riding on the back of the beast, which we were introduced to in Revelation 13. This is the same beast that rose up out of the sea, with seven heads and ten crowns, signifying that he also has his origins in mankind – at least in part. However, the text describes this beast as having some very intriguing differences that the other beast, the False Prophet in chapter 13, does not have.

The beast of Revelation 13 has a deadly wound to the head, which had been healed. This, of course, is an obvious reference to the False Messiah's (i.e., the Antichrist's) false claim to have power over death by appearing to rise from the dead. If it were real this would be a very convincing power to have. Its deceptive appearance will fool many. The False Messiah will flaunt this sign in mankind's face, thereby convincing millions that he truly is the Messiah.

How ironic that when the real Messiah actually *was* resurrected, the world of that era (as it still does today) only scoffed and came up with numerous contrary theories, thus attempting to whitewash this historical fact to justify their unbelief. Among those false theories would be the "Swoon" theory, the "Yeshua Never Existed" theory, and the "Romans Stole His Body" theory.

In contrast, the Scriptures are very clear that, when the False Messiah makes his appearance after his false resurrection, the world will fall down and worship him. For a time, as previously described in Revelation 9, this will allow them, metaphorically, to ride on the back of the beast along with the harlot. In both places we see mankind uniting its forces with devils to accomplish the goals of the False Messiah.

The position that the harlot has, on the beast's back, indicates that they have a relationship of sorts. She is momentarily in control, but as we will soon see, any such "control" is only temporary. The beast has a different plan and will use the harlot to bring it about, by tricking her into thinking that she can have this position of power forever. In the end the beast will discard and destroy her when she's no longer useful to him. But for the time being he needs her charms to deceive the unbelieving world into giving him mankind's authority, as illustrated in our story at the beginning of this chapter. This comes about when mankind chooses to worship the beast by falling for the harlot's deception.

The Hebrew words describing the colors of her clothing are blue/purple, scarlet/red, and gold/yellow, and her clothing is adorned with various gemstones. Ironically, these colors and gemstones are the very same ones worn by the priests of God, as detailed in Exodus 28. Thus this woman is acting as a false priest and represents all the religions of the world that are anti-Torah. She is using the persuasions of false religions to deceive people into worshipping her and the beast. These three colors mirror the colors of covenant. Unfortunately, her colors are soil-based while the true bride's colors are light-based.

In Satan's kingdom we have now been introduced to three beings – Satan, the False Messiah; Abaddon, the False Prophet; and the whore, the false high priest. Together they represent a collective counterfeit of the true messiah. In reality, Yeshua *is* the *true* Messiah, is the *true* king prophet, and is the *true* high priest.

Who's Who in the Final Years?

The book of Revelation sometimes uses more than one title for some of the characters who interact with each other in the end times. This list may not be exhaustive but it should be helpful. Titles from Revelation are in boldface, followed by definitions.

God's Bride = the wheat

The Whore = Astarte; Satan's bride; the harlot; the false high priest; the weeds

Satan = the Dragon

Abaddon = the angel of death; the star that falls from heaven with the keys to the abyss

The False Messiah = Antichrist; Satan plus the fourth type of nephilim, called the beast from the sea

The False Prophet = Abaddon plus the fourth type of nephilim; the wolf in lamb's clothing; the beast from the land. This is also a nephal.

The beast in Revelation 17 is not the false prophet/wolf. It is a beast that mirrors the False Messiah, but also represents the seven evil kingdoms. It reveals the spirit behind these seven kingdoms throughout history, which is always Satan. Satan is the seven-headed beast as described in both Revelation 13 and 17.

He is the bull figurine/idol that we have seen unearthed in the Mideast, representing a god that was worshiped by the ancients. From an Hebraic point of view he represented Ba'al/Satan. And Astarte, the whore in Revelation 17, was usually riding on his back.

The beast that comes out of the sea in Revelation 13, and the one that comes out of the abyss in Revelation 17 – rather than being different beasts – are actually the same one, who is simply revealing its multifaceted nature and source.

The origin of the first implies that it comes from mankind/sea; the origin of the second implies that it is a devil that was bound in the abyss. Same beast; different origins, just as evil in our own society – and throughout all of recorded history as well – has arisen (and still arises!) from many different sources.

All Dressed Up in the Colors of Covenant

In Volume 1 of this series we examined some of the fundamental truths about the various relationships enshrined in godly covenant. There we explained that the three primary colors – red, yellow, and blue – represented the three covenants that God offers to man. We also learned that Satan also offers these same covenants, which we've called *counter*-covenants in the previous volumes in this series. Of course, Satan has different motives and an entirely different purpose for everything he offers to mankind.

Red represents the servant covenant, yellow represents the friendship covenant, and blue represents the inheritance covenant. In ancient times, wearing blue/purple was often a sign of royalty. The king, the queen, and their sons and daughters were adorned with blue and purple clothing. Blue dye was very rare, and clothing colored with it had great value.

> Purple was indeed extracted from the marine gastropod mollusk, known as the "murex," which has a spiny shell and lives near the coasts of the Mediterranean sea (length up to 8 cm for the largest species). The use of murex as a dye is attested since the first half of the second millennium at Ugarit, but mainly during the first millennium on the coast of Phoenicia, where Tyre and Sidon exerted a monopoly on fabric dying. These cities were stopovers on the Silk Road, not only for transportation reasons but also because silk could be dyed there. To extract the dye, shells were broken and the mollusks were macerated in basins. The obtained dye could vary from pink to violet through crimson as a result of different sun-drying times. Piles of shells have been found near ancient dying places near Tyre and Sidon, and also

Athens and Pompeii. Basins of the ancient Carthagenese city of Kerkouane are still colored by red dye.

Because of the resistance of the dye and difficulty in harvesting the animal, purple fabrics were expensive and highly estimated. They were only used for the cloth of noblemen, kings, priests, and judges. The purple color, similar to that of blood, symbol of life, became a sign of temporal and spiritual power. Under the Roman Republic, the chief commanders of the armies wore the "paludamentum," a purple coat. The toga, sign of Roman citizenship, had a purple stripe. The toga of triumphators was fully purple and had a golden border. The tunic worn by Senators under the toga had a wide purple stripe, and was called "laticlava." The stripe of the knights' tunic ("angusticlava") was narrower. Under the Roman Empire, the "paludamentum" was the privilege of the Emperor. The Roman Catholic Church still uses the purple color for cardinals ("pourpre cardinalice"). Nowadays, the main component of the dye (dibromo-indigo) can easily be obtained through chemical synthesis.[1]

In Satan's never-ending effort to copy God, this woman/harlot represents the worldly religions and those who have believed in their deceptions. He is honoring them by allowing them to wear these same symbols of relationship and honor. Unfortunately for them, the associated colors now reveal their choice of king: Satan. The end result is that, by virtue of worshipping false gods, these people fall away from the one true God and become the false bride/harlot who is riding on the back of the beast.

What Does Color Have to Do with It?

Have you ever wondered what causes things to be certain colors? Mankind and the creation that surrounds him do not give off colors that originate within themselves. They have only the capacity to reflect light, which usually comes from the sun. They absorb most of the color spectrum in white light and reflect just a small portion of certain parts of the color spectrum.

> That reflected light is what our eyes pick up. In other words, things that are blue are blue only because they reflect blue light while absorbing the other colors.
>
> Because God dwells in His people we should act as conduits for His light – not reflectors. Reflectors only pretend to be sources of light, but God's people should know that their thoughts and actions can be conduits of His light, to the world, revealing Truth. Truth should be the focus for His people. They should not think that they are the light's origin but should humbly recognize the true source.

Embedded within the concept of covenant are the levels of personal relationships, each of which also represent different types (or aspects) of the color spectrum while simultaneously revealing different functions of God. Recall that we saw the False Prophet, the whore, and the beast/False Messiah all emulating the attributes of Yeshua, the *true* Messiah. The true Messiah acts as a prophet, as the high priest, and as the real Messiah.

As these three positions correlate with the three types of covenant – blood, salt, and sandal respectively – so do their colors. In Hebraic understanding the prophet's color was red because his symbols were water and blood. The tribe of Levi, from which the priests came, was represented by a topaz gemstone, whose color is yellow. The Messiah Himself will come and rule forever as the King, the ultimate inheritor. And, as we learned above, the color blue is the symbol of royalty.

The Ultimate Weed

In verse 5 we are told that this harlot also has *Babylon the Great* inscribed on her forehead, and that it has a symbolic meaning. In Hebrew, the forehead (or the head) symbolizes authority. That this name is on her forehead could also mean that her mind, her thoughts, and her commitments have been given over to Babylon the Great. So the question then becomes, What *is* Babylon the Great?

The word *babel*, in Hebrew, is spelled *bet/bet/lamed*, and it means *confusion by mixing*. In Volume 1, we explained that when we mix the primary and secondary colors of light back together we produce white light again. But, with respect to soil-based colors, which are only reflecting light, when we mix those pigments together we get a murky brown/black result. In Hebrew thinking, white is the equivalent of truth, purity, clarity, and understanding, while blackness is the equivalent of confusion, amounting to the exact opposite of truth.

Furthermore, the root word for babel is *balal*, which also means *to be anointed with oil*, but in a bad sense as in *stained* or *soiled*. Here, the text makes it clear that this whore has been anointed/stained by a greater authority. But the things that she is worshipping and serving – opposite to the things of righteousness – have brought on her own destruction.

The Physics of Light and Color[2]

God is light (I John 1:5) and is clothed in light (Psalm 104:2). His object is to restore man back to the fullness of white light, to make us as mature in Him as we are willing to be.

The goal of covenant is restoration of relationship with our Creator. The three primary types of covenant – blood, salt, and sandal – correspond to the three primary colors (red, yellow, and blue). God initiates these covenants.

The secondary colors (orange, green, and purple) show man's positive response to God's offer of covenant. The ultimate covenant, marriage covenant, is a combination of the three primary types and should correspond to the color white. However, physics teaches us that the three primary colors do not combine to give white light as we would expect. Why is this?

White light is composed of all colors, but red, green, and blue are the minimum that can combine to give white light. In fact, with light, green is said to be a primary color, not yellow. Why is green a secondary color in pigment but a primary color in light?

This is true for the same reason that the Son lowered Himself to a state below even that of the angels (Hebrews 2:9), yet is still the Sovereign of the Universe. The three primary colors of light represent God and the order of the work that is done for the process of restoration (the Spirit must draw you to the Son so that you can receive from the Father – Ephesians 2:18).

> Red = the Spirit
> Green = the Son
> Blue = the Father

The Son is green instead of yellow because He is a combination of the divine and the earthly. The second part of the Godhead came to earth as both God and man. He became a "secondary color" in terms of earthly pigment out of His great love for us, but will always be a primary color in terms of light.

Who Was Ephraim?

> Ephraim mixes himself with the nations;
> Ephraim has become a cake not turned. (Hosea 7:8)

Ephraim was the name given to one of the sons of Israel. However, in this particular passage this word refers to the northern ten tribes of Israel who separated themselves from Judah. Thus this passage in Hosea is a perfect example of what God accused Ephraim of doing, at which the whore has also excelled.

In this context the word *mixes* means *to mix sexually*. Thus Ephraim had perverted himself and made himself unclean by physically mingling himself with idolatrous nations, and with their religions. God specifically told the Israelites never to do this, yet they had started to integrate various evil religious practices into their own daily lives.

In Revelation 12 and 13, we were introduced to a great dragon/beast that had seven heads. These heads represented seven evil kingdoms that have ruled the earth, sequentially, from the beginning of time. The goals of these kingdoms have been to promote the purposes of the

Adversary, confronting and opposing the will of God by attempting to destroy the faith of His chosen people. If Satan couldn't destroy their faith he would attempt to kill, rob, or subvert their godly intentions through the use of these evil kingdoms, created by him for this very purpose.

Some Things Almost Never End

Recall the relationship between Nimrod and the original whore of Babylon, Nimrod's mother. She was also his wife. This perverse arrangement was very similar to the relationship we find in Revelation 17, between the whore and the False Messiah. Ishtar (Nimrod's mother), beyond her sexual perversion with her son, had authority over him as well just as the whore has authority over the False Messiah.

The biggest difference is that the end-times relationship between the whore and the False Messiah will culminate in Satan's plan to rule the earth. In contrast, the ancient Ishtar/Nimrod relationship ended when they died. Even so, they represented a kind of perversion that has existed throughout time . . . but will soon come to an end.

On the seven evil kingdoms mini-menorah, the name of Babylon appears three different times. It appears in the first, the fourth, and the seventh positions. Recall that the fourth position on the menorah is also called the *shamash,* which is the word used to refer to the sun as well as the true Messiah. This light is in the central position. If Babylon represents Satan's attempts throughout time to oppose, resist, and destroy God's plans, this shamash position tells us that he desires to be recognized as the central source of light for mankind.

Babylon has a symbolic meaning in the biblical text. It sometimes represents all that is evil in opposition to God. It certainly was the source of rebellion after the Flood. Is it accidental that Satan represents himself and his kingdom as the first and the last and the light of the world (shamash), again copying God?

The name of Nimrod's kingdom, *Babylon*, is the source of our word *babble*. God made it clear right up front that the words and deceptions offered to man by Satan are nothing but nonsense. They counter truth and oppose logic, just like the string of letters a monkey might type on a keyboard. The question then is, why is man so prone to believe these lies?

The Babel Babble

Some commentators have confused (1) the babble of Babel with (2) speaking in tongues at Pentecost. But they are not remotely the same thing. In effect, the Babel babble was a curse, inflicted by God because of mankind's rebellion and leading to tremendous confusion among the people who were trying to build a tower that would reach up to heaven so they could challenge God directly. Their God-induced linguistic confusion led to their dispersion all over the world, which was God's way of preventing an even more tragic outcome had they continued their joint construction efforts.

In contrast, those who spoke in tongues on Pentecost were doing God's will by speaking eternal truths in various real-world languages. All of the languages were legitimate even though many of the speakers could not understand what they were saying without the help of translators. Their words absolutely were not "babble" of any kind whatsoever – they were words that God wanted spoken, in the languages God chose to use.

Ironically, these two examples – different as they are – both demonstrate God's infinite ability to use ordinary resources to bring about extraordinary results. No need to smack and smash – in these two cases He simply used our own languages, first to diversify arrogant humans and second to unify willing worshippers.

Amazing.

More Than One Babylon?

The second Babylon (see Figure 3-3) was led by king Nebuchadnez-zar. His kingdom was in the shamash position, or head, on the mini-menorah that charts the seven evil kingdoms we introduced in chapter 3 of this volume. This king's exploits are recorded in the book of Daniel, the second chapter of which reveals a dream Nebuchadnezzar had. It was shown to the king by God that he and his kingdom were the head of a very large statue. The rest of the statue represented three additional kingdoms that would follow his.

The last kingdom, representing the very foundation of worldly opposition to God, was destroyed by the hand of God, which ushered in the restoration of the kingdom of God and His reign on earth. In this prophetic book we learn that a great dragon/beast will rule this last Babylon for 3½ years before the coming of Messiah. Thus these beasts in Daniel and Revelation are one and the same.

The foundation of this beast rests on the unity of the forces of mankind and devils in opposition to God. The harlot, representing the first post-flood rebellion against God, continues operating to this day. This kingdom will attempt to replace God, the true source of light, with a reflector, named Babylon for a good reason (Revelation 18:2).

But Babylon (which has always been here) will ultimately fail and will be destroyed for the final time in the end, at the hands of the true Messiah. From the beginning Satan has offered up to mankind a counterfeit way for us to live our lives, built on the biggest lie of all time – the notion that we can become gods if we will only give our worship and obedience to Satan. And we do this, of course, by ignoring the one true God and the principles He has given to mankind.

Never forget that this False Messiah will come in the context of religion. In the end he will claim to be the God of most belief systems, including Christianity, Judaism, and Islam. He will offer up just enough truth and false miracles to convince many to believe. But at the root of all he says will be Babylon, founded on rebellion and confusion.

In Revelation 17:8 we learn this beast's origin: the abyss. The abyss is also called the bottomless pit. In Volume 2 in this series we learned about another group that came out of this same pit. These were the fallen angels (teraphim) that were locked away by God because of their depraved actions as described in Genesis 6, II Peter 2, and the book of Enoch. These were the ones who lusted after the women of mankind and produced offspring the biblical text called *nephilim*, which usually gets translated as *giants* in our English texts.

The Three Levels of Hell

Scripture contains three words that describe the three levels of the underworld, or the "afterlife" for the wicked. The first is Sheol (the grave); the second is Gehenna (a place of fiery torment, the lake of fire, i.e., hell), and the third is Abaddon (the abyss).

Who Is in the Book of Life?

Before we continue, let's review two important verses from Revelation 17. We have added italics in two different places:

> [7]And the angel said to me, "Why do you wonder? I will tell you the mystery of the woman and of the beast that carries her, which has the seven heads and the ten horns. [8]The beast that you saw *was, and is not, and is about to come up out of the abyss* and go to destruction. And those who dwell on the earth, whose name has not been written in the book of life from the foundation of the world, will wonder when they see the beast, *that he was and is not and will come.* (Revelation 17:7–8, italics added)

Who are those who are referred to here as "those who dwell on the earth" and whose names "have not been written in the Book of Life?" They do not include mankind. In Hebrew thinking, all people start with their names written in the Book of Life. Some of us just happen to be so perverse that we literally tell God to erase us from the book. Thus we are removed from the Book of Life by our own evil actions and our rejection of God's invitation for relationship with Him.

This verse is sometimes used to support the unbiblical doctrine of predestination commonly known as Calvinism. Some prognosticators believe that these verses are evidence that God predestines some for hell and some for heaven. However, the Hebraic perspective on which the Bible is based is that all mankind is predestined for salvation. Yet they are still free to determine their own eternal destiny by either accepting or rejecting God's plan for their lives.

So . . . who are those "who dwell on the earth"? They are the nephilim, whom we have referred to and defined extensively in the previous two volumes in this series. Remember, the nephilim can never receive salvation. They have never been written in the Book of Life because they lack the key component God gave to mankind. They do not have a God-breathed spirit.

As Peter made very clear in one of the books that bears his name:

> But these, like unreasoning animals, born as creatures of instinct to be captured and killed, reviling where they have no knowledge, will in the destruction of those creatures also be destroyed, [13]suffering wrong as the wages of doing wrong. They count it a pleasure to revel in the daytime. They are stains and blemishes, reveling in their deceptions, as they carouse with you, [14]having eyes full of adultery that never cease from sin, enticing unstable souls, having a heart trained in greed, accursed children; [15]forsaking the right way, they have gone astray, having followed the way of Balaam, the *son* of Beor, who loved the wages of unrighteousness. (II Peter 2:12–15)

Thus they are the ones who would truly be astonished to see this beast/teraphim return, especially from the dead. Remember, this beast is the very personification of Satan, their lord and master.

What's in a Name?

The ancients, especially the eastern nations (including the Hebrews), used names to describe some interesting event or attribute connected to (or describing) the person in question. God used this same idea when he named the Hebrews *Israel*. In Hebrew, *Israel* means *the prince or warrior of God*. Therefore, those who are His should act their part, representing the King and realizing they have responsibilities and work to do for Him.

The Beast That Was, Is Not, and Is About to Come

The beast referred to in Revelation 17:8 (and also in the heading directly above) is the same beast that rose up out of the sea in Revelation 13. He is identified here, again, as having seven heads and ten horns. But now we get a new piece of information about him, whom we have already identified as the False Messiah as impersonated by Satan.

From that perspective, this beast is a composite of Satan (a cherubim) and the fallen teraphim released from the abyss, and is a nephal. Plus, it represents a picture of a satanic plan that is now coming to fruition, which was hatched 6,000 years ago.

Remember, the book of Revelation was written at the end of the first century AD. By the time the Apostle John wrote Revelation the same composite entity "was" when it was involved with the rebellion described in Genesis 6. In John's time, the same entity "was no more" because he was still locked away in the abyss. But in the future, from that perspective, he will be set free once more and thus would "come again."

In pictorial terms, the image of this beast represents the plans of Satan via his seven heads and ten crowns. Recall that, in Revelation 9, in describing the events of the fifth trumpet, Abaddon falls from heaven with the key to the bottomless pit and releases locusts, or teraphim. The beast with the woman riding on his back gains his freedom at that point.

Verse 9 reveals some information about the location of the woman. It says that the seven heads of the beast on which she sits represent seven hills where she can be found. As most of us know, the city of Rome sits on seven hills and has been the center of pagan religions for thousands of years. Rome was taken over by the Roman Catholic

Church about 1,500 years ago, at which time it took on many pagan ideas and mingled them with biblical principles. The resulting mixture (babble) of "religious truths" has since infiltrated the mind of man, distracting him from the pure Truth created by God. God can still be found in Catholicism, but through its association with paganism it has seriously diluted His Word.

In any case, Catholicism still has worldwide influence. It is possible that in the coming days it might be taken over totally by the enemy, to help usher in Satan's kingdom and play his part in opposing God at the very end of time.

The Adversary's Final Days

In the Adversary's final days he will present himself as the messiah and will try to fulfill the prophecies of the Jews, the Christians, and the Muslims, as contained in the Old Testament, the New Testament, and the Koran. All three prophesy a messiah who will perform many miracles and will usher in what will appear to be worldwide peace. He will tell the world that he is the one true God and that all religions of the world now have one purpose – to unite mankind and usher in peace. In fact he may even tell the world that all the world's religions were *created* by him, and that they all point to and inform mankind about the one true God: himself.

> [10]" . . . and they are seven kings; five have fallen, one is, the other has not yet come; and when he comes, he must remain a little while. [11]The beast which was and is not, is himself also an eighth and is one of the seven, and he goes to destruction. [12]The ten horns which you saw are ten kings who have not yet received a kingdom, but they receive authority as kings with the beast for one hour.
>
> [13]"These have one purpose, and they give their power and authority to the beast. [14]These will wage war against the Lamb, and the Lamb will overcome them, because He is Lord of lords and King of kings, and those who are with Him are the called and chosen and faithful." [15]And he said to me, "The waters which you saw where

the harlot sits, are peoples and multitudes and nations and tongues.

[16]"And the ten horns which you saw, and the beast, these will hate the harlot and will make her desolate and naked, and will eat her flesh and will burn her up with fire. [17]For God has put it in their hearts to execute His purpose by having a common purpose, and by giving their kingdom to the beast, until the words of God will be fulfilled. [18]The woman whom you saw is the great city, which reigns over the kings of the earth."
(Revelation 17:10–18)

The remaining verses of Revelation 17, shown above, continue to explain what is meant by the seven heads of the beast whom we have identified as personified by Satan. The beast's body has a different source, coming from the pit, but the spirit inside is *personified evil*. It is important to differentiate between these two, for one is just a physical body while the evil satanic spirit is the animating force that controls everything that body does.

Recall that a nephal comes from the union of a fallen angel (teraphim) and a human woman. Since the teraphim were locked away in the abyss, because half of a nephal's genetic code comes from a teraph it's as if its body comes from the abyss.

Two Different Paths of Judgment

Later on we shall see that the two parts of this composite entity have different paths of judgment that God will pour out on them. But for now, this passage further explains the meaning of the beast's seven heads, which represent seven evil kingdoms that Satan has created over the last 6,000 years. These kingdoms have ruled the world through their tyrannical machinations.

Those kingdoms also represent seven hills (i.e., Rome) on which this woman sits. In addition to Catholicism the city of Rome has multiple religious "connections," via which various worldly powers have attempted to control and exploit mankind by taking advantage of man's innate interest in spiritual things.

From the Hebraic perspective it's also not accidental that Satan's realm centers itself on top of seven hills. A hill signifies a place of authority, and seven means perfection. Satan will not be perfect in righteousness, however – he will be perfect in deception.

Verse 10 tells us that these seven heads reveal even more. They represent seven kings that have existed in the past but also exist as this prophecy unfolds. We are told that five of these kings have fallen, one still exists and is reigning, and the other has not yet appeared. But when he does he will have a short reign. At the same time, the beast that "was and [now] is not" is an eighth ruler yet is "of the seven" and belongs to them.

These seven kings represent the evil kingdoms referred to earlier. At the time of the writing of the book of Revelation, five had fallen. The count would be as follows: Babylon, Egypt, Assyria, Babylon again, Medo-Persia, and Greece. This list includes Babylon twice, so the list really includes just five separate evil kingdoms.

The kingdom existing in the first century, when Revelation was written, was the first half of the Roman kingdom, represented by the calves of iron in the second chapter of Daniel. However, remember that this prophecy splits up the last evil kingdom into two halves, each existing within different time periods – (1) the Roman empire that existed at the time of Yeshua's life, death, and resurrection, and (2) another that will come to power just before the second coming of Yeshua, the real Messiah.

This latter one will spring out of the European land mass that the earlier Roman Empire conquered and ruled. It will rule at the time of the end and is the kingdom that has not yet appeared. In Daniel it is described as a terrible beast that will crush its opponents and destroy many, just as the previous six did. The seven-headed beast will also create a false peace by appealing to the lust of the flesh.

As we explained above, these pronouncements make it clear that Satan, the originator of all these kings and their kingdoms, is making his final push to bring the plan he hatched in the Garden of Eden, 6,000 years ago, into fruition. He was the one with the original idea that he (and we, too) could become gods, and that is what he is going to proclaim to the world from the very throne of God in Jerusalem: *I am God, so fall down and worship me!*

In verse 12 we are told that the ten horns on this beast represent an additional ten kings, and that they give their power to the beast. Some have suggested that these ten kings are the ten nations of the European Union, while others have proposed that, in the end times, the world and its people will be divided into ten regions with rulers for each. The beast will govern and control them all, thereby ushering in a one-world government.

Most important, these ten kings will be the primary conduits for worldly opposition to the one true God. In the final war these ten will be destroyed and will lose their places, and God and His followers will be victorious.

It's also confirmed here that the waters on which the whore is seated represent the nations and tribes of mankind (Revelation 17:15). She will be given authority to control and manipulate them as she sees fit. However, even though she is helping to set up the kingdom of Satan, behind the scenes she will be hated by her own cohorts, the ten horns/kings. These ten will strip her, eat her flesh, and utterly consume her with fire.

Let's Try That Again!

Many of the devil's earlier schemes will be tried again during the end times. For example, just as Jezebel ruled over ten tribes in the 9th century BC she will again rule over ten kings, who will rule over the world.

The original ten tribes were chosen by God but made their own choice to rebel. Likewise in the end times – the ten rulers will also be in rebellion.

Jezebel Again

The above is also very reminiscent of what happened to Jezebel. During the 9th century BC she was the queen over the ten northern tribes of Israel. She and her husband, Ahab, committed many evil deeds in the sight of the Lord. For example, Jezebel brought the Babylonian gods into Israel and promoted their worship. Together, Jezebel and Ahab confronted Elijah, forcing him to expose and destroy the prophets of Ba'al by proving that they didn't have enough authority to confront God and win. They certainly did not have enough power to call down fire from heaven and burn up a sacrifice, *as the true God was able to do.*

This bit of biblical history is even more interesting in light of what will happen in the book of Revelation. In Revelation 13 the beast's False Prophet is able to call down fire from heaven, supposedly as a witness to mankind that the beast is God Himself. Also, consider the two witness in Revelation 11, one of whom we suggested, in Volume 2 in this series, could be Elijah. Remember, Elijah did not die but was taken up in a chariot to be with God.

He might still have work to do in the end times. During the 3½ years that God gives the two witnesses they will cause drought over the face of the earth to focus mankind's attention on their fallen spiritual state, just like Elijah of old. They will also confront the False Prophet of the beast, but this time God will allow them to be defeated and killed by the enemy's prophet. Or will he? Actually, Elijah, Enoch, and God win in the end; the two witnesses' bodies are resurrected in the face of the beast, ascending back to God.

Jezebel's father was the king of Tyre. In Ezekiel 28 the king of Tyre is described as being in the Garden of Eden, perfect in beauty and filled with wisdom. He was covered with precious stones and was anointed to be the covering cherub (see Volume 1). In other words, this cherub was intended to focus his power (he was one of the most powerful angels) on relationship and covenant. But he was consumed with admiration for his own wisdom and beauty and was thrown out of the presence of God.

This cherub was none other than Satan himself. He, of course, was the one who was in Eden and brought on the downfall of mankind. Satan, in this passage, is being metaphorically described as the king of Tyre. Jezebel is said to be the daughter of the king of Tyre. These two have been working together for centuries to deceive and destroy God's people. Long ago their target was Israel and is now Israel once again.

As is true today, Israel was hated in the past and will be hated even more in the end. The ten kings will take up the cause by leading the charge to destroy God and His people. But they will implement the beast's plan, which had been hidden from Jezebel, his daughter, for all this time. That plan will include using her by allowing her to have a place of authority in Satan's kingdom. That place is symbolized in Revelation 17 by her position on the beast's back. But now, verse 16 reveals that she will come to her final destruction, just as she came to her physical end back in the 9th century BC, when she was thrown off the city walls and the dogs ate her flesh.

The Destruction of the Woman

Revelation 17:18 reveals that she also represents that great city that dominates and controls the rulers and leaders of the earth. This is the very reason she will be hated by these same rulers. They have grown tired of playing second fiddle. Once given the go-ahead by the beast they will consume her and destroy her with fire.

In Revelation 18:2 we learn that this great city/woman is Babylon. Chapter 18 is a further description of the destruction of this great city. But where does this destruction occur on our time line?

In our study of the angelic proclamations in Revelation 14, we learned that the second angel to appear with a message from the throne of God was instructing us that Babylon the Great had fallen. Revelation 14:8 says that she made all nations drink of the wine of her passionate unchastity.

This feminine reference sounds a lot like references to the whore we meet in chapter 17. In fact, they are one and the same! The city of

Babylon, and these female references in Revelation 14 and 17, are all describing the same thing – a worldly presence that promotes sin in all its abominable forms. The proclamation of the first angel in Revelation 14, and the warnings of Revelation 18 by another angel from heaven, are very similar as well:

> [7]"Fear God, and give Him glory, because the hour of His judgment has come; worship Him who made the heaven and the earth and sea and springs of waters." [8]And another angel, a second one, followed, saying, "Fallen, fallen is Babylon the great, she who has made all the nations drink of the wine of the passion of her immorality." (Revelation 14:7–8)

> [3]"For all the nations have drunk of the wine of the passion of her immorality, and the kings of the earth have committed acts of immorality with her, and the merchants of the earth have become rich by the wealth of her sensuality." [4]I heard another voice from heaven, saying, "Come out of her, my people, so that you will not participate in her sins and receive of her plagues; [5]for her sins have piled up as high as heaven, and God has remembered her iniquities." (Revelation 18:3–5)

In other words, all those who are partaking of her sin will not go unpunished and will suffer greatly at the hand of God.

The angelic proclamations will occur during the seven evil kingdoms. At the demise of the last evil kingdom at the hand of God, Yeshua will usher in a thousand-year reign in which He will live on earth and will govern with His Bride in Jerusalem.

These proclamations will occur just before the seventh trumpet is sounded and the first of the bowls is poured out onto the earth. Remember, that trumpet will usher in the harvest of the Bride as described in the fifth angelic proclamation. It will also end the 3½-year reign (1,260 days) of the two witnesses and will initiate the last 3½ years (42 months).

This last period, we know, will be the time that God has given over to the beast and Satan to rule the earth. But it will not be a time of fun and peace for the beast and those who inhabit the earth. The bowl judgments will occur during this time, and those who dwell on the earth will suffer greatly.

To make the above clear, this great city, portrayed metaphorically as the woman in Revelation 17, will be destroyed at the end of the first 1,260-day period, during which the two witnesses will reign. At the end of their reign the seventh trumpet will blast, initiating the final 3½ years during which the bowl judgments will be poured out, and the beast will be allowed to rule and reign over God's creation for 42 months. At the end of those months the thousand-year reign will begin.

So, Revelation 18 describes the destruction of Babylon (Rome), which will occur just before the seventh trumpet is sounded and will leave only 3½ years remaining before the final coming of the true King.

Chapter 17 closes with a last allusion to whom and what this woman actually will be: a great city. The name "Babylon" is clearly delineated by the inscription on her forehead in Revelation 17:5: ". . . and on her forehead a name was written, a mystery, 'BABYLON THE GREAT, THE MOTHER OF HARLOTS AND OF THE ABOMINATIONS OF THE EARTH.'"

This woman, the beast, and now Babylon will all have something in common. As we have seen in our review of the history of Nimrod's Babylon, and in the biblical use by God of this city to describe Satan's intentions, Babylon has been the source and center of perversion and deception throughout all time. Obviously, based on her description in chapter 17, the whore builds on this satanic perversion by being called "THE MOTHER OF HARLOTS AND OF THE ABOMINATIONS OF THE EARTH." She has opposed righteousness and godly principles at every turn, but so has the father of lies, Satan, and the mother of perversion, Babylon.

Gee . . . we wonder who their kids are.

Satan Was the Original Cause

Isaiah 14 and Ezekiel 28 make it clear that Satan has been the original cause of all of this perversion and deception. Isaiah 14 also contains a very interesting prophecy about Babylon. It reveals a coming judgment that will be poured out upon this great ancient city because of her tyrannical ways. Then, in verses 6 through 23, the Babylonian rulers will morph into Satan. Here he is referred to as the *Bright Star*.[3]

The Hebrew root is *Halal (hay/lamed/lamed)*, which means *light* or *brilliant*. It also means *to be proud, boastful,* and *foolish*. Ultimately, this is God's opinion of Satan. So this will give us a signpost of things to watch for in Satan's kingdom – people who *are* these things are foolish and are operating with the authority of Satan.

In the Amplified version of the Bible, verses 13 and 14 say, "And you said in your heart, I will ascend to Heaven; I will exalt my throne above the stars of God; I will sit upon the mount of assembly in the uttermost north; I will ascend above the heights of the clouds, I will make myself like the Most High."

This has been Satan's endgame from the beginning. In Revelation 13 we see Lucifer incarnating as a beast and doing exactly that! During his last 3½ years, he will temporarily attain his ancient goal: sitting on the throne of God.

But here in Isaiah 14 these kingly tyrants of Babylon are equated with Lucifer/Satan. Then, beginning in Ezekiel 26 a string of prophecies begins, all of which tell of the city and people of Tyre and their destiny. These passages describe in great detail the coming destruction of a city that was once a great center of sea trade. Sadly, traders from all over the earth will wail and cry bitterly at Tyre's destruction, as in Isaiah 23.

Recall that in Revelation 18:11 we again see sea traders weeping and grieving when their city is destroyed. But in Ezekiel 28, the king of Tyre morphs into Satan again, as in Isaiah 14, but this time Satan is described as a covering cherub that "was in Eden." As Ezekiel said:

"Your heart was lifted up because of your beauty; you corrupted your wisdom by reason of your splendor. I cast you to the ground; I put you before kings, that they may see you. [18]By the multitude of your iniquities, in the unrighteousness of your trade you profaned your sanctuaries." (Ezekiel 28:17–18)

This same cherub that was cast to the ground is the same dragon that Revelation 12 describes as being thrown down to the earth after trying to destroy the child that was Yeshua. This dragon and the proud cherub, both falling from heaven, are one and the same: Satan.

The Historical Jezebel

Here are brief passages from two other sources that further illuminate the above events from a slightly different historical perspective:

> Let's take a quick historical review of Queen Jezebel. The story of Jezebel, the Phoenician wife of King Ahab of Israel, is recounted in several brief passages scattered throughout the Books of Kings. Scholars generally identify I and II Kings as part of the Deuteronomistic History . . . One of the main purposes of the entire Deuteronomistic History, which includes the seven books from Deuteronomy through II Kings, is to explain Israel's fate in terms of its apostasy. As the Israelites settle into the Promised Land, establish a monarchy and separate into a northern and a southern kingdom after the reign of Solomon, God's chosen people continually go astray. They sin against Yahweh in many ways, the worst of which is by worshiping alien deities.

> The first commandments from Sinai demand monotheism, but the people are attracted to foreign gods and goddesses. When Jezebel enters the scene in the ninth century B.C., she provides a perfect opportunity for the Bible writer to teach a moral lesson about the evil outcomes of idolatry, for she is a foreign idol worshiper who seems to be the power behind her husband. . . .

> As the books of Kings recount, the princess Jezebel is brought to the northern kingdom of Israel to wed the newly crowned King

Ahab, son of Omri (I Kings 16:31). Her father is Ethbaal of Tyre, king of the Phoenicians. The Bible writer's antagonism stems primarily from Jezebel's religion. The Phoenicians worshipped a swarm of gods and goddesses, chief among them Ba'al, the general term for 'lord' given to the head fertility and agricultural god of the Canaanites. As king of Phoenicia, it is likely that Ethbaal was also a high priest or had other important religious duties. According to the first-century A.D. historian Josephus, who drew on a Greek translation of the now-lost Annals of Tyre, Ethbaal served as a priest of Astarte, the primary Phoenician goddess. Jezebel, as the king's daughter, may have served as a priestess as she was growing up. In any case, she was certainly raised to honor the deities of her native land.

When Jezebel comes to Israel, she brings her foreign gods and goddesses – especially Ba'al and his consort Asherah (Canaanite *Astarte*, often translated in the Bible as 'sacred post') – with her. [Ed. Note: "Sacred post" is more often translated as "Asherah poles."] This seems to have an immediate effect on her new husband, for just as soon as the queen is introduced we are told that Ahab builds a sanctuary for Ba'al in the very heart of Israel, within his capital city of Samaria: 'He took as wife Jezebel daughter of King Ethbaal of the Phoenicians, and he went and served Ba'al and worshiped him. He erected an altar to Ba'al in the temple of Ba'al which he built in Samaria. Ahab also made a 'sacred post' (I Kings 16:31-33).[4]

The name Jezebel finds its meaning from the character's native Syro-Phoenician language. It may be rooted in the word *ba'al* (lord), referring either to the Syro-Phoenician god, the "King of Heaven," or simply the royal title "lord." Thus, *Iz-ba'al* [Jezebel] may mean "the Lord (Ba'al) exists/exalts" or "where is the prince," a name known from liturgies of the Syro-Phoenician Ba'al cults.[5]

The Lord Ba'al exists/exalts as the meaning for *Jezebel* is exactly what we see being played out in Revelation 17. Ba'al/Satan, in the form of this many-headed beast, is lifting Jezebel up on his back and allowing her to have authority "for a time."

The biblical Hebrew for Jezebel is *Ezehvel* and may be rooted in a Hebrew word for *prince/nobility* or *husband* (*bul/ba'al*). This is combined with the word for *naught/none* (in Hebrew, '*iy*). When these words/concepts are combined they would render the meaning of the name as *there is no prince/nobility/husband*, suggesting a lack of chastity and also implying a lack of character or morality, further implying adultery or fornication.

The Ancient Gods of Babylon

The great city of Tyre worshipped the same gods created by ancient Babylon – Ba'al and Astarte. The meaning of the word *Ba'al* is *lord* or *master* or *husband*, but it also refers to the ancient deity known as the *Lord of Heaven*. Of course, in the Hebrew Bible, Ba'al is known as a false god.

> In Babylonia it [i.e., Ba'al] was the title specially applied to (the god) Merodach of Babylon, which in time came to be used in place of his actual name. The Babylonian Bel-Merodach was a sun-god, and so too was the Can-baal whose full title was Ba'al-Shemaim, 'lord of heaven.' The Phoenician writer Sanchuniathon (Philo Byblius, Fragmenta II) accordingly says that the children of the first generation of mankind in time of drought stretched forth their hands to heaven toward the sun; for they regarded him as the sole lord of heaven, and called him Beel-samen, which means *Lord of Heaven* in the Phoenician language and is equivalent to *Zeus* in Greek. A temple to Ba'al-Shemaim had stood at Umm el-Awamid between Acre and Tyre, and his name is found in inscriptions from the Phoenician colonies of Sardinia and Carthage."[6]

Thus the kings of Tyre and Babylon both represent Satan. Jezebel, represented by the whore in Revelation 17, in the ninth century BC promoted the worship of the gods of these two cities. Such worship included human sacrifice and prostitution, the very things God accuses her of in the book of Revelation.

More Warnings . . .

Revelation 2:20, in the letter to the congregation of Thyatira, also warns the people about tolerating the woman Jezebel. Here she is called a prophetess and is accused of leading God's servants astray and beguiling them into practicing sexual vices.

In all these kingdoms, Satan and Jezebel either have devilish origins and purposes or are actually devils, all of which have led mankind away from God. Their roots go back to very ancient times.

For example, the king of Tyre was the leader over the Phoenicians. As we've indicated elsewhere in this volume, these ancient people were known as seafarers, trading far and wide along the coast of the known world. They established colonies wherever they went, such as the Philistine cities south of ancient Israel. Many historical stories are recorded in the Bible about God's people interacting with these colonies. Battles and confrontations in the lives of King David and Samson come immediately to mind.

The word *Phoenicia* is derived from a Greek word. In Hebrew, these people were called *Sidonians*, named after their capital, Sidon, located north of Tyre and originally named after its founder, Sidon. In the table of nations found in Genesis 10, Sidon is the first son of Canaan, the son of Ham. Remember, Canaan was the son Noah cursed after his father was found looking at the nakedness of Noah. The word here in Genius 9:25 for *cursed* is *arar* and means *to be made a curse* or *to be cursed*. However, this usage of the word does not mean to use inappropriate language but refers, instead, to a "spell" or "the curse of an enchanter."

Because of this weakness in their souls, like Ham's son in the reference above, various people have pursued evil destinies throughout the ages. They have opposed God at every hand. After the Flood, they migrated down to the land that God had reserved for His chosen people. Israel and his descendants were to be given the Promised Land, but the Canaanites ("the cursed ones") were living in the land reserved for Israel when Joshua showed up.

More important, even as the Canaanites attempted to steal the Promised Land 3,500 years ago, Satan himself will attempt to steal the throne of God, located in the center of the same land, in the future. Clearly the land of Israel is somehow very important. It has been the center of major battles throughout time, and will be the center of three more world wars before the coming of the true King.

In Summary . . .

Revelation 18 tells us that Babylon will once again become great, only to be destroyed just before Satan sits upon God's throne in Jerusalem. In fact, this may be one of the reasons for the beast's move to the city. His city, called Babylon in Revelation, will be destroyed just as the two witnesses are killed and he comes to power.

He will then move the center of his power to the city in the land he has coveted for all time, where he will sit upon a throne he has also coveted. Israel and Jerusalem are Satan's final goals. Jerusalem itself is the center of three major religions, and ruling from this location while claiming to be the God of all three of those religions has long been Satan's most cherished desire.

What we want to accomplish in this chapter, via this somewhat wide-ranging history lesson, is to reveal Satan's final endgame. But we also need to understand that he's a broken record. Everything he will do in the end times will be a repeat effort, only then he will be rallying all his friends, forces, authority, and power to realize his deepest desires.

What caused the Flood was the same kind of thinking, via which Satan tried to pervert mankind. But God wasn't having any part of it. Nonetheless, Satan never seems to learn. Each of his evil kingdoms has represented another attempt at pushing God aside and ruling His creation. In the final kingdom, via his final endgame, he will actually accomplish his original goal. But only for a time.

Chapter 9

The True Bride

THE PREVIOUS TWO CHAPTERS OF REVELATION (17 AND 18) FOCUSED ON the bride of Satan. We want no part of her destiny. Fortunately for us there is another destiny and another bride with which we can align ourselves. Before we take a closer look, let's read this very important text from the beginning of Revelation 19:

> [1]After these things I heard something like a loud voice of a great multitude in heaven, saying, "Hallelujah! Salvation and glory and power belong to our God; [2]BECAUSE HIS JUDGMENTS ARE TRUE AND RIGHTEOUS; for He has judged the great harlot who was corrupting the earth with her immorality, and HE HAS AVENGED THE BLOOD OF HIS BOND-SERVANTS ON HER." [3]And a second time they said, "Hallelujah! HER SMOKE RISES UP FOREVER AND EVER."
>
> [4]And the twenty-four elders and the four living creatures fell down and worshiped God who sits on the throne saying, "Amen. Hallelujah!"
>
> [5]And a voice came from the throne, saying, "Give praise to our God, all you His bond-servants, you who fear

Him, the small and the great." [6]Then I heard something like the voice of a great multitude and like the sound of many waters and like the sound of mighty peals of thunder, saying, "Hallelujah! For the Lord our God, the Almighty, reigns. [7]Let us rejoice and be glad and give the glory to Him, for the marriage of the Lamb has come and His bride has made herself ready."

[8]It was given to her to clothe herself in fine linen, bright and clean; for the fine linen is the righteous acts of the saints. [9]Then he said to me, "Write, 'Blessed are those who are invited to the marriage supper of the Lamb.'" And he said to me, "These are true words of God." [10]Then I fell at his feet to worship him but he said to me, "Do not do that; I am a fellow servant of yours and your brethren who hold the testimony of Jesus; worship God. For the testimony of Jesus is the spirit of prophecy." (Revelation 19:1–10)

Satan's bride, which has been described in the last two chapters, is destroyed by her groom. Now, in the next two chapters, almost simultaneously God elects to rescue and redeem His *own* Bride. In these verses one could almost envision a young, excited bride in a room with all her attendants around her. In contrast, the other bride would now be a smoldering ash heap, with all her attendants weeping around her and kicking up her ashes (Revelation 18:9–11).

Who would you like to be associated with? It's not accidental that God put these four chapters in a row. In graphic imagery, God is portraying a choice of destines. Which do you want for yourself and your loved ones?

The scene then changes from earth to heaven, and the Apostle John now witnesses a large crowd including twenty-four elders, four living creatures, and the Bride of the Lamb. First, let's identify these groups.

Group One: The Guests at the Wedding

Revelation 15:2–4 identifies a large congregation of people. Here they are described as a glassy sea. Remember, in Hebrew thinking, mankind is sometimes referred to as a sea. In this text, this group of people is accompanied by another group described as being victorious over the beast.

They are seen standing beside the glassy sea with harps of God in their hands. They are praising and worshiping God with the song of Moses and the song of the Lamb – and recognizing His omnipotence and his righteousness. This glorification of God occurs just after the harvesting of the Bride in the fifth angelic proclamation but before the first of the seven bowls of judgment are poured out upon the earth and the kingdom of the beast.

These voices of praise, joined by angels, are also recorded in Revelation 7:9–17 and 11:15–18. All of these texts, in chapters 7, 11, 15, and 19, make it clear that God is now in charge. He has reclaimed His right to rule all of His creation and has begun to do exactly that. Chapters 11 and 15 also tell us that the doors to the Temple in heaven have now been thrown open.

In all of these texts, the group of people who are described as a sea are also before the throne of God, or are holding palm branches and singing songs of praise to God. These are the guests who have been invited to the wedding of the Lamb. Remember, in a Hebrew wedding the guests are always *before* the throne (i.e., the *chuppah*) where the wedding will take place. At the same time the Bride is *under* the chuppah, or *on* the throne but *not before* it.

The guests honor the wedding couple by laying palm branches before them. Recall that, in ancient times, palm branches were laid down before both kings and newlyweds.[1]

Group Two: The Twenty-Four Elders

The twenty-four elders and the four living creatures have been described in detail in Volumes 1 and 2 in this series. To recap, here is a short passage that actually appears in *both* volumes:

Next John sees twenty-four elders, wearing white (the color of marriage), crowned with gold and seated on twenty-four thrones. Who are these elders? Are they ancient rabbis?

Let's begin with the following quote of Yeshua addressing His disciples:

> And Jesus said to them, "Truly I say to you, that you who have followed Me, in the regeneration when the Son of Man will sit on His glorious throne, you also shall sit upon twelve thrones, judging the twelve tribes of Israel." (Matthew 19:28)

This passage strongly suggests that half of the twenty-four elders will be his twelve disciples. Ancient rabbinic writings suggest that the other twelve could well be the twelve tribal leaders of Israel, which certainly makes sense.

In contrast, modern Christianity seems to believe that the twenty-four elders are angelic beings with unknown qualifications. This understanding is very ancient and has its roots in *de Coelesti Hierarchia, pseudo-denys,* by Dionysius the Areopagite, going back to the 5th century AD. But here again, the church is deriving its interpretations from people, however well-meaning, who are nonetheless Greek or Latin rather than from Hebraic people with Hebraic models of analysis.

Group Three: The Four Living Creatures

Next, with respect to the four *living creatures* that John saw, we are inserting below a short passage from Volume 1 of this series. The original passage was much longer and describes the three types of angels. If you haven't read it recently we highly recommend doing so at this point.

This is an abbreviated version of the portion that discusses the cherubim, of which the four that we specifically name (paragraph six in the following quotation) are almost certainly the four that John saw surrounding God's throne. He saw each of them from one of four different perspectives, which thereby revealed one of the four different faces that each one had:

As we know, God created all things. But even before God created all the life forms on earth He also created a huge host of heavenly beings, commonly called *angels*. They were dedicated to eternal service to Him. In a sense, from their moment of creation they have been God's hands and feet, for they are the ones who carry out many of His missions throughout His creation.

But not all angels are equal, for Scripture tells us that God created three separate "orders," each one having a unique form, function, and purpose. In the Hebrew singular their titles were *teraph*, *seraph*, and *cherub*. The Hebrew plural forms are as follows.

The *cherubim*, also called *archangels*, are angels of the highest and the most powerful order. They literally surround the throne of God. Cherubim have six wings, four faces, and are quite large. The four faces (Revelation 4:7, Ezekiel 1:10) are a man's face, a lion's face, a bull's face, and an eagle's face. They are also covered with eyes.

We are introduced in the Bible to four cherubim. The most commonly known are the Archangel Michael (the Prince of Israel), the Archangel Gabriel, and the two who fell, one called *Lucifer* in the *King James Version* of Isaiah 14:12 . . . and one called *Abaddon*, now the angel of Death (see below). The other two, *Uriel* and *Raphael*, are referred to in extra-biblical writings – the Talmud, Mishnah, and apocryphal books.

Here are the meanings of the names of the four cherubim/ archangels who did not rebel and thereby kept their positions around the throne of God:

- **Michael** Warrior (prince) of God
- **Gabriel** Redeemer of God
- **Raphael** Healer of God; Bringer of God's Healing
- **Uriel** Light of God; Bringer of God's Light

All these names end with "el," which is a Hebrew word (or suffix) meaning *God*. Each of these four angels represents some attribute, characteristic, or service that originates with God.

The four living creatures are these four cherubim – Michael, Gabriel, Raphael, and Uriel.[2]

Why So Many Eyes?

In several places the Bible tells us that God is light. Could it be possible, then, that the cherubim who surround God and do His bidding would be covered with eyes to enable them to become the best possible processors of His instructions? After all, only one organ in the body actually deals with light.

It's also interesting to note that, in Revelation 1:11 and 1:19, the Apostle John was told to write down *only what he saw*.

Group Four: God's Bride

Finally this leaves the Bride and the Lamb. Of course, we know that the Lamb is Yeshua. The lamb metaphor is used many times to describe the Messiah. For example, John 1:29 says, "The next day he [John] saw Jesus coming to him and said, 'Behold, the Lamb of God who takes away the sin of the world!'" Revelation 5:6 again refers to Yeshua as the Lamb that had been slain.

Then, in Revelation 19:7, the text reads, "for the marriage of the Lamb has come and His bride has made herself ready."

Revelation 19:8 then describes the Lamb's Bride in this way: "It was given to her to clothe herself in fine linen, bright and clean; for the fine linen is the righteous acts of the saints." She has been allowed to wear these garments because of her works. She has run the race as referred to by Paul in this familiar passage:

> I have fought the good fight, I have finished the course,
> I have kept the faith; [8]in the future there is laid up for

me the crown of righteousness, which the Lord, the
righteous Judge, will award to me on that day; and not
only to me, but also to all who have loved His appearing.
(II Timothy 4:7–8)

The crown that Paul refers to here is the Crown of Jerusalem – the
Bride's crown. It was certainly not the gift of salvation, for salvation
is something that is *given* to us whereas this crown Paul speaks of is
something that one earns by running the race and living righteously.
We doubt very much that Paul was running any race for salvation.
That would imply that salvation could be earned and we know that
it cannot. It is a gift from God for those who believe, as stated clearly
in these familiar passages:

> For God so loved the world, that He gave His only begot-
> ten Son, that whoever believes in Him shall not perish,
> but have eternal life. (John 3:16)

> For the wages of sin is death, but the free gift
> of God is eternal life in Christ Jesus our Lord.
> (Romans 6:23)

Furthermore, we know from this passage in I Corinthians 3 that salvation can be likened to a foundation.

> [10]According to the grace of God which was given to
> me, like a wise master builder I laid a foundation, and
> another is building on it. But each man must be careful
> how he builds on it. [11]For no man can lay a foundation
> other than the one which is laid, which is Jesus Christ.
> (I Corinthians 3:10–11)

As detailed in the rest of I Corinthians 3, on this foundation we can
erect works made of gold, silver, precious stones, wood, hay, and straw.
These materials represent different types of works that we choose to
build in our lives. All will be tested by fire, but only those who have
works made of gold, silver, and precious stones, that survive the
flame, will receive a reward. However, even those who earn nothing,
because none of their "good works" survived the fire, will still have
the gift of salvation.

For example, the thief on the cross typifies this concept – Jesus saw him that day "in paradise" but his earthly works earned him no heavenly rewards.

The Wedding Ceremony

So, given that all members of the wedding party are assembled together, when does the celebration start? We know that the wedding ceremony occurs in the Holy of Holies, under the chuppah. With all the players now assembled the wedding is about to begin.

To remind ourselves of how an ancient Hebrew bride and groom were joined together in marriage, here's a short passage from Volume 1 in this series:

> As he escorted her to the *chuppah*, a dome of bright crimson cloth, its color symbolizing their covering by a blood covenant, the groom would also be wearing a wreath of fresh myrtle and roses, thorns included, a symbol that their love would bring him both joy and pain. (Does this sound familiar?) Somewhat earlier, a broad circlet of gold, shaped into the silhouette of the city of Jerusalem, would have been placed on the bride's head.
>
> The couple would perform the wedding ceremony themselves, during which the groom would pronounce his bride pure, holy, and set apart for him alone. They would speak seven blessings over each other and vow their eternal faithfulness and love. After completing their vows they would share the fourth cup of wine together, the final step in the long betrothal process which began with the groom's proposal perhaps more than a year ago.
>
> When they finished this fourth cup the groom would place it on the ground and put his foot on it. The bride would rest her foot on his and together they would stomp the cup to pieces, assuring that no one else would ever drink from it, thus signifying the exclusivity of their relationship.
>
> Next the bride and groom would take a triple-braided loaf of *challah* bread, bless it, break it, dip it in salt, and feed it to each

other as a further pledge of their friendship and a renewal of the salt covenant. Then the groom would give his bride a new inheritance by removing her old, worn-out sandals, washing her feet, and putting on a new pair. Both of these customs clearly reinforce the pillars of covenant, the foundation underlying ancient Hebrew marriages on which modern marriages as well should stand.

At that point the bride and groom would sometimes exchange rings, placing them on their right hands. The bride and groom were considered a king and queen for a week, starting with their wedding day. As the queen stands at the king's right hand, so the bride must always symbolically be at her groom's right hand.[3]

But Revelation 15:8 says that no one is allowed to enter the sanctuary in heaven until the seven bowls of wrath have been poured out on the earth. So the wedding must occur *after the bowls are poured out.*

The Groom Cannot Be Fooled!

In ancient and modern Jewish custom, contrary to Western tradition, the bride and the groom were (and still are) required to see each other just prior to the ceremony. This custom is based on the deception that Laban perpetrated on Jacob by substituting Leah for Rachel, which he could do only because Leah was covered up.

In the current Hebraic custom, a small ceremony called the "unveiling" is conducted prior to the actual wedding ceremony itself, in which the bride and the groom and the wedding party go into a separate room so the groom can verify that the person he is about to marry truly is his desired bride, in contrast to a false bride.

In heaven, at this moment in the Revelation text, we believe this is what is taking place. The wedding invitation is being extended here, but the actual ceremony itself does not occur yet. In the next chapter of Revelation we see the Groom coming with the Bride, mirroring a king and queen's triumphant entry back to the earthly Temple in Jerusalem to conduct the wedding ceremony.

Yes, the wedding ceremony will occur on earth, not in heaven. And, it will occur on Yom Kippur, the Day of Atonement, after His return on Feast of Trumpets.

Antiochus Epiphanes is foretold in Daniel's prophecy. As you may recall, he was a monster who defiled the Temple in Jerusalem and was a prophetic archetype of the False Messiah. In response to this abomination the Jews rebelled, won their freedom from tyranny, and cleansed and rededicated the Temple.

This is the basis of the modern Hebrew feast called *Hanukkah*. At that time (165 BC), the Hebrews, following the customs and instructions of Torah, took seven days to cleanse and purify the Temple. Then, on the eighth day they were allowed to rededicate the Temple and reinitiate the sacrificial services.

In this particular rededication, the ancient Hebrews saw the celebration of Hanukkah mirroring Sukkot, which is the seventh feast and lasts for seven-plus-one days. Is the same thing occurring in this case? Is God coming back and finding a defiled Temple, which requires a cleansing process before He can conduct his marriage ceremony?

Happy Hanukkah!

When viewed through an Hebraic lens the text of Daniel 12:10–12, plus Revelation 11:2 and 13:5, present us with an intriguing insight into what's happening in Revelation. Here in Revelation 19 we see an obvious allusion to the Bride, referencing her white garments for purity and refinement. In turn, this is an obvious allusion to the ultimate wedding ceremony itself.

Meanwhile, the Revelation text refers to the time period during which the beast will rule and reign. The angel instructing the Apostle John tells him that the beast will be allowed to reign for 42 months, which equates to 1,260 days. We believe that this time period will terminate on Feast of Trumpets, when Yeshua returns with His Bride.

However, the Daniel text tells us that those who wait for 1,335 days (an extra 75) alludes to the same thing that happened during the Maccabean rebellion. Antiochus Epiphanes' occupation of Israel ended with a giant battle, followed by a cleansing and rededication of the Temple as explained above.

Is the Daniel text implying a similar scenario? Is God honoring Hanukkah, the man-made festival? Many believe that He might be recognizing this holiday, established to honor God Himself, by holding His own wedding to His Bride on the same day.

Is it also accidental that Hanukkah occurs 75 days after Yom Kippur, which would fulfill the additional 75 days in Daniel's prophecy? Yom Kippur is recognized by many Jewish rabbis as the feast that celebrates the day of the wedding between God and man.

The seven bowls of judgment are poured out on the inhabitants of the earth during this last 3½ years, during the reign of the beast, which has been established in Jerusalem. The judgment itself is fulfilling a promise Yahweh made to Israel specifically, and to the world generally, more than thirty-four hundred years earlier as contained in the writings of Moses in Deuteronomy 27 and 28.

Yahweh makes it clear that He wants His people to love and obey Him. If they did, as we have explained numerous times in these three volumes, He would bless them, protect them, and provide for them. Otherwise He would send a curse. The word for curse here is *kalal* and means *to curse*. But because God does not curse, as in "put a hex on someone," this word reveals what God will do when He is ignored, profaned, disregarded, and discarded.

Kalal also means *to be diminished, to be despised, to be of little account, to be lightly esteemed,* and *to bring contempt*.[4] The idea here is that when we ignore God, try to make Him insignificant, and otherwise discard our Creator we literally bring the same insignificance upon ourselves. Rejection of God and His ways brings judgment, resulting in the ultimate curse – perpetual and permanent separation from Him.

In Summary . . .

The best description of our current state of being is that we are alive but also dead, hopeless and forever without access to God. This is the state mankind found itself in immediately after Adam and Eve sinned in the Garden of Eden. We had access to the Tree of Life but we died. That is, we were separated from our Creator.

This is also the reason why God barred the way to the Tree of Life in the Garden of Eden. God knew that in our fallen state, while we could still claim access to perpetual physical life here on earth, He could never save us from our hopeless situation. It amounted to eternal life but also included eternal separation from Him. By cutting off access to the Tree of Life He enabled His Son to come as a man, to die, and thereby to pay the price for our sins. This was the only way God could save us from our fallen state.

In heaven the situation will be quite different. As this wedding party gets going – the one that lasts all night just before the ceremony – it will be attended by all the close friends of the Bride and Groom. Certainly the groomsmen and the bridesmaids will be there. It is a time of joyous celebration just prior to the wedding ceremony itself.

These events both occur after the pouring out of the seventh bowl. At this point God's ultimate goal is coming to fruition. He is being reunited with mankind. The precious relationship that mankind threw to the ground more than 6,000 years ago has now been restored.

Chapter 10

The Return of the True King

IN THE LAST HALF OF REVELATION 19 THE SCENE DRASTICALLY CHANGES.

> [11]And I saw heaven opened, and behold, a white horse, and He who sat on it is called Faithful and True, and in righteousness He judges and wages war. [12]His eyes are a flame of fire, and on His head are many diadems; and He has a name written on Him which no one knows except Himself. [13]He is clothed with a robe dipped in blood, and His name is called The Word of God.

> [14]And the armies which are in heaven, clothed in fine linen, white and clean, were following Him on white horses. [15]From His mouth comes a sharp sword, so that with it He may strike down the nations, and He will rule them with a rod of iron; and He treads the wine press of the fierce wrath of God, the Almighty. [16]And on His robe and on His thigh He has a name written, "KING OF KINGS, AND LORD OF LORDS."

> [17]Then I saw an angel standing in the sun, and he cried out with a loud voice, saying to all the birds which fly in midheaven, "Come, assemble for the great supper of God, [18]so that you may eat the flesh of kings and the flesh

of commanders and the flesh of mighty men and the flesh of horses and of those who sit on them and the flesh of all men, both free men and slaves, and small and great."

[19]And I saw the beast and the kings of the earth and their armies assembled to make war against Him who sat on the horse and against His army. [20]And the beast was seized, and with him the False Prophet who performed the signs in his presence, by which he deceived those who had received the mark of the beast and those who worshiped his image; these two were thrown alive into the lake of fire which burns with brimstone. [21]And the rest were killed with the sword which came from the mouth of Him who sat on the horse, and all the birds were filled with their flesh. (Revelation 19:11–21)

Our Groom – the One on the white horse – has everything under control. The angels' declaration at the seventh trumpet is being fulfilled before our very eyes. The kingdoms of this world are now becoming the kingdoms of our Lord!

He is conquering and destroying all the armies and forces that have ruled the world up to this point. No longer will He allow them to deceive the nations. No longer will He allow them to lead people astray and pervert what is rightfully His. No longer will He allow His people to be separated from Himself.

The Army from Heaven

He is accompanied by an army from heaven. These troops certainly include His Bride, all decked out in dazzling white garments. In fact, the language used in Revelation 19, to describe her clothing, is also used here to describe the clothing His army is wearing.

Recall Paul's description of the armor of God in Ephesians 6:10–17. This was a description of how He sees His Bride adorned. However, the message is not that we procure our defense from any kind of man-made armor. The passage in Ephesians (remember, think Hebrew) is an excellent description of the garments that a priest wore when he served in the Temple of God. We form the most powerful army against the forces of evil when we are serving God.

Other members of the dazzling white army following the King would certainly include the angels. All of these now go into battle against the worldly forces opposing God. This could include rebellious mankind, devils, demons, and especially Satan and Abaddon. And the only thing they have is worldly armor. Guess who wins?

In fact this fight doesn't really look at all like a fight that Hollywood might produce. No great war scenes are needed; no shots of flames leaping high and explosions going off. No swords clashing or great loss of life on both sides. In fact this is an extremely lopsided battle. Most everyone on one side is killed while everyone dressed in white survives. The damage is all done by a single sword that comes out of the mouth of the King – obviously a Hebrew metaphor for the Word of God. With it He wins the day and defeats the armies, powers, and principalities arrayed against Him.

This King will bring to an end the evil government that has ruled over His creation, the same way that He started His government over His creation back in Genesis 1. He once spoke His creation into existence, and with this same voice God (for this sword represents the words of God) will destroy this opposing government and restore His right to rule. The power of God's spoken Word will once more take precedence over any other opinion or authority.

The Name on His Thigh

In Revelation 19:16 we read that His name is inscribed on the King's garment and on His thigh. From a western perspective we might not question this. It is not unusual for important people to have their names written on their lapels.

However, why does this name also appear on this horse rider's thigh? From a Hebrew perspective, this is more understandable. Two thousand years ago, when the book of Revelation was written, it was common practice for men to wear a talit. This garment had four corners and was used as a wrap or outer covering. At each corner, Hebrew men would attach tzit tzit, following the instructions of the Torah (Numbers 15:38; Deuteronomy 20:12).

> Hanging from the corners of the talit are the tzit tzit, what most people call "fringes" but which are actually four cords doubled over and knotted in a distinct pattern, numerically spelling out the name of God.[1]

These four strings would be tied together to form a single strand. In the process, they would be tied into five separate knots. The number of wrappings in the four spaces between the five knots would correspond to the numerical values of the Hebrew letters forming the name YHWH (in English letters).

These tzit tzit would hang down from the four corners of the talit and would end up resting on the thighs of the person wearing it when that person was seated. So the name YHWH was on both his garment and His thigh as He rode out with His army.

Next we see a huge gathering of birds that have been called to come and feast on the flesh of all these fallen enemies of the kingdom of heaven. It is common knowledge in the Mideast that Israel serves as a migratory flyway for countless birds, many of which come out of Europe in the fall and head toward Africa for the winter. They then fly north to breed each spring, back into Europe and various parts of Russia. The text tells us that they are now called to participate in a great "feast."

The word for *supper* (or *feast* in some versions of the Bible) in Revelation 19:17 also means *sacrifice*. The funny thing about these birds is that – when you think of birds that will be eating flesh – what comes to mind are birds of prey such as eagles and hawks, or birds that eat carrion such as vultures. But the word here is *zipor*. This is not the usual word for eagles or vultures, such as *azneah* or *aiah*. Zipor is the Hebrew word for *sparrow* or *dove*. These kinds of birds, especially doves, were themselves used as sacrifices in the Temple and were definitely not birds that would feast on flesh.

Obviously, God is making a point here. Mankind can accept salvation through the blood of Yeshua, which is sometimes represented in the Temple as a dove. Or, the "unsacrificed sacrifice" will come and consume those who reject salvation and remain unrepentant. This is reminiscent of the seven bowls of judgment that were earlier poured out on all those who refused to repent, including those involved with the kingdom of the beast. This is also a symbolic image of life consuming death.

These bowls of judgment contained wine, which represents the blood of sacrifices. However, instead of this sacrifice and its blood being offered up humbly, on the altar at the Temple of God, this blood was thrown out upon the earth causing the carnage earlier described and recognized as the final judgment of God. Mankind has the choice to allow God's sacrifice, His Son, to do the work of cleansing us and making us whole, or the sacrifice Himself will judge and will expunge all our impurities.

Unfortunately, the cleansing in the latter case removes the man. What a terrible reality many people will face. Hearing on that day that the Creator never knew them will echo in their memories throughout eternity, which they will spend separated from God in a place no one would want to be. It's called hell.

Confronting the Leaders

The war between the rider of the white horse and His army, named in Revelation 19:11, and the beast and his army, comes to a head when God confronts the leaders of the rebellion. The beast with ten horns and seven heads that we met back in Revelation 13, who rose up out of the sea, and the False Prophet who deluded mankind with all kinds of deceptive miracles, will now be confronted by their Creator. After allowing them to reign over His creation for forty-two months God intends to bring His own plan to completion, which includes throwing the beast and his False Prophet into the lake of fire.

However, this is not the end of Abaddon and Satan. Unfortunately, for those who continue to live out their lives during the thousand-year reign, Abaddon still lives. In fact, we know that he does because those who remain on the earth, living in bodies of flesh, will still die. Granted, they will live longer than we do today, as Isaiah tells us in the following verse:

> "No longer will there be in it an infant *who lives but a few* days,
> Or an old man who does not live out his days;
> For the youth will die at the age of one hundred
> And the one who does not reach the age of one hundred
> Will be *thought* accursed. (Isaiah 65:20)

Even so, Abaddon will still have control over the unbelieving people when they die during the thousand-year reign, because death will still be present. But at the end of that time period we will learn of Abaddon's final destiny.

Satan was represented as the Dragon we met in Revelation 12. He is the enemy of God who stood before the woman who represented Israel, God's Bride. He was seen losing his place in heaven and being thrown down to earth. There Satan pursued the woman to destroy her, but God swept her up and took her to a place in the wilderness to protect her from the wrath of the Dragon.

The Adversary was the one who possessed the beast that rose up out of the sea in Revelation 13. Satan, represented by the Dragon, gave all of his power to that same beast, who then ruled the earth for forty-two months from the Temple in Jerusalem, proclaiming that he was God. In a moment we will see what happens to Satan. He will take a little detour rather than the direct route the beast takes.

The last verse in Revelation 19 tells us that the sword that comes from the mouth of the One who is mounted on the white horse will kill all the remaining participants of the beast's army. On that day we will witness the awesome power of His spoken word.

Revelation 10 told us about seven thunders. As God's principles for holy living are spoken by the *actual* creator of these words, they immediately identify, judge, and kill those who oppose His plan. Unfortunately for the condemned they will have chosen the wrong team.

In this case, "See you later, alligator!" just doesn't apply anymore. This will be "Game over!" in the most literal sense.

The Enemy Chained

> [1]Then I saw an angel coming down from heaven, holding the key of the abyss and a great chain in his hand. [2]And he laid hold of the dragon, the serpent of old, who is the devil and Satan, and bound him for a thousand years; [3]and he threw him into the abyss, and shut it and sealed it over him, so that he would not deceive the nations any longer, until the thousand years were completed; after these things he must be released for a short time. (Revelation 20:1–3)

Satan, instead of going directly to the lake of fire at the *beginning* of the thousand-year reign, takes a small detour. An angel of God chains him up and throws him into the abyss. Here he waits, in darkness, to be released at the *end* of the thousand-year reign.

During that time, all the nations of the earth are now free from the accusations and deceptions of the Adversary. Unfortunately, when he returns, he will immediately incite a final worldwide rebellion to test the hearts of men again.

Who Is Who?

At the very beginning of the Messiah's thousand-year reign, as He comes back to take command of His creation, four groups that should be identified will still remain.

- First will be the Bride of the One who is riding on the white horse. The Bride includes all the people who were resurrected as the beast that came out of the sea was beginning his forty-two-month reign. During this time they were with their Groom and formed part of the army, dressed in white, that accompanied Him as He descended to earth to confront the armies of the beast.

These people will partner with God during the thousand-year reign, in their eternal bodies.

- Second, some people will remain on the earth. However, not every one of them will be part of the beast's army, to be destroyed by the sword that comes from the mouth of the Groom. Some of these may even be believers, but we suspect that most will not be. Either way, all will be judged at the Great White Throne Judgment that will occur at the end of the thousand-year reign.

- Third, those who died prior to His return but chose not to receive the free gift of salvation offered up by their Creator during their lifetimes, will still be in the grave during the thousand-year reign. They will then rise again during the Great White Throne Judgment, to receive their eternal bodies and their reward. Unfortunately, we don't believe they will want what they have earned.

- Fourth, some believers died in the past but were not resurrected at the fifth angelic proclamation to become part of the Bride. They were not considered worthy to be counted among the Bride, but they have lived with God in heaven since Yeshua's victory over death two thousand years earlier. They were the guests at the wedding – the ones waving palm branches who saw the Bride in heaven when she was given her white garments. They accompanied the Bride, with praise, and exalted the Groom.

  The members of this last group will live as spirits, without their restored bodies, during the thousand-year reign. They will not be given the same reward or the same responsibilities as the Bride, for the Bride comprises those who did have works that stood the test of fire (I Corinthians 3:12–15).

Thus, for believers there will be two distinct resurrections of the dead. First will come the Bride's resurrection, which will occur at the fifth angelic proclamation/seventh trumpet. Second will come the Great White Throne Judgment during which all remaining believers will be resurrected and will receive their restored bodies.

There will also be two groups of non-believers – those who have died and those still living in their earthly bodies. The dead will be in the grave, separated from God. The living will continue to dwell on the earth and will still have the opportunity to receive the gift of salvation. And both groups will receive God's final verdict on the Great White Throne Judgment day.

That judgment day will bring us to the close of the God-ordained time of man. Mankind will have had seven thousand years, from creation to the end of the thousand-year reign, to get it right. Whether we like it or not, our time will be up. The curses and blessings will now be distributed according to God's plan – not Satan's, not ours, and not anyone else's.

God's Infinite Patience

The thousand-year reign offers us one more beautiful picture showing how God gives people every possible opportunity to choose to serve Him, as differentiated by Rosh Hashanah (Feast of Trumpets) and Yom Kippur (Day of Atonement).

Rosh Hashanah was recognized as a celebration for those who had their names written in the Book of Life, while Yom Kippur, which occurs ten days later and represents the ten-hundred-year reign, enables God to extend to mankind another period of time during which they can get it right and correct their lives. However, the end of this final ten days absolutely terminates their final chance to get their names rewritten in the Book of Life.

Are We There Yet?

In chapter 20 we are re-introduced to two groups of people who are sitting on thrones. We have met them before. The first group, described in verse 4, is given the authority to judge others during the thousand-year reign. God will entrust these individuals to provide government over those who are still alive – the ones who did not die during the bowls or Armageddon. This first group includes those who were resurrected as the Bride of Yeshua during the fifth angelic proclamation/ seventh trumpet in Revelation 14:16 and 11:15–19.

The second group also seems to have the same authority, but they are more clearly described. They are martyrs who have been beheaded because they refused to pay homage to the beast. They also did not accept the mark of the beast on their hands or their foreheads. They now live again and rule with Messiah.

We have met this second group of people before. They were the group of souls who were beneath the altar in Revelation 6. At that time, during the days of the fifth seal, they cried out to the Lord and asked Him how long it would be before their blood would be avenged upon those who still lived on the earth. They were told to wait a bit longer because others would still be martyred for their faith before God would come back to avenge them all.

Both of these two groups have now been resurrected and are living eternally, ruling with their Groom during the thousand years. They will no longer be concerned with the coming second death. This second death will occur at the end of the thousand-year reign, but there will be one last test for those living on the earth who have not been resurrected and are still living in their fleshly bodies.

Satan, the deceiver, will be released from the bottomless pit where he has been chained up during the thousand-year reign. Once more he will attempt to deceive mankind, and once again some people will fall for his deceptions. It's hard to believe that many people still cannot seem to figure out who the real King is even though the Messiah Himself is now dwelling with them. But this will fulfill the prophecy foretelling their lack of passion . . . and their even greater lack of discernment.

Hot, Cold, or Lukewarm?

Revelation 3 describes Laodicea, the last of seven congregations that will now exist on the earth. In Volume 2 in this series – and also in chapter 8 in this volume – we explained how two different types of springs were located in this city, some hot and some cold. But eventually the streams from both flowed together, creating lukewarm pools. Soaking in either the hot or cold springs could bring healing for various types of ailments, but the lukewarm pools were worthless.

This passage was not talking about wishy-washy believers. It was referring to people who had deceived themselves into thinking that they were saved and doing good, but their works testified against them because they did not have any faith and were actually self-serving and ungodly. As Yeshua's own brother said, "For just as the body without the spirit is dead, so also faith without works is dead" (James 2:26).

It is well known that the most vibrant congregations, filled with spiritually mature people who truly love the Lord, are sometimes found in situations in which they are under great persecution, often where their very own survival is in question. During the thousand-year reign that kind of persecution will not exist. No one will be harassing believers. Freedom will reign.

In that environment some people will come to know God, but others will fail the test of faith and find themselves falling for that ancient lie, to the effect that someone other than God is the Creator and King. They will pay with their eternal lives for their lack of attentiveness.

Those who are now sitting on thrones, ruling God's creation, were raised at the last trumpet. The last trumpet was described in Revelation 11. There we are told that the kingdoms of this world are now the kingdoms of God. With that seventh and last trumpet blast, the fifth angelic proclamation also occurred simultaneously. Revelation 14 described that proclamation, which is the first resurrection.

There the Messiah, the Groom, appears in the clouds with a sickle and is instructed to harvest the earth. This event describes the taking of God's Bride, who are then seated on thrones and given the authority to judge those who still dwell on the earth.

The members of the Bride, now living in their immortal, glorified bodies, are also now immune from dying a second death or entering the lake of fire. In contrast, Revelation 20:5 informs us about the remainder of the dead who were not included when the Bride was raised at the first resurrection. Those people (i.e., those not raised with the Bride) will not be resurrected until after the thousand-year reign. At that point they will be joined by those who died during the last thousand years. All of these will then be subject to the second-death judgment.

One Final Try

Satan's one last attempt to overthrow the kingdom God will end in disaster. As in the days of Elijah, when God destroyed the prophets of Ba'al, fire will fall from heaven and destroy Ba'al, an ancient pagan name for Satan himself. This Dragon has gone by many names, but all of them have represented the same fallen cherub. He is referred to here, in Revelation 20:8, as Gog and Magog, the same name by which he was referred to in Ezekiel 38 and 39.

Those chapters in Ezekiel describe a war in which Russia and some allies attack Israel during the days that lead up to the two witnesses. Gog and Magog represented Satan's heart then, and they also represent Satan's heart here. In both cases they are destroyed by miraculous means, by fire coming from the hand of God. Sadly, those who will join Satan's ranks will number as the sands of the sea.

The devil now receives his final reward, and we can't say that he hasn't earned it – the lake of fire in which he joins his buddies, the beast and False Prophet. Remember, they were thrown into this lake at the beginning of the thousand-year reign. All of them will be tormented there, day and night, for eternity.

But wait, isn't one more monster left? His name is Abaddon, who was referred to as the angel of death – the one who fell from heaven with the key to the bottomless pit back in the fifth trumpet. He released the locusts from the pit and led an attack on the people of the earth that consumed one-third of mankind.

The Great White Throne Judgment is the last of the events that will deal with the fallen nature of man and angels. Those who have died over the last seven thousand years, who were not counted worthy to be resurrected at the beginning of the thousand-year reign, will finally be raised from the dead and will be judged accordingly. Books will be opened, including the Book of Life, and millions of people will be judged by what they did while they were alive. Their works will try them. Their faith will be judged to see if it was true. Those that are found without faith, without their promised covering, will be thrown into the lake of fire.

Given what the Bible says in Revelation 20:14, have you ever wondered how He could throw "death" into the lake of fire? The answer is fairly simple. The word describing death in this verse implies an actual person and not a vague concept. It's referring to the *angel* of death, Abaddon. He was the one who had authority over all who died in the past, because of their sins. He had the power to lock them away from God until Yeshua came and set the captives free, as He did in the following verses from I Peter.

> For Christ also died for sins once for all, *the* just for *the* unjust, so that He might bring us to God, having been put to death in the flesh, but made alive in the spirit; [19] in which also He went and made proclamation to the spirits *now* in prison. (I Peter 3:18-19)

This fallen cherub now joins his companions of deception in the lake of fire. Revelation 20:14 then tells us: "Then death and Hades were thrown into the lake of fire. This is the second death, the lake of fire."

In Hebrew, the idea of death includes the concept of separation from our Creator. Thus we all died the *first* death when we were separated from Him by being born into a world that contaminated us with sin the moment we arrived. But then He came into the same world and paid the consequences for that sin by offering up Himself as the ultimate sacrifice for all of mankind.

Each us has therefore been given the opportunity to accept His free gift. However, on the day of judgment, those who turned His salvation down while they were on this earth will then suffer eternal separation from God, amounting to a second death in the lake of fire.

Unfortunately, no more payments will be offered up for them for the forgiveness of their sins. They will spend eternity permanently separated from their Creator.

In Summary . . .

Here is the actual text of Revelation, which we have just described:

> [1]Then I saw an angel coming down from heaven, holding the key of the abyss and a great chain in his hand. [2]And he laid hold of the dragon, the serpent of old, who is the devil and Satan, and bound him for a thousand years; [3]and he threw him into the abyss, and shut it and sealed it over him, so that he would not deceive the nations any longer, until the thousand years were completed; after these things he must be released for a short time.
>
> [4]Then I saw thrones, and they sat on them, and judgment was given to them. And I saw the souls of those who had been beheaded because of their testimony of Jesus and because of the word of God, and those who had not worshiped the beast or his image, and had not received the mark on their forehead and on their hand; and they came to life and reigned with Christ for a thousand years.
>
> [5]The rest of the dead did not come to life until the thousand years were completed. This is the first resurrection. [6]Blessed and holy is the one who has a part in the first resurrection; over these the second death has no power, but they will be priests of God and of Christ and will reign with Him for a thousand years.
>
> [7]When the thousand years are completed, Satan will be released from his prison, [8]and will come out to deceive the nations which are in the four corners of the earth, Gog and Magog, to gather them together for the war; the number of them is like the sand of the seashore. [9]And they came up on the broad plain of the earth and

surrounded the camp of the saints and the beloved city, and fire came down from heaven and devoured them.

¹⁰And the devil who deceived them was thrown into the lake of fire and brimstone, where the beast and the false prophet are also; and they will be tormented day and night forever and ever.

¹¹Then I saw a great white throne and Him who sat upon it, from whose presence earth and heaven fled away, and no place was found for them. ¹²And I saw the dead, the great and the small, standing before the throne, and books were opened; and another book was opened, which is the book of life; and the dead were judged from the things which were written in the books, according to their deeds. ¹³And the sea gave up the dead which were in it, and death and Hades gave up the dead which were in them; and they were judged, every one of them according to their deeds.

¹⁴Then death and Hades were thrown into the lake of fire. This is the second death, the lake of fire. ¹⁵And if anyone's name was not found written in the book of life, he was thrown into the lake of fire. (Revelation 20:1–15)

Chapter 11

Renewed Heaven and Earth

⌒

THE LAST TWO CHAPTERS OF THE BOOK OF REVELATION ARE UNIQUE. They describe events that are rarely revealed anywhere else in the Bible. These events immediately follow the thousand-year reign that ends with the Great White Throne Judgment. They describe our ultimate destiny and the hope of the Bride. They reveal the purpose, gift, and the restored life God is still offering to all of mankind.

Unfortunately, they reveal only a tiny tidbit of what God has in store for us; for example, they tell us very little about our daily activities. But one thing will be certain – we will be given responsibility over various portions of God's vast creation. This time we will manage it with wisdom and love.

From here on the text no longer refers to unbelievers. In His great wisdom God will redirect our attention so that productivity and management of the creation will become our focus. We will re-member the past and those who failed to choose God will come to mind. This memory will serve as a reminder and a guide to keep our eyes on righteous principles and the One who gave them to us centuries before.

> [1]Then I saw a new heaven and a new earth; for the first heaven and the first earth passed away, and there is no longer any sea. [2]And I saw the holy city, new Jerusalem, coming down out of heaven from God, made ready as a bride adorned for her husband.
>
> [3]And I heard a loud voice from the throne, saying, "Behold, the tabernacle of God is among men, and He will dwell among them, and they shall be His people, and God Himself will be among them, [4]and He will wipe away every tear from their eyes; and there will no longer be any death; there will no longer be any mourning, or crying, or pain; the first things have passed away."
>
> [5]And He who sits on the throne said, "Behold, I am making all things new." And He said, "Write, for these words are faithful and true." [6]Then He said to me, "It is done. I am the Alpha and the Omega, the beginning and the end. I will give to the one who thirsts from the spring of the water of life without cost. [7]He who overcomes will inherit these things, and I will be his God and he will be My son." (Revelation 21:1–7)

The first verse reveals that, immediately after the thousand-year reign, God is going to clean house. In fact, let's talk a bit about this "house" before we go on. Many people in the church suggest that the believer's ultimate destiny will be with God in heaven. They suggest that our ultimate goal will be to spend eternity with Him in the heavenly realms. Yet nothing could be further from the truth.

The idea of a heavenly end goal has its roots in Gnostic thinking. These ideas permeated the world at the time of the early church, precisely as it was losing its original Hebrew roots. As a result the church took on the thinking of the early Greek Fathers. Unfortunately, the people who became the leaders of the early church, in the second and third centuries, did not have biblical Hebraic backgrounds.

Remember, the Jews had been summarily removed and had lost most of their influence over the messianic believers by this time. These congregations had started out as a sect or a "branch" of Judaism. But given the expulsion of their original Jewish majorities, leadership, and perspective, plus the introduction of Greek ideas, many pagan concepts infiltrated into and corrupted the thinking of the messianic congregations. The evidence of this can still be seen permeating the views of some believers and teachers yet today.

According to the Gnostics . . .

The Gnostics believed that it was incumbent upon man to usher in God's return by making the world more righteous. Making the world more righteous is certainly a good idea. However, the biblical view is that the Messiah's presence is needed in order for the manifestation of righteousness to occur. In fact, God says that in spite of mankind's or even Israel's behavior, He will come back *because of His promise*, not because we have fixed the world all up and made it into an acceptable place for Him to dwell.

The Gnostics also believed in a remote God – one who was not interested in personal relationships and certainly not interested in any daily interactions with us. Again, this conflicts with the concept of a God who walked in the Garden, chose to dwell in the midst of the Israeli camp, and then came and lived in our midst. This desire to be with us culminated in His death on the cross, His resurrection, and a promise to come and dwell with us again.

The church's idea of three persons making up one God also has its roots in Gnostic teachings. As the Gnostics knew him, God was a leader of gods – not the one and only. There is no support in the Hebrew text for the idea that three beings make up the one Godhead. This is polytheism at its core.

Yes, there are different aspects to God, just as man, made in His image, has different aspects. The attributes and aspects of body, mind, and soul in man copy the attributes and aspects of the Father, Son, and Holy Spirit, which is God in His fullness. But all together are still just one being or person (Isaiah 43:10).

Also central to Gnostic belief was the view that one of the lesser gods would come and usher in benevolence and peace to mankind. This is nothing more than an echo of the stated goals of the False Messiah.

These ideas also suggest that our bodies are evil. It is our conscience that is good yet needs to reach a higher plane of spirituality. We can even awaken the divine nature trapped within mankind if we can overcome the evil nature of our bodies. These sound like ideas taught in some churches today, yet none of these are sourced in the Bible. Such thinking comes from pagan Gnosticism.

The "heavenly goals" for mankind came from these same ideas. Heaven forbid that we have to come back down to earth when it is all over, some would suggest. But that is exactly what God has promised and it will not be a disappointment.

Yes, God will clean house – His house, the one He lent to mankind back in Genesis. We were supposed to manage it, not destroy it. The usual translation here is that God will establish a "new heaven and a new earth." But, on the contrary, the underlying Hebrew for *new* suggests that it should be *renewed* not *new*. In other words, God is going to reestablish His creation and restore it back to its original state. He will not destroy it completely and replace it with a new one, held offstage in the wings like the next set of scenery waiting for the curtain to come down before the next act can begin.

The fifth chapter of Matthew has something to contribute to the above scenario:

> Do not think that I came to abolish the Law or the Prophets; I did not come to abolish but to fulfill. [18]For truly I say to you, until heaven and earth pass away, not the smallest letter or stroke shall pass from the Law until all is accomplished (Matthew 5:17–18)

In this passage Yeshua is explaining that *Torah* (the Hebrew word here for *Law*) will not pass away but will be fulfilled, not at the death and resurrection of the Messiah but at the end of the thousand-year reign. We suggest that God will reestablish the same laws of righteousness that He gave Adam and Eve. We know that God and His Word do not change. In other words, to think and act righteously after the thousand-year reign our knowledge of the old ways will function like the foundation of the renewed ways.

> Then I saw a new heaven and a new earth; for the first heaven and the first earth passed away, and there is no longer any sea. (Revelation 21:1)

We also read here in the first verse that there will not be any sea. This revelation has many implications. Certainly the weather – and what causes it to change in the renewed world – will be totally different. No longer will there be hurricanes to dodge or great storms to be concerned with. Certainly our surroundings will be more stable – God may even restore the weather that existed before the fall of man.

A Truly Unique Rainbow

We believe that, prior to Noah's time, the earth was watered by springs rather than by storm systems. After the Flood Noah saw a rainbow, given to him as a sign that God would never again destroy the earth with a flood. The following text from Genesis 9 strongly implies that this was the first rainbow Noah had ever seen:

> "I set my bow in the cloud, and it shall be for a sign of a covenant between Me and the earth. [14]It shall come about, when I bring a cloud over the earth, that the bow will be seen in the cloud, [15]and I will remember My covenant, which is between Me and you and every living creature of all flesh; and never again shall the water become a flood to destroy all flesh. [16]When the bow is in the cloud, then I will look upon it, to remember the everlasting covenant between God and every living creature of all flesh that is on the earth." [17]And God said to Noah, "This is the sign of the covenant which I have established between Me and all flesh that is on the earth." (Genesis 9:13–17)

> The words God spoke to Noah also suggest that it had never significantly rained before. Rainbows are caused by the refraction of light from the sun as it interacts with the water in raindrops. Surely this would have happened before had rain been a common phenomenon before the Flood began.

The City of God

Jerusalem is then seen descending from heaven, adorned like a bride. She and her Groom, the Messiah, are given the earth to reign over and Jerusalem to rule from. The Bride is described here as Jerusalem, which has its roots in very ancient times. This is the city that King David ruled from. He was described as the apple of God's eye.

This city was also where God chose to dwell. It was the place He directed that His house, the Temple of God, should be built. Here He placed His presence in the midst of His chosen people, Israel. If it isn't so important, why is everybody still fighting over it today? It's not accidental that Satan, in the form of the beast and the False Messiah, will choose to rule and reign from God's throne in Jerusalem.

Revelation 21:3 gives us some interesting information about the dwelling place of God. It says that now God's abode is with man here on earth. Well, we thought that He was already dwelling on earth with His Bride during the thousand-year reign. Didn't He come back riding on a white horse with a great army to destroy the beast and then set up His kingdom here on earth?

The word translated here as God is *Elohim* in the original Hebrew. This word is used many times in the Tanakh (Old Testament) to identify "God in His totality." For example, here is one passage showing how God describes Himself:

> "You are My witnesses," declares the LORD, "And My servant whom I have chosen, so that you may know and believe Me and understand that I am He. Before Me there was no God formed, and there will be none after Me. [11]I, even I, am the LORD, and there is no savior besides Me." (Isaiah 43:10–11)

In Revelation 21:3, God calls Himself by the actual name by which He often referred to Himself, *YHWH* in Hebrew but *Yahweh* with vowels added so we can pronounce it. Here Elohim says about Himself that "I am Yahweh, and besides Me there is no Savior." Here He is describing and referring to the many aspects of Himself.

We see these aspects coming to the forefront when we examine the plan of restoration unfolding before our eyes. First, after the death and resurrection of Yeshua, God is able to send the Holy Spirit to comfort us and to lead us into all truth, as detailed in Paul's first letter to the congregation at Corinth:

> [12]Now we have received, not the spirit of the world, but the Spirit who is from God, so that we may know the things freely given to us by God, [13]which things we also speak, not in words taught by human wisdom, but in those taught by the Spirit, combining spiritual *thoughts* with spiritual *words*. (I Corinthians 2:12–13).

Dwelling Within Man

Two thousand years ago, after He started the process by which He would restore mankind, the Spirit of God was able to come and dwell within man from that time forward. That is, the people who chose to accept the gift of salvation and become believers *invited* and *allowed* him to dwell within them.

Now we wait for the return of our Groom, the event that kicks off the thousand-year reign. When He returns He will confront and remove Satan, the one who has deceived mankind from the start. Our minds, under Satan's influence, have been barraged with deceptions, confusion, and untruths. During the thousand-year reign, Yeshua the Son also never leaves or abandons us, and only truth will rain down into the minds of man.

After the thousand-year reign the physical bodies of all men and women will be the last aspect of mankind that will be restored to its original state. Mankind will then be a 777, and with his wholeness then established forever, our God, immortal and without sin, will arrive and complete the plan He initiated more than seven thousand years ago. From that point on Elohim will abide with men. And they shall be His people and God Himself will personally be their God.

In both Revelation 1 and 21, God calls Himself the Alpha and the Omega. Or, in Hebrew, the *Aleph* and the *Tav* – the Beginning and the End. He shows Himself to be the source of all life and the lover of mankind. In Revelation 21:8 He gives us a list of the types of behaviors that are abominable to Him:

> "But for the cowardly and unbelieving and abominable and murderers and immoral persons and sorcerers and idolaters and all liars, their part will be in the lake that burns with fire and brimstone, which is the second death."

He then warns us again of the destiny of those who practice such things, which Revelation 20:14 had already made very plain.

A description is also given of His new Bride, whom He refers to again as Jerusalem. A clear reference to His Bride being Israel is included. This would include the Israel of the Tanakh, but also all those Gentiles who loved the same God and accepted their redemption too.

There is no temple here in this city. There is no need for a separate dwelling place just for God. Given the restoration of mankind, God can now dwell with us. There will also be no need for the light of the sun or the moon for God Himself will illuminate the whole city. However, this does not mean that the new creation will have no sun and no moon, but remember – God was literally the only light in the universe before He created the sun and the moon on the fourth day.

The River Runs Through It

The last chapter in the book of Revelation introduces us to a river that flows through the middle of Jerusalem. In fact, its course is probably similar to the stream that intermittently flows through the Kidron Valley in Jerusalem today. This small stream courses its way from the eastern side of the Temple and then eventually flows to the Dead Sea.

The stream here in Revelation 22 originates from the throne of God. Its life-giving waters support the growth of many trees, one of which is the Tree of Life.

Each month this tree grows different types of edible fruit, twelve varieties in all, and its leaves are for the healing of the nations. This prophecy finds its equivalent in Ezekiel 47. More detail is given about the increasing flow of water and its ultimate destiny. In verse 8 the river is said to flow into the Arabah Valley. This is a very ancient name for the valley that the Dead Sea is found in, which also included the valley to the south. Here is a small portion of Ezekiel 47 in which God speaks to Ezekiel and gives him a fascinating tour. We highly recommend that you read all of it, and the surrounding chapters as well!

> 6Then he brought me back to the bank of the river. 7Now when I had returned, behold, on the bank of the river there *were* very many trees on the one side and on the other. 8Then he said to me, "These waters go out toward the eastern region and go down into the Arabah; then they go toward the sea, being made to flow into the sea, and the waters *of the sea* become fresh. 9It will come about that every living creature which swarms in every place where the river goes, will live. And there will be very many fish, for these waters go there and *the others* become fresh; so everything will live where the river goes.

> 10And it will come about that fishermen will stand beside it; from Engedi to Eneglaim there will be a place for the spreading of nets. Their fish will be according to their kinds, like the fish of the Great Sea, very many. 11But its swamps and marshes will not become fresh; they will be left for salt. 12By the river on its bank, on one side and on the other, will grow all *kinds of* trees for food. Their leaves will not wither and their fruit will not fail. They will bear every month because their water flows from the sanctuary, and their fruit will be for food and their leaves for healing." (Ezekiel 47:6–12)

No Longer Dead!

In other words, the water referred to in these verses brings renewed life to the Dead Sea except for some shore line marshes and swamps. This sea will now become the source of food for the people who fish there. In contrast, nothing edible lives in its waters today. So much salt is found there that people find it very difficult to dive beneath the surface, but they can easily float because of the buoyancy caused by the extreme concentrations of salt.

It seems that, after the thousand-year reign, God's intention is to restore the earth back to its original vitality (Isaiah 46:10; 48:3; 41:22). As Revelation 22 explains in detail, He will restore the Tree of Life that was once in the Garden of Eden. Also, He will again allow mankind to eat its fruit, which will have the same effect as before, providing life and sustenance. The waters that flow from God's throne are symbolic of His character. All things that have their source in Him bring blessing and life, even if sometimes we can't see this immediately.

It is also interesting to compare this passage to Genesis 2. Both texts talk about a river that flows from the presence of God. In each of these cases we believe that His presence is in Jerusalem. Both of these rivers grow lush plant life and also provide the water needed by many kinds of animals to thrive. Both rivers also flow east.

If it is true that God has not changed the location in which He desires to dwell, then what would lie to the east of Jerusalem would be the Dead Sea in the post-thousand-year-reign prophecy. Yet what apparently lay to the east of the presence of God in Genesis was the Garden of Eden.

So . . . Is the location of the Dead Sea actually the ancient location of the Garden of Eden? If so, that would help explain why God does not completely restore the Dead Sea. He wants us to always remember the chaos that we perpetrated on His holy and pure creation. Salt is a cleanser but it's also a life killer. Just a little bit of residual salt, left around the edges of the Sea, will act as a reminder of the deadly consequences we brought upon ourselves and His creation. It will also serve to help us recall the purifying response that God made by sending His Son to clean up the mess.

After the thousand-year reign, God tells us that He will be the light of the world. There will be no need of the sun to provide light, for He will provide all that will be needed. Again this is reminiscent of the state of affairs during the creation of the world. In Genesis 1:3 it tells us that God, on the very first day, provided the light without the need of the sun. The sun was not created until the fourth day.

The sun and the stars were made to be signs for us. Obviously, one of the signs that the sun will proclaim is that it only emulated its Creator, but in so doing it provided a clear picture of the nature of God to mankind. He revealed, by the sun's characteristics, His warmth and His intensity. It also mirrors His desire to walk with man and provide a constant presence that will give guidance and direction for our lives.

In Revelation 22:7 God repeats His admonition from the first chapter of Revelation: "Blessed is he who heeds the words of the prophecy of this book." Revelation 22:18 then gives us a very interesting warning. It tells us that we should not add or subtract from the statements that are made in His book. Some think that, because Revelation is at the end of the Bible, this verse is referring to the whole thing. However, it seems clear that this particular warning refers to the book of Revelation, for in the very next verse (Revelation 22:19) it literally calls itself "the book of this prophecy."

In Summary . . .

Many biblical books are not prophetic. The above description (from Revelation 22:19) should help us understand that God is elevating the importance of the words of Revelation above others. This certainly confronts head-on another idea floating around today, that the book of Revelation is not very important. Unfortunately, because of this false impression, people rarely give it the attention and concern it deserves, often ignoring it completely.

In fact, there are only two other places in the entire Bible where this same warning is used by God. It is stated twice but both passages refer to the same principle, in Deuteronomy 4:2 and 12:32. God warns His people not to add or diminish the statutes and judgments that He gave them. Clearly, two very important ideas are presented in the Bible that He does not want changed or misrepresented under any circumstances.

Isn't it interesting that many believers in the Christian church today attack or disregard these two issues? They claim that the law has been abolished and the book of Revelation is no longer applicable, both of which God told us not to add to or subtract from.

Chapter 12

Coming to a Close

In this conclusion to the three volumes in this series we'd like to remind you of something we said way back near the beginning of Volume 2.

Back to that Stool

> Our goal is to show you, in graphic terms, how the book of Revelation rests on three solid supports . . . . When you see that foundation and understand how the pieces fit together, your ability to comprehend both the individual elements and their relationships to each other will be vastly increased. Only then will Revelation be readily comprehensible.

Here are the three supports.

1. **First,** the book of Revelation is a thoroughly Hebraic text and therefore communicates on four levels at the same time . . . to the student who is looking at the text through Hebrew eyes, the words of Revelation also communicate other far deeper and more intimate understandings.

2. **Second,** in terms of its actual construction, the book of Revelation arrays itself naturally onto a very simple, solid, structural foundation, based on the menorah. God has taken an image that was thoroughly familiar to the ancient Hebrews and expanded it as only He can do, to serve as an underlying framework.

This particular image is no longer familiar to most modern non-Hebraic audiences, and is therefore not usually part of any teachings on how to diagram and understand Revelation. And yet, once you put that framework in place you can hang every major event in Revelation in its appropriate spot and thereby see exactly where every major event fits in relation to every other major event.

In addition, the beauty of Revelation is that every end-times biblical prophecy can *also* be hung on the same framework, such that you now see this detailed, chronological panorama of biblical eschatology laid out with breathtaking clarity. It all comes together in Revelation.

Books such as Daniel and Zechariah, end-times prophecies as old as those in Deuteronomy and Genesis, and all the late-dated prophecies as well can be overlaid on this structure. Thus Revelation itself provides a brief outline and some details about the events that lead up to the second coming of Messiah. Meanwhile, other biblical prophecies embellish these events along the way, so you get a much more detailed description – when you overlay them on the menorah – of other events that lead to the big one.

To repeat, that structural foundation – which we have also called its *structural metaphor* – is based on the menorah . . .

3. **Third,** an accurate understanding of Revelation requires an understanding of the basic types of covenant. As we've said so many times already, if you don't know covenant you don't know Scripture. However, to fully understand Revelation

you must be especially familiar with the ultimate covenant that God desires all of mankind to enter into with Him – its mechanics, its terms, and all of its standard requirements.

The primary *conceptual metaphor* on which Revelation rests is the ancient Hebrew marriage covenant. . . .

Revelation also functions like a *roadmap*, a *timetable of events*, and a *traveler's guide* all rolled into one. It shows you *where you are*, *where you're going next*, and *what you should be watching for* as you journey from the present day to the time of Yeshua's return. Revelation does all that by giving you a list of milestones that have to be passed, in the proper order, before you can move from one spot to another on the map – or, on the timeline.[1]

To Summarize All the Above . . .

As we hope these three volumes have demonstrated, more than anything else the book of Revelation is a chronology of events that lead to the glorious second coming of the Messiah, as outlined on the right side of the master menorah. The letters, seals, and trumpets on the right side are followed by the bowls on the left side, containing the wrath of God, with the seventh bowl bringing in the kingdom of God after the Battle of Armageddon.

Meanwhile, the two remaining mini-menorahs on the left side (i.e., the evil kingdoms and angelic proclamations mini-menorahs) do not add to the basic chronology. They occur simultaneously with the events of the letter, seal, and trumpet mini-menorahs. On the other hand, the thunders are the shamash of the master menorah itself and show mankind the standard by which God separates the wheat from the weeds, the true Bride from the false bride.

The right side of the master menorah represents God's desire to restore His Bride through an ever-more-intimate relationship. And yet, by consistently loving *all* people God continues to reach out, in many cases even to the ones who repeatedly reject Him.

In contrast, some of the events represented on the left side of the master menorah are distorted mirror images of God's plan for mankind. Satan wants the same position and power that God already has, but for separate reasons and different purposes. On the left side we see the Adversary establishing his kingdom on earth, then deceiving and dominating mankind so that we will serve him.

Only God Offers a True Reward

In the end God will reward faithful service and punish the disobedient. This is what we would expect to find in the closing pages of God's message to mankind, as contained within the Bible. We need to understand the Bible to be one continuing plan that reveals God's goals, passions, and purposes in their totality. It is a mosaic rather than completely separate Old and New Testaments in which the newer one replaced the older one, as many churches of today teach. Therefore, it should come as no surprise to find His plan beginning in the very first book of the Bible. And it should be even less of a surprise to find it nearing completion in the very last book of the Bible.

It should also come as no surprise to discover that the New Testament portions of His plan connect back to the Old Testament in numerous ways. For example, through the Israelites, His chosen people, God gives to mankind a complete, highly detailed scenario that reveals how we as individuals can become part of His eternal kingdom. God provides us with the means and asks us to be holy, just as He is.

Meanwhile, although His instructions for holy living are detailed throughout His Word they have their foundation in Torah, the first five books of the Bible. For example, in Deuteronomy 27–28 God tells His people that if they choose to be holy and obey His instructions He will send blessings to them. However, if they choose to disregard His ways and His instructions He will send curses instead. At the same time, the judgments described in Revelation, which will befall mankind if they choose to disobey, are contained in great detail, hundreds of pages earlier, in those two chapters in Deuteronomy.

On the other hand, through the New Testament history of His Son's life and testimony on earth, combined with the stories of those who knew Him and believed in Him, God provides us with proof that loving and serving Him can help us achieve the relationship with Him that He desires for us. At that point the books of Hebrews and Jude, plus the letters and admonitions of Paul, Peter, James, and John, simply reinforce the message that God, in His infinite wisdom, has already made plain. Have you ever wondered why so many authors in the New Testament quote extensively from the Old?

Some may choose to dislike God because they do not like the way He runs the world. How dare He punish people for not obeying Him? They seem not to realize that they are neither the Master nor the Creator. Thus, by choosing to believe the ancient lie that they can be like gods and not be subject to any higher authority, they will bring judgment onto themselves. They simply cannot go unpunished in spite of His boundless love for them. Therefore they inherit the curses and wind up being part of the wrong story.

Two Story Lines at the Same Time

As we first explained in Volume 2 in this series, the book of Revelation contains two different stories unfolding at the same time. The *shamash* sections reveal God's plans to fulfill His promise by bringing ultimate blessings to those who accept the free gift of salvation and live their lives according to His ways. The *mini-menorahs* and the events they describe promise the exact opposite. We can choose to covenant with only one of two different kingdoms – the choice is up to us.

Satan's goal – which he has been very successful in accomplishing – is to deceive mankind into believing that his ways offer the keys to happiness, completion, and godliness. Those serving in his kingdom believe that if they can win enough of mankind over to Satan's belief system they will gain enough authority to force the real God to move aside. They think it's a contest with the outcome still up in the air.

Good luck with that! Sadly, nothing could be further from the truth. God has everything under control. He gives each person many chances to make the choices that will lead him back to the Creator. This is not a contest for control of the world, with mankind's will and mankind's behavior determining the outcome. Likewise, no matter how many people Satan may convert to his own ends Satan also has no control over his own destiny. As Yeshua Himself said:

> "Enter through the narrow gate; for the gate is wide and the way is broad that leads to destruction, and there are many who enter through it. [14]For the gate is small and the way is narrow that leads to life, and there are few who find it." (Matthew 7:13–14)

Earthquakes, Famines, and Pestilence

Earthquakes, famine, pestilence, failed harvests, floods, and intense storms are occurring with increasing frequency all over the earth. Certainly we also see the social and political tensions between various countries increasing as well. All of this will end poorly.

At the same time, most of the economies of the world are sitting on a knife's edge and are ready to fail. We believe that they will continue to get worse and worse. All of these kinds of catastrophes – and many more – will continue to increase in frequency in the months and years ahead.

For example, on the economic front the world's debt problems cannot be solved by borrowing more money. Debt is never resolved by multiplying itself. Only paying off debts will bring positive resolutions. We do not believe that our own government officials have the will, the foresight, and the courage to seriously pursue this option. And neither do other government officials around the world.

Most worldwide currencies – including our own dollar – will become worth less and less as time marches on. As a result, many everyday commodities, such as food and fuel, will continue to go up in price. These increases will gain momentum over time and become one of the biggest concerns for the average person. At the same time, the value of large ticket items, such as homes, will continue to decline.

In response to the current recession, over the last few years some of the governments of the world have bought the bad debts of troubled corporations, financial institutions, and even other countries. They paid full price for these investments and now their balance sheets are encumbered with mostly worthless assets. In addition, the governments who did this bought these so-called assets mostly with trillions of dollars of newly created currency, and then continued to spend far more than they could take in. For example, for every dollar the United States government is currently spending we are borrowing 43 cents or more. Who knows what that ratio will become in the next few years?

On a personal level, what would be the result if you managed your own finances in the same way? Our politicians have convinced many voters that we can continue to spend in the name of fairness and need, without prudence. Unfortunately, though it's good to give to others to meet legitimate needs, it serves no one when we mismanage our finances until the giver becomes destitute himself. To paraphrase something that Margaret Thatcher said a few years ago, "Socialism is great until you run out of other people's money."[2]

And, of course, none of this will be limited to the United States. Europe will continue to borrow and print new money to pay off the debts of the weaker member nations. Eventually the euro may begin sliding in value if several weaker member countries decide to leave the European Economic Union. They know it's easier to pay off your debt when you can print your own money. At the same time, the European Union might respond to the falling value of the euro by raising interest rates. This will shut down any remaining economic activity in Europe, but it will "save" the value of the euro.

Even the Powerhouse Falters

China, the economic powerhouse that many experts expect to keep the world's economy going, will also falter. Chinese banks have loaned huge amounts of money to their local magistrates, developers, businesses, and the politically connected, not to mention (of course) the United States government. This has precipitated a building boom in

China, which might sound good except that sellers are now finding very few buyers. Entire Chinese cities go mostly unoccupied because of this over-investment, which has caused commodity inflation and a huge temporary bubble in real estate values in China.

As of the summer of 2011, the Chinese government began raising interest rates and making money less available in order to slow the rate of inflation and get control of the markets again. This effort will probably fail. Reducing the availability of money by shutting down the loan markets will cause a collapse in demand. The ballooning real estate markets will then blow up, leaving the banks with loans on properties that are then valued way below their cost of construction as reflected in the original construction loan amounts. Chinese banks will then face bankruptcy.

This mess will parallel our own housing market disaster, except that it will be much worse. Even though China has the strongest economy in the world today, it will soon find itself in an economic disaster of its own making.

[Ed. Note: As we go to press, the above has already started to occur. Housing prices in China have begun to collapse, in some cities by as much as 40-50 percent. The Chinese are buying precious metals in fear that their government has inflated away the value of their currency. And all their other economic numbers have begun to plummet as well.]

Worldwide chaos will be the result. Social programs that aim to help the underprivileged, seniors, and the disabled will be unable to provide the benefits they've promised. At the same time, millions of people will not understand why their government payments buy so little. Why food is in short supply, or so expensive. Why jobs are virtually nonexistent, and why things are so unfair.

The gap between the haves and the have-nots will then become bigger than ever. The middle class will become scarce, all of which will cause worldwide unrest and chaos at a time when governments can ill afford such disasters. Likewise, most investors big and small will grow tired of the complete mismanagement of sovereign finances that is now occurring around the world. All this will lead to riots that will dwarf anything we've seen so far.

The Center of Upheaval

The Middle East will continue to be the center of these upheavals. Eventually, in the midst of all this unprecedented instability the Arabs will unite and attack Israel, as detailed in Volume 2 in this series. This may result from the world's dealing with the Iranian nuclear issue. Whether the western powers initiate an attack on Iran, or Iran attempts to force the issue beyond any reasonable forbearance, either one will certainly cause increased instability in that region.

As we have suggested previously, we believe that the anti-Israel animus could well become worldwide in its effect. The price of oil will skyrocket. This will occur in the midst of the economic, geological, and food crises we've already mentioned, in fulfillment of the first six seal events.

This war (the second seal war) will be won by Israel and will usher in a time of peace during which the Jews will be able to rebuild the Temple. This will take several years, a time period that will include the events of the first five trumpets. Unfortunately, as we are told in Ezekiel 38, this constructive period for Israel will also set up the environment for the Gog war involving Russia and its allies (the sixth trumpet war).

Israel will win this war as well, but at a huge cost. The first few chapters of the book of Joel detail this "victory" – it sounds like Israel will suffer greatly at the hands of an army described by Joel as locusts. However, after their second major victory the Jews will use this time to reestablish their government and re-institute the workings of the Temple. During this time the two witnesses will begin their temporary reign.

By now you know the rest of the story. Satan, masquerading as the Messiah, and Abaddon, claiming to be his prophet, will kill the two witnesses. The False Messiah will then claim to be the real God and will take God's place in His own Temple. He will then attempt to conquer the entire world and put it under his control.

Coming in the clouds of heaven, God will then snatch away His Bride soon after the False Messiah makes these false claims about his own godhood. Fortunately for those who remain on the earth, Satan's reign will then last just 3½ years, but what a horrific time this will be. His perverted claim of godhood, and his insults to the real Creator, will usher in part of Satan's preordained punishment as defined in the seven bowls of judgment. All this will be terminated at last by the Battle of Armageddon.

Armageddon will bring this last 3½ years to a close, ending with much loss of life. It will also bring about the end of the time God has given mankind to make correct choices about who they will worship and serve. All of these events will then arrive at their inevitable conclusion with the coming of the true King and the setting up of His kingdom, during which He will rule and reign over His creation for a thousand years.

These final events, leading up to the snatching away of God's Bride and introducing the seven bowls of judgment, are certainly years away. But they are not so far away that you don't need to make plans to get yourself spiritually ready. In the meantime the more current events will try every believer on earth, ultimately testing our faith in Him and causing us to draw away or rush toward Him all the more.

In our opinion, all believers need to immediately take the next few months to seek God's direction on how they should make preparations. Given that we will not be "raptured" out of all the troubles that the book of Revelation prophesies, you might need to make plans and acquire supplies just as God instructed Noah and Joseph to do. As Proverbs 22:3 says: "The prudent sees the evil and hides himself, but the naive go on and are punished for it."

Often a bit of preplanning before a crisis occurs can go a long way toward improving your ability to meet the needs of your family, and perhaps other people as well.

A Thousand Years Until Judgment Day

We are often asked who will be living on the earth during the thousand-year reign. As we have already indicated, the "ordinary" or "regular" (to be explained momentarily) folks who will live on the earth during that time will still be living in their mortal bodies. The Bible even informs us that some of them will live very long lives, even though others will die during this period.

> [17]"For behold, I create new heavens and a new earth;
> And the former things will not be remembered or come to mind.
> [18]But be glad and rejoice forever in what I create;
> For behold, I create Jerusalem for rejoicing
> And her people for gladness.
>
> [19]"I will also rejoice in Jerusalem and be glad in My people;
> And there will no longer be heard in her
> The voice of weeping and the sound of crying.
> [20]No longer will there be in it an infant who lives but a few days,
> Or an old man who does not live out his days;
> For the youth will die at the age of one hundred
> And the one who does not reach the age of one hundred
> Will be thought accursed." (Isaiah 65:17–20)

Meanwhile the Bride – now in her immortal body – will be ruling and reigning with Yeshua on the earth. Those who managed to survive the final tribulation, yet are not part of the Bride, will be the only ones living on the earth at the time of Yeshua's second coming.

At the same time, those who have died but have not yet been raised from the dead because they were not part of the Bride – and therefore have not yet received their immortal bodies during the harvest described in the fifth angelic proclamation – will still be waiting to be judged.

It is very likely that the thousand-year reign will be recognized, in biblical renderings of time, as the seventh thousand-year period. We know that the number seven, from a Hebraic perspective, represents a sabbatical or a time of rest. It also represents the concept of completion and ushers in perfection. All of this mirrors the concepts introduced in the Garden of Eden. When God completed His work He called it very good (perfect), and entered into a time of rest.

For many years after the Israelites entered the land of Canaan, every seventh year was called a sabbatical year. God instructed His people to rest from their labors and allow their land to rest too, during this entire year. All slaves were set free from bondage as well.

God then instructed His people to celebrate a year of Jubilee after seven sets of seven years. During the Jubilee year, all debts were to be terminated. The fiftieth year was also a Sabbath of Sabbaths in which the people were to rest from their labors again.

On the forty-eighth year they would rely on God for a bountiful harvest to tide them over for the next three years. These three years would include:

- The forty-ninth year, which was a traditional, no-work sabbatical year

- The fiftieth year, which was a Jubilee year in which no work was done

- The fifty-first year, during which they still had to eat until the next crop could be harvested

We believe it is highly likely that the Second Coming will occur during a sabbatical year, and possibly even a Jubilee year.

Wiping the Slates Clean

If all the above is true, will the people who survive into the thousand-year reign benefit from the principles God established to be put into effect for these two types of special years? Will God usher in a time of rest for those living on the earth? Will He set the captives free by forgiving their sins in spite of their previous ways of living? Will He wipe their slates clean, just as Adam and Eve's were before they fell?

And, will all their debts be forgiven? Today our debt to God is the bondage of sin we carry around. The only one who can pay it off is

Yeshua via the shedding of His blood. We accept that free gift as a payment for our debt and we are then set free. But most of the folks who will survive into the thousand-year reign will not have been set free. They will never have accepted the free gift Yeshua offered.

Is it possible that God, wanting to restore His creation back to the way it was before sin and death entered into the world, will be recreating the conditions and the situation that existed in the Garden of Eden before man fell? If so, these people would have the opportunity to live their lives in the presence of God, living in obedience to Him . . . or not. They would have the opportunity to try again, but this time – unlike their ancestors – without the distractions and temptations of the deceiver we know as Satan.

On the other hand, Satan could no longer be blamed for any sin they might choose to commit. It would all be on their own slate. It would all be their own doing. So – will salvation be offered to them if they do fall during this time? We think that makes sense.

But that's still not the whole story! Just before the end of the thousand-year reign, Satan will be released from the bottomless pit where he has been chained. He will come to the people living on the earth and will deceive them once again. Revelation 20:8 describes their numbers as the sands of the sea, meaning many and most.

How could this possibly happen? The living God is dwelling on earth. The nations of the world are being managed in a holy and righteous way by emissaries sent from the throne of God Himself. People can come and visit and hear their Messiah anytime they want. His blessings will surround anyone who pays attention.

What's the problem here?

Laodicea Revisited

We believe that the congregation of Laodicea,[3] described in Revelation 3:14–22, best represents these people. The letter to Laodicea addresses a group of people who think they have grown wealthy but are actually poor. Their works are described as worthless or lukewarm.

Today we sometimes find people suffering from this same malaise. Typically it occurs in congregations that are not suffering from persecution or troubles of most kinds. In fact, these congregations often appear to be wealthy. Won't this be the situation during the thousand-year period? Satan will not be around, deceiving people and causing them to hate, steal, and kill each other. It should be a time of bliss, of peace and blessing, of men loving and serving God and mankind.

Sadly, even people who have acquired such great wealth will not realize that human beings, with the ability to make their own choices, don't acquire the attributes of their Creator simply by close proximity. Yes, being close to God Himself represents great riches, but in order to truly own those riches we have to live in submission to Him.

Have you ever lived next to someone who was wealthy? If so, you know firsthand that close proximity to wealth does not automatically increase your balance sheet. You have to *do* something! Associating with the wealthy may feel good but only your own actions can make you wealthy too.

Return of the Sacrificial System

Some also think that after the second coming of the Messiah there will be no need for a Temple, and definitely no need to start up the sacrificial system again. They believe that God will have nothing to do with all of that because those ancient sacrifices have been replaced by Yeshua's blood, once and for all.

The only problem with that assumption is that it is not scriptural. For example, in Isaiah 66 Yahweh assures us that there will be a Temple in Jerusalem, and that surviving Levites will be available to make the sacrifices. This is further supported by many other prophecies about the millennial reign.

We suggest that you read some of the following passages – all in Appendix A at the back of this volume – to get a better picture of the Temple and the situations affecting people during this time: Zechariah 14:21; Ezra 3:1–7; Jeremiah 17:24–27, 33:14–18; Ezekiel 20:40;

Isaiah 56. All these passages offer examples of various types of offerings and the sacrificing of animals at the Temple during the Millennium.

Also, despite the different words used in different translations of the Bible, most of the original words for offerings, or for sacrifice, meant *a blood* offering in contrast to a *grain* or *oil* offering. Likewise, many people do not seem to understand that the sacrifices offered in God's Temple, at His request, never did take away sin. All they did was remind the people of the One who would come and offer up Himself as the perfect sacrifice.

In addition, they should remind us of our duty. That, of course, consists of offering up to God our own will, sacrificing our own ways, and transforming them into His ways. The giving of Yeshua's life paid the price that we are unable to pay on our own no matter how many animals we offer or how obedient we might be to Him. The world's only perfect man, by making the ultimate sacrifice for each one of us, has provided a way to complete His plan – restoration of His people back to Himself.

> "For this is My blood of the covenant, which is poured out for many for forgiveness of sins." (Matthew 26:28)

> Therefore, brethren, since we have confidence to enter the holy place by the blood of Jesus, [20]by a new and living way which He inaugurated for us through the veil, that is, His flesh, [21]and since we have a great priest over the house of God, [22]let us draw near with a sincere heart in full assurance of faith, having our hearts sprinkled clean from an evil conscience and our bodies washed with pure water. [23]Let us hold fast the confession of our hope without wavering, for He who promised is faithful . . . (Hebrews 10:19–23)

> If we say that we have fellowship with Him and yet walk in the darkness, we lie and do not practice the truth; [7] but if we walk in the Light as He Himself is in the Light, we have fellowship with one another, and the blood of Jesus His Son cleanses us from all sin. (I John 1:6–7)

The Temple and its sacrifices perfectly illustrate all of this.

The End of the End

From the authors' standpoint it's never easy to come to the end of a book, especially when the book in question is actually the third in a series that has been "in the preparation stage" for ten years. Not to mention, of course, the years and years of intensive study, for John Klein and Adam Spears, that preceded the actual writing itself.

At the same time, it's hard not to admit to a sense of relief at knowing that we have done as God Himself has so strongly encouraged us to do, by fully exploring the book of Revelation with Him looking over our shoulders at every turn. That has always been the key element for us. It simply would not have been possible even to *begin* this project entirely on our own.

At the same time, we recognize that much of what we've poured into the pages of these three volumes may not always concur with what has come to be accepted by many others as the "official" and "correct" interpretation of the book of Revelation. This includes the works of several best-selling, well-meaning authors. Our only response to that claim remains the same as it was when we began.

We believe that the only way to truly understand Revelation is to look at it through Hebrew eyes. The Bible is not a Greco-Roman-Western book. To repeat what we have said several times in these three volumes:

> The entire Bible was written down by Hebrew authors inspired by a Hebrew God, using Hebrew idioms that reflected Hebrew customs and Hebrew cultural understandings. In other words, it was keyed to a mindset that was relentlessly Hebraic on every level. And it still is.[4]

Ultimately, in its own final pages the Bible makes it very clear that we need not guess at what's coming next. To repeat one more short passage from Revelation that we have examined before:

> [1]Then I saw a new heaven and a new earth; for the first heaven and the first earth passed away, and there is no longer any sea. [2]And I saw the holy city, new Jerusalem,

coming down out of heaven from God, made ready as a bride adorned for her husband.

[3]And I heard a loud voice from the throne, saying, "Behold, the tabernacle of God is among men, and He will dwell among them, and they shall be His people, and God Himself will be among them, [4]and He will wipe away every tear from their eyes; and there will no longer be any death; there will no longer be any mourning, or crying, or pain; the first things have passed away."

[5]And He who sits on the throne said, "Behold, I am making all things new." And He said, "Write, for these words are faithful and true." [6]Then He said to me, "It is done. I am the Alpha and the Omega, the beginning and the end. I will give to the one who thirsts from the spring of the water of life without cost. He who overcomes will inherit these things, and I will be his God and he will be My son."

(Revelation 21:1–7)

These words, written down by John the Beloved at God's clear direction, tell us how our lives will turn out if we live them in obedience to Him. These words tell us what He has promised. These words tell us how He will reward us.

May that reward be yours and that of your loved ones as well.

Appendix A

The Temple Offerings

The following biblical passages detail how the Temple offerings will come about during the millennial reign of Yeshua.

Zechariah 14:21
Every cooking pot in Jerusalem and in Judah will be holy to the LORD of hosts; and all who sacrifice will come and take of them and boil in them. And there will no longer be a Canaanite in the house of the LORD of hosts in that day.

Ezra 3:1–7
[1]Now when the seventh month came, and the sons of Israel were in the cities, the people gathered together as one man to Jerusalem. [2]Then Jeshua the son of Jozadak and his brothers the priests, and Zerubbabel the son of Shealtiel and his brothers arose and built the altar of the God of Israel to offer burnt offerings on it, as it is written in the law of Moses, the man of God. [3]So they set up the altar on its foundation, for they were terrified because of the peoples of the lands; and they offered burnt offerings on it to the LORD, burnt offerings morning and evening. [4]They celebrated the Feast of Booths, as it is written, and offered the fixed number of burnt offerings daily, according to the ordinance, as each day required; [5]and afterward there was a continual burnt offering, also for the new moons and for all the fixed festivals of the LORD that were consecrated, and from everyone who

offered a freewill offering to the LORD. [6]From the first day of the seventh month they began to offer burnt offerings to the LORD, but the foundation of the temple of the LORD had not been laid. [7]Then they gave money to the masons and carpenters, and food, drink and oil to the Sidonians and to the Tyrians, to bring cedar wood from Lebanon to the sea at Joppa, according to the permission they had from Cyrus king of Persia.

Jeremiah 17:24–27

[24]"But it will come about, if you listen attentively to Me," declares the LORD, "to bring no load in through the gates of this city on the sabbath day, but to keep the sabbath day holy by doing no work on it, [25]then there will come in through the gates of this city kings and princes sitting on the throne of David, riding in chariots and on horses, they and their princes, the men of Judah and the inhabitants of Jerusalem, and this city will be inhabited forever. [26]They will come in from the cities of Judah and from the environs of Jerusalem, from the land of Benjamin, from the lowland, from the hill country and from the Negev, bringing burnt offerings, sacrifices, grain offerings and incense, and bringing sacrifices of thanksgiving to the house of the LORD. [27]But if you do not listen to Me to keep the sabbath day holy by not carrying a load and coming in through the gates of Jerusalem on the sabbath day, then I will kindle a fire in its gates and it will devour the palaces of Jerusalem and not be quenched."

Jeremiah 33:14–18

[14]"'Behold, days are coming,' declares the LORD, 'when I will fulfill the good word which I have spoken concerning the house of Israel and the house of Judah. [15]In those days and at that time I will cause a righteous Branch of David to spring forth; and He shall execute justice and righteousness on the earth. [16]In those days Judah will be saved and Jerusalem will dwell in safety; and this is the name by which she will be called: the LORD is our righteousness.' [17]For thus says the LORD, 'David shall never lack a man to sit on the throne of the house of Israel; [18]and the Levitical priests shall never lack a man before Me to offer burnt offerings, to burn grain offerings and to prepare sacrifices continually.'"

Ezekiel 20:40

"For on My holy mountain, on the high mountain of Israel," declares the Lord GOD, "there the whole house of Israel, all of them, will serve Me in the land; there I will accept them and there I will seek your contributions and the choicest of your gifts, with all your holy things."

Isaiah 56

[1]Thus says the LORD, "Preserve justice and do righteousness, for My salvation is about to come and My righteousness to be revealed. [2]How blessed is the man who does this, and the son of man who takes hold of it; who keeps from profaning the sabbath, and keeps his hand from doing any evil." [3]Let not the foreigner who has joined himself to the LORD say, "The LORD will surely separate me from His people." Nor let the eunuch say, "Behold, I am a dry tree." [4]For thus says the LORD, "To the eunuchs who keep My sabbaths, and choose what pleases Me, and hold fast My covenant, [5]to them I will give in My house and within My walls a memorial, and a name better than that of sons and daughters; I will give them an everlasting name which will not be cut off.

[6]"Also the foreigners who join themselves to the LORD, to minister to Him, and to love the name of the LORD, to be His servants, every one who keeps from profaning the sabbath and holds fast My covenant; [7]even those I will bring to My holy mountain and make them joyful in My house of prayer. Their burnt offerings and their sacrifices will be acceptable on My altar; for My house will be called a house of prayer for all the peoples."

[8]The Lord GOD, who gathers the dispersed of Israel, declares, "Yet others I will gather to them, to those already gathered." [9]All you beasts of the field, all you beasts in the forest, come to eat. [10]His watchmen are blind, all of them know nothing. All of them are mute dogs unable to bark, dreamers lying down, who love to slumber; [11]and the dogs are greedy, they are not satisfied. And they are shepherds who have no understanding; they have all turned to their own way, each one to his unjust gain, to the last one.

[12]"Come," they say, "let us get wine, and let us drink heavily of strong drink; and tomorrow will be like today, only more so."

Endnotes

Introduction

[1] That's why we devoted so much space to explaining biblical covenant in *Volume 1* of this series.

[2] Gaddafi was killed in 2011 by his own people, who captured him while he was trying to escape in a caravan driving across the Libyan desert.

[3] www.dictionary.reference.com/browse/weed.

Chapter 1 — Three Wars Ahead

[1] John Klein and Adam Spears, with Michael Christopher, *Volume 2, Lost in Translation, The Book of Revelation Through Hebrew Eyes* (Bend, OR: Covenant Research Institute, Inc., 2009), p. 51.

Chapter 2 — Shamash of the Seven Evil Kingdoms

[1] See "What Are 'Shamash' Chapters?" p. 52–56, in *Volume 2, Lost in Translation*.

[2] See "What Is a Ketubah?" p. 25–27, in *Volume 2, Lost in Translation*.

[3] *Volume 2, Lost in Translation*, p. 227.

[4] This particular statement is usually attributed to Edmund Burke but no one can positively identify the precise source. It might be based on a paraphrase of various ideas that he put forth both in speaking and writing.

[5] Gesenius, H.W.F., *Gesenius' Hebrew-Chaldee Lexicon to the Old Testament* (Grand Rapids: Baker Books, 1979), p. 376.

[6] *Volume 2, Lost in Translation*, p. 275.

[7] Ibid., p. 292–293.

[8] Michael Christopher, *James – Faith Without Works* (Nashville: Thomas Nelson Publishers, 2005).

Chapter 3 — The Seven Evil Kingdoms

[1] Adapted from "Evil Kingdoms," *The Ten-Foot Pole*, (Bend, OR: Covenant Research Institute, Inc.), volume 8–1, p. 1.

[2] *Pirke Avot* 1:10 III B. This is known in English as *Wisdom of the Fathers*.

[3] *Pirke Avot* 2:3 III A.

[4] Section 267 of the *Code of Hammurabi*.

[5] The book of Enoch is available in several modern volumes. The one we used here is *The Book of Enoch the Prophet*, translated by Richard Laurence (Kempton, IL: Adventures Unlimited Press, 2000).

[6] John Klein and Adam Spears, with Michael Christopher, *Volume 1, Lost in Translation, Rediscovering the Hebrew Roots of Our Faith* (Bend, OR: Covenant Research Institute, Inc., 2007), p. 89. (Note, also, that the last paragraph in this quotation was actually footnote #6 in chapter 4 in the referenced volume.)

[7] Ibid, p. 79–81.

[8] *Gesenius*, p. 751–752.

[9] Ibid, p. 649.

[10] Note that Babylon appears twice on the list but is not given a separate number at the second listing.

[11] *Gesenius* (*sheker*), p. 849.

[12] *Volume 2, Lost in Translation,* p. 170–172.

[13] *Gesenius*, p. 710.

[14] Jodi Klein, *Hanukkah Covenant Seder* (Bend, OR: Covenant Research Institute, Inc., 2007), p. 39–40.

[15] *Volume 2, Lost in Translation,* p. 186–189.

Chapter 4 — Shamash of the Seven Angelic Proclamations

[1] These were the very gleanings that Ruth gathered in Boaz's field, which then provided food for herself and for Naomi, her mother-in-law.

Chapter 5 — The Seven Angelic Proclamations

[1] *Volume 1, Lost in Translation,* p. 134–135.

[2] The words for "son of man" in Daniel 7:13 are in Aramaic and are *bar enash*.

[3] *Volume 2, Lost in Translation,* p. 291–293.

[4] Ibid, p. 123, 279–280.

Chapter 6 — Shamash of the Seven Bowls

[1] "But Moses and the children of Israel sang on the other side of the sea a song of thanksgiving and triumph, which, repeated every Sabbath in the Temple, when the drink-offering of the festive sacrifice was poured out, reminded Israel that to all time the kingdom was surrounded by the hostile powers of this world; that there must always be a contest between them; and that Jehovah would always Himself interpose to destroy His enemies and to deliver His people. Thus that great event is really not solitary, nor yet its hymn without an echo. For all times

it has been a prophecy, a comfort, and a song of anticipated sure victory to the Church. And so at the last, they who stand on the 'sea of glass mingled with fire,' who have 'gotten the victory,' and have 'the harps of God,' 'sing the song of Moses, the servant of God, and the song of the Lamb.'"

Tradition informs us that the "Song of Moses" was sung in sections (one for each Sabbath) in the Temple, at the close of the Sabbath-morning service. The Song of Moses consists of three stanzas (Exodus 15:1-5, 6-10, and 11-18), of which the first two show the power of Jehovah in the destruction of His enemies, while the third gives thanks for the result, in the calling of Israel to be the kingdom of God, and their possession of the promised inheritance.

Albert Edersheim, *Bible History, Old Testament, Volume 2* (Peabody, MA: Hendrickson Publishers, Inc., 1995), chapter 7.

"... At the close of the additional Sabbath sacrifice, when its drink-offering was brought, the Levites sang the 'Song of Moses' in Deuteronomy 32. This 'hymn' was divided into six portions, for as many Sabbaths (v 1-6; 7-12; 13-18; 19-28; 29-39; 40-end). Each portion was sung in three sections with threefold blasts of the priests' trumpets, the people worshipping at each pause. If a Sabbath and a 'new moon' fell on the same day, the Sabbath hymn was sung in preference to that for the new moon; if a feast day fell on the Sabbath, the Sabbath sacrifice was offered before that prescribed for the day. At the evening sacrifice on the Sabbath the song of Moses in Exodus 15 was sung."

Alfred Edersheim, *The Temple: Its Ministry and Services* (Peabody, MA: Hendrickson Publishers, Inc., 1994), chapter 9.

"The Jews have a notion, that the very song of Moses itself will be sung in the world to come, in the days of the Messiah; for they say, there are in it the times of the Messiah, and of Gog and Magog, and of the resurrection of the dead, and the world to come..."

Larry Pierce, *The New John Gill's Exposition of the Entire Bible* (Paris, AR: The Baptist Standard Bearer, 2010).

Chapter 7 — The Seven Bowls of Wrath
[1] Gesenius also confirms the modern location of Armageddon.

Chapter 8 — The Whore/False Bride
[1] http://www.crwflags.com/fotw/flags/xf-dye.html
[2] *Hanukkah Covenant Seder*, p. 37–38. For additional explanation, please see *Volume 1, Lost in Translation,* p. 179–188. Also, p. 33–51.
[3] *Gesenius*, p. 222: Lucifer (*Halal*, which means "lightbearer").
[4] http://phoenicia.org/jezebel.html
[5] http://en.wikipedia.org/wiki/Jezebel
[6] http://www.conservapedia.com/Ba'al

Chapter 9 — The True Bride

[1] *Volume 2, Lost in Translation*, p. 201.
[2] Ibid., p. 135-138. Also includes material from *Volume 1*.
[3] *Volume 1, Lost in Translation*, p. 70–71.
[4] *Gesenius*, p. 733.

Chapter 10 — The Return of the True King

[1] *Volume 1, Lost in Translation*, p. 72.

Chapter 12 — Coming to a Close

[1] *Volume 2, Lost in Translation*, p. 42–44.
[2] During an appearance on a television program called *This Week*, on February 5, 1976, Thatcher actually said, "Socialist governments traditionally do make a financial mess. They always run out of other people's money." However, the quote we used was "extracted and condensed" from the original and has been quoted widely in this version.
[3] *Volume 2, Lost in Translation*, p. 117–119.
[4] See the final paragraphs of the *foreword* in this volume.

Bibliography

Christopher, Michael. *James – Faith Without Works*. Nashville: Thomas Nelson Publishers, 2005.

Edersheim, Alfred. *Bible History, Old Testament, Volume 2*. Peabody, MA: Hendrickson Publishers, 1994.

Edersheim, Alfred. *The Temple: Its Ministry and Services*. Peabody, MA: Hendrickson Publishers, 1994.

Gesenius, H. W. F. *Gesenius' Hebrew-Chaldee Lexicon to the Old Testament*. Grand Rapids: Baker Books, 1979.

Klein, John; Spears, Adam and Christopher, Michael. *Volume 1, Lost in Translation: Rediscovering The Hebrew Roots of our Faith*. Bend, OR: Covenant Research Institute, Inc., 2007.

Klein, John; Spears, Adam and Christopher, Michael. *Volume 2, Lost in Translation: The Book of Revelation Through Hebrew Eyes*. Bend, OR: Covenant Research Institute, Inc., 2009.

Recommended Reading

Aharoni, Yohanan. *The Land of the Bible*. Philadelphia: Westminster Press, 1962.

Aharoni, Yohanan and Avi-Yonah, Michael. *The MacMillan Bible Atlas*. New York: MacMillan, 1968.

Archer, Gleason L. *A Survey of Old Testament Introduction*. Chicago, IL: Moody Publishers, 2007.

Backhouse, Robert. *The Kregel Pictorial Guide to The Temple*. Grand Rapids: Kregel, 1996.

Berkowitz, Ariel and D'vorah. *Torah Rediscovered*. Hampton, VA: Shoreshim Publishing, Inc., 2004.

Bivin, David. *New Light on the Difficult Words of Jesus*. Holland, MI: En-Gedi Resource Center, 2005.

Bivin, David. *Understanding the Difficult Words of Jesus*. Shippensburg, PA: Destiny Image Publishers, Inc., 1994.

Black, Naomi (Ed.). *Celebration: The Book of Jewish Festivals*. Middle Village, NY: Jonathan David Publishers, 1989.

Bowles, Warren, L. *Christianity Reconsidered.* Denver, CO: Montgomery-Porter Publishing, 2008.

Brown, William. *The Tabernacle, Its Priests and Its Service.* Peabody, MA: Hendrickson Publishers, 1996.

Byers, Marvin. *The Mystery: A Lost Key.* Miami: Hebron Press, 2000.

Charles, R. H. *The Book of Enoch.* San Francisco: Weiser Books, 2003.

Church, J. R. and Stearman, Gary. *The Mystery of the Menorah.* Oklahoma City: Prophecy Publications, 1993.

Cohen, Abraham A. *Everyman's Talmud: The Major Teachings of the Rabbinic Sages.* New York: Schocken Books, 1995.

Cohen, Shaye J. D. *From the Maccabees to the Mishnah.* Philadelphia: Westminster Press, 1987.

Crossan, John D. and Reed, Jonathan L. *Excavating Jesus.* New York: Harper, 2001.

Donin, Rabbi Hayim Halevy. *To Be a Jew.* Jackson, TN: Basic Books, 1982.

Donin, Rabbi Hayim Halevy. *To Pray as a Jew: A Guide to the Prayer Book and Synagogue Service.* Jackson, TN: Basic Books, 2001.

Dunn, James D. G. *Jews and Christians, the Parting of the Ways.* Grand Rapids: Eerdmans, 1992.

Edersheim, Alfred. *Sketches of Jewish Social Life.* Peabody, MA: Hendrickson Publishers, Inc., 1994.

Edersheim, Alfred. *The Life and Times of Jesus the Messiah.* Peabody, MA: Hendrickson Publishers, Inc., 2000.

Edersheim, Alfred. *The Temple.* Peabody, MA: Hendrickson Publishers, Inc., 1994.

Finto, Don. *Your People Shall Be My People.* Ventura, CA: Regal Books, 2001.

Free, Joseph and Vos, Howard. *Archaeology and Bible History.* Grand Rapids: Zondervan, 1992.

Friedman, David. *They Loved the Torah.* Baltimore: Lederer Books, 2001.

Frydland, Rachmiel. *What Rabbis Know About the Messiah.* Columbus, OH: Messianic Literature Outreach, 1991.

Frymer-Kensky, Tikva, Novak, David, Ochs, Peter, Sandmel, David F., and Signer, Michael A. *Christianity in Jewish Terms.* Boulder, CO: Westview Press, 2000.

Gruber, Daniel. *Copernicus and the Jews.* Hanover, NH: Elijah Publishing, 2005.

Howard, Kevin, and Rosenthal, Marvin. *The Feasts of the Lord.* Orlando, FL: Zion's Hope, Inc., 1997.

Kasdan, Barney. *God's Appointed Customs.* Clarksdale, MD: Messianic Jewish Publishers, 1996.

Kasdan, Barney. *God's Appointed Times: A Practical Guide for Understanding and Celebrating the Biblical Holidays.* Baltimore: Messianic Jewish Publishers, 1993.

Kenyon, E.W. *Blood Covenant.* Lynnwood, WA: Kenyon's Gospel Publishing Society, 1981.

Kohlenberger, John R., III. *The Interlinear NIV Hebrew English Old Testament.* Grand Rapids: Zondervan, 1979.

Lamm, Maurice. *Jewish Way in Love and Marriage.* New York: Jonathan David Publishers, 1980.

Lash, Jamie. *The Ancient Jewish Wedding and the Return of Messiah for His Bride.* Ft. Lauderdale: Jewish Jewels, 1997.

Lattimore, Richard. *The Odyssey of Homer.* New York: HarperCollins, 1991.

Laurence, Richard. *The Book of Enoch the Prophet.* Kempton, IL: Adventures Unlimited Press, 2000.

Levy, David M. *The Tabernacle: Shadows of the Messiah.* Bellmawr, N J: The Friends of Israel Gospel Ministry, 1993.

Martin, Richard P. *Bulfinch's Mythology: The Age of the Fable, The Age of Chivalry, Legends of Charlemagne.* New York: HarperCollins, 1991.

Mason, Steve. *Josephus and the New Testament.* Peabody, MA: Hendrickson Publishers, 1992.

Moseley, Ron. *Yeshua.* Clarksville, MD: Lederer Books, 1996.

Murray, Andrew. *The Two Covenants.* Fort Washington, PA: CSC Publications, 2001.

Nanos, Mark D. *The Mystery of Romans.* Minneapolis, MN: Augsburg Fortress Press, 1996.

Nanos, Mark D. *The Irony of Galatians.* Minneapolis, MN: Augsburg Fortress Press, 2002.

Neusner, Jacob. *The Mishnah: A New Translation.* New Haven, CT: Yale University Press, 1988.

Olitzky, Rabbi Kerry M., Judson, Rabbi Daniel, editors. *The Rituals & Practices of a Jewish Life.* Woodstock, VT: Jewish Lights Publishing, 2002.

Philips, Neil. *Myths & Legends: The World's Most Enduring Myths and Legends Explored and Explained.* New York: DK Publishing, 1999.

Richmond, Barbara. *Jewish Insights into the New Testament.* Woodland Park, CO: For Your Glory, 1996.

Rosen, Ceil and Rosen, Moishe. *Christ in the Passover.* Chicago: Moody Press, 2006.

Scott, Bruce. *The Feasts of Israel.* Bellmawr, NJ: Friends of Israel Gospel Ministry, 1997.

Seekins, Frank T. *Hebrew Word Pictures*, Phoenix: Living Word Pictures, Inc., 1994.

Shanks, Hershel. *Understanding the Dead Sea Scrolls.* New York: Random House, 1992.

Stern, David H. *Messianic Judaism.* Clarksville, MD: Lederer Books, 2007.

Stern, David H. *Restoring the Jewishness of the Gospel.* Clarksville, MD: Jewish New Testament Publications, 1990.

Trumbull, H. Clay. *The Blood Covenant.* Kirkwood, MO: Impact Christian Books, 1975.

Trumbull, H. Clay. *The Salt Covenant.* Kirkwood, MO: Impact Christian Books, 1975.

Trumbull, H. Clay. *The Threshold Covenant.* Kirkwood, MO: Impact Christian Books, 1975.

Vernes, Geza. *The Religion of Jesus the Jew.* Minneapolis, MN: Augsburg Fortress Press, 1992.

Wilson, Marvin R. *Our Father Abraham.* Grand Rapids: Eerdmans, 1989.

Winkler, Gershon. *The Way of the Boundary Crosser: Introduction to Jewish Flexidoxy.* North Vale, NJ: Jason Aronson, 1998.

Young, Brad H. *The Parables.* Peabody, MA: Hendrickson Publishers, 1998.

CPSIA information can be obtained at www.ICGtesting.com
Printed in the USA
BVOW06s1117110116

432402BV00002B/133/P